Contents

SO-BDY-445

List of Figures

FOUNDATION FUNDAMENTALS

A Guide for Grantseekers
Third Edition

Edited by Patricia E. Read

The Foundation Center
1986

Foreword

Seeking National Support for Local Projects

James Richmond
Vice-President, W. K. Kellogg Foundation

The following remarks are drawn from a presentation Mr. Richmond made at a conference on "Strategies for Successful Fundraising" sponsored by the Clearinghouse for Mid-Continent Foundations in Kansas City, Missouri.

O N several occasions, I've read through the *History of Philanthropy in Kansas City*, published by the Clearinghouse for Mid-Continent Foundations; it is probably the most comprehensive, interesting, and enlightening profile of philanthropy in one city ever published. What always impresses me about this history is that it tells the story of how private giving has flourished in Kansas City with relatively few large family fortunes or large foundations, but with extremely broad community support. It seems to me that Kansas City's history tells us much about what types of funding are most appropriate, and obtainable, for local projects.

How many of you have developed proposals which have been funded by national foundations like Ford, Carnegie, Rockefeller, or Kellogg? How many have had proposals funded by foundations located right here in the Kansas City area? There's a common, if understandable, misperception that it's the large, "big-name" national foundations that represent the best chances, the best avenues for funding of local projects. Realistically, that's only the case if those large foundations are based in your own community.

Out of the approximately 24,000 active grantmaking foundations in the United States, only 166 have assets of $50 million or more. The vast majority of foundations, over 80 percent, have assets of less than $1 million. Most of these smaller foundations tend to limit their funding by geographic areas, and as local foundations, they are particularly oriented to and concerned with local needs. The outstanding work of the Kansas City Association of Trusts and Foundations over the past 30-plus years is a good example. It has awarded more than $20 million in grants for local initiatives during that period, whereas the Kellogg Foundation, as a national foundation, has only awarded grants totaling $1.1 million in the Kansas City area and $7 million in all of Missouri.

In most cases, the funding source for a project should be directly related to the population that will be served by that project: local population—local funding; state population—state funding; national population—national funding. That approach has been used successfully by a number of organizations and institutions here in Kansas City. Projects with *only* local impact have been funded by major contributions from local donors, including individuals, corporations, and foundations. Many projects, of course, have drawn upon all three sources of private funding, as well as drawing on public or government resources.

In seeking support from national foundations, the key words are *national impact*, *evaluation*, and *replication potential*. For example, the Kellogg Foundation provided over $500,000 over the past decade to the Kansas City Regional Council for Higher Education (KCRCHE) to improve and coordinate educational services and faculty development among higher education institutions in the Kansas City region. Kellogg was concerned about Kansas City's local educational needs, but the primary reason for our support was that the project addressed faculty development problems found at colleges and universities in many other communities across the nation. KCRCHE developed an unusual approach to solve these problems and proposed ways to measure the impact of its programs on area colleges. Our funding was based to a significant extent on the potential that this pilot approach would be picked up, adapted, and used by other communities facing similar problems.

An emphasis on project evaluation and the potential for replication—for solving a problem that is larger than just one neighborhood or even one city—is often a key consideration in funding decisions at the Kellogg Foundation as well as many other national foundations. Come up with a good idea that benefits your institution. One that will solve your problem. That can be evaluated as to its effectiveness. *And* which has replication potential for other communities.

That sounds simple, but of course, it's not, and the competition for limited foundation dollars is intense. At Kellogg, we receive about 5,000 written requests each year, but we have resources to fund only about 130 new projects annually. More than 65 percent of those requests are *outside* our areas of programming priority, even though those priorities are described in our annual report and in the reference publications available in The Foundation Center's 160 cooperating libraries across the country. This indicates that many organizations still follow the "shotgun" strategy for foundation fundraising which states: "Send proposals to as many foundations as your paper supply, envelopes, and postage stamps will allow, and hope that one will hit the foundation funding jackpot."

It may be possible to get a foundation grant through that kind of gambling, but the odds are not much better than they are for hitting the Michigan state lottery. Chances are much better if an organization takes the time to research foundation funding priorities and match its proposal to the right foundation.

Although replication potential is a key consideration for most national foundations, there are a number of national foundations that have an historical commitment to community-based problem solving all across the United States and which fund national demonstration projects that might match up with your organization's or community's needs. It's important to keep abreast of the programs at these foundations, and it's also important—if you're serious about on-going funding by national foundations—to keep informed on general foundation funding trends.

There are scores of publications and directories available from The Foundation Center, Grantsmanship Center, Taft Corporation, and many others that detail current foundation funding patterns. Publications issued by foundations, including annual reports and newsletters, are also a key source of information about funding interests and trends. For spotting the emerging trends and important new funding programs, I recommend *Foundation News*, the bimonthly magazine of the Council on Foundations, the national trade association for foundations.

Once you've researched your foundation prospects, it's also crucial to be aggressive in your approach to them. The meek may inherit the earth, but they don't get large grants from foundations very often. Use your research and your personal and professional contacts to find out which people within those foundations should receive your proposal. If possible, discuss your proposal idea with those people over the phone before you mail the actual proposal. After you've sent the proposal in, be aggressive in following up your request with a telephone call.

What I've outlined then is a relatively simple, four-point strategy for national foundation funding:

1. Come up with a good idea that solves a problem, serves people or serves a community, that can be evaluated for its effectiveness, and that has replication potential for other communities.

2. Do the necessary homework to research foundation priorities.

3. Target your proposal to foundations with similar program priorities.

4. Be aggressive in approaching foundations by contacting the right people at the foundation and following up mailed proposals with telephone or personal contact.

Beyond these four points, there are some other key considerations you should take into account when soliciting funding from a local or national foundation or, for that matter, from an individual donor or a corporation. At Kellogg, we use the following checklist as we review proposals for funding:

1. Appropriateness of the project for the foundation.

2. Assurance of Treasury Department and IRS requirements.

3. Defense of why this plan is needed.

4. Importance and utility of the venture to the community or to society.

5. Originality and creativity of the proposed venture.

6. Prospects for leverage and pattern-making effects.

7. The organization's trustees and staff:
    —lists
    —dedication and commitment
    —competence
    —cooperation
    —integrity
    —references
    —overall personnel rating.

8. Financial planning:
    —budgets submitted
    —soundness and quality of the budgets
    —report on funds pledged to date
    —time and liquidation planning.

9. Provision for project evaluation.

10. Feasibility and realism of the proposal.

Each funding source will undoubtedly have its own application requirements and funding criteria, and it will be useful to learn as much about those criteria before submitting a request for funding. Almost every funder will want to see evidence that grant applicants have taken these ten items into consideration in planning their program and preparing their proposals.

I mentioned the importance of being aggressive with foundations. It's also important to be positive in your approach and attitude toward the whole process of foundation solicitation. Remember that foundations need *you* almost as much as you need them. Most foundations look to nonprofit organizations for creative, problem-solving initiatives. Foundations are *looking* for good ideas and exciting, meaningful projects to support. The challenge is to meet their needs and yours.

Introduction

EVERY YEAR thousands of nonprofit organizations receive grant support from foundations that enables them to provide cultural programs, educational services, health care, social services, and a vast array of other charitable activities essential to their communities. Unfortunately, a far greater number of nonprofits are unsuccessful in their appeals for foundation funding support. Many worthy appeals must be declined simply because there are not enough foundation dollars to meet the full funding needs of nonprofits. Other worthy requests are rejected because they fall outside of the program and geographic interests of the foundations approached. Some of the applications declined are poorly prepared and do not reflect a careful analysis of the applicant organization's needs, its credibility, or its capacity to carry out the proposed project. The organization may not have asked itself if it is especially suited to make a contribution to the solution of the problem or to provide the service proposed.

Although it is impossible to eliminate the possibility of rejection entirely, grantseekers can further their causes by undertaking a careful analysis of their organization and its needs, learning more about the foundation funding process, and relating their funding needs to the interests of specific grantmakers. This guide is designed to help both novice and experienced grantseekers begin the process of understanding the world of foundations and identifying appropriate funding sources.

This third edition of *Foundation Fundamentals* has been fully revised and updated, adding new materials suggested by users of the first two editions developed by Carol M. Kurzig and introducing new resources developed over the last four years. We have prepared new worksheets to help readers through the process of identifying and researching funders who would be most likely to be interested in their programs. Several appendices have also been added, including more detailed bibliographies for further reading and study, two special sections on how to find information on grants to individuals and corporate grantmakers, and a listing of national organizations providing information or services to grantmakers and grantseekers.

The first section of this guide, Understanding the World of Foundations, describes the various types of foundations, the regulations that govern their activities, the relationship of foundations to other funding sources, and who gets foundation grants. Although this book focuses primarily on foundation grants, we recommend strongly that grantseekers also consider other sources of funding, such as individual contributors, government grants, earned income programs, and so on. Although foundations are an important source of support for nonprofits, their total giving represents a relatively small percentage of the total private philanthropic dollars contributed annually, and an even smaller percent of the total support for nonprofit activities when government funding and earned income are included. Chapter 2 describes some of these other funding sources and how to learn more about them, and Appendix D outlines in more detail how to find out more about corporate funding.

In Section II, The Search for Appropriate Funders, we describe the resources available and how grantseekers can use them to learn about the foundations most likely to be interested in their proposals. The resources and search strategies we recommend are based upon The Foundation Center's 30 years of service to both funders and fundraisers and reflect the questions most frequently asked by visitors to our libraries. The primary focus is on materials produced by The Foundation Center in cooperation with grantmakers, although a number of other reference tools and fundraising guides are referred to in the text and described in Appendix A. Judging which of these resources will have value to your work can require a considerable investment of time and money, but we've attempted to provide guidelines for determining the types of resources you should investigate and many of the specific materials can be examined free of charge at Foundation Center cooperating libraries.

Since The Foundation Center first opened its New York library in 1956, well over a million individual grantseekers and representatives of nonprofit organizations have visited the four Center-operated libraries in New York, Washington, D.C., Cleveland, and San Francisco and its 160 cooperating libraries across the country. Each of these libraries provides free public access to the basic directories, indexes, and funding guides published by the Center, in addition to other fundraising reference tools. These cooperating libraries are listed in Appendix G and should be the first stop for grantseekers as they begin their search for funding sources.

Although this edition of Foundation Fundamentals bears the name of one editor, it is truly the result of many people's efforts. This third edition relies heavily on the concept and materials developed by Carol M. Kurzig, former Director of Public Services at the Center, for the first two editions of this guide. Special credit also goes to Donna Dunlop, former Coordinator of Cooperating Collections at the Center, who contributed many of the initial materials and recommendations for revision; Kim Clarke and Elise Linden, who compiled the basic entries for the listing of national organizations and the bibliographies which appear in the appendices; Robert Kilbride, who developed the special section on funding for individuals; Lydia Motyka, who compiled the listing of state and regional directories of foundations; Rick Schoff, who designed the text and worksheets and offered invaluable editorial assistance; and all of the staff of the The Foundation Center who work to ensure the accuracy, timeliness, and comprehensiveness of our information resources. I also want to thank James Richmond of the Kellogg Foundation for the insights and advice to grantseekers he offers in the Foreword to this edition. Finally, I want to express special thanks to our customers and library users who have waited so patiently through the long process of preparing this third edition.

Patricia Read
Editor

Section I

Understanding the World of Foundations

1

What Is
a Foundation?

THE FOUNDATION CENTER defines a private foundation as a nongovernmental, nonprofit organization having a principal fund of its own, managed by its own trustees and directors, and established to maintain or aid charitable, educational, religious, or other activities serving the public good, primarily by making grants to other nonprofit organizations.

Some private foundations are organized as operating foundations that conduct their own research program or provide a direct service. Operating foundations generally make few, if any, grants to other organizations. Community foundations function in much the same way as private foundations, but because their funds are drawn from many donors, they are usually classified as "public charities."

Some foundations may use different words in their names, such as "fund," "trust," or "endowment," but these terms indicate no legal or operational differences. On the other hand, there are organizations that use the term "foundation" or "trust" in their names but that do not operate as foundations, although in some cases they may make grants to other organizations. The nomenclature can be confusing, but the significant distinction is that those nonprofits actually classified by the Internal Revenue Service as private foundations must be organized and operated under specific regulations.

Foundations are usually created and organized as corporations or charitable trusts under state laws and receive their federal tax-exempt status under the

Internal Revenue Code. The Tax Reform Act of 1969, the first major legislation dealing with foundations, introduced the term "private foundation" and defined the phrase only by the exclusion of other nonprofit organizations. David Freeman, former President of the Council on Foundations, explains the Code's definition in his book *The Handbook on Private Foundations*:

> "Starting with the universe of voluntary organizations described in Section 501(c)(3), the Code excludes broad groups, e.g., churches, schools, hospitals, governmental units, publicly supported charities and their affiliates. Public supported charities are those which derive much of their support from the general public and reach out in other ways to a public constituency. All of the above kinds of excluded organizations are commonly and conveniently referred to as 'public charities.' Section 501(c)(3) organizations remaining after these exclusions are, without more precise definition, 'private foundations.'"*

Within the category of private foundations, the 1969 Tax Reform Act distinguishes between operating foundations—that is, foundations that are established primarily to operate specific research, social welfare, or other charitable programs—and non-operating foundations. The category of non-operating private foundation includes independent grantmaking foundations, company-sponsored foundations, and a variety of non-grantmaking organizations that function in similar ways as operating foundations do or as "public charities" but that do not meet the legal requirements for those tax statuses.

In this handbook and in its publications, The Foundation Center covers only grantmaking private foundations, community foundations, and operating foundations that have been so designated by the Internal Revenue Service.

TYPES OF FOUNDATIONS

There are a number of ways foundations are classified, and you should familiarize yourself with the terms most commonly used because they generally imply certain operational differences.

Independent foundations, which comprise the largest segment of the foundation universe, are grantmaking organizations whose funds are generally derived from an individual, a family, or a group of individuals. They may be operated under the direction of the donor or members of the donor's family or they may have an independent board of directors that manages the foundation's program.

Typically, independent foundations have broad charters, but in practice they often limit their giving to a few fields of interest. Their broad charters,

---

*Freeman, David F. *The Handbook on Private Foundations*. Washington, DC: The Council on Foundations, 1981, p. 6.

however, allow them to move into new fields in response to changing social priorities. Dependent on the range of their giving, they may also be known as "general purpose" or "special purpose" foundations.

Company-sponsored foundations, also called corporate foundations, are created and funded by a business corporation for the purpose of making grants and performing other philanthropic activities, but are separate legal organizations from the sponsoring corporation. Company foundations are generally managed by a board of directors often composed of corporate officials, but which may also include individuals with no corporate affiliation. In some company-sponsored foundations local plant managers and officials are also involved in grantmaking and policy decisions. Their giving programs often focus on communities where the company has operations and on research and education in fields related to company activities.

Company-sponsored foundations should be distinguished from corporate contributions or direct giving programs that are administered within the corporation. Direct giving programs are under the full control of the corporation and funds drawn solely from the corporation's pre-tax earnings. Direct giving programs may encompass "in-kind" contributions, such as donations of equipment, office space, supplies, or staff time, as well as monetary grants. A company-sponsored foundation, on the other hand, is an independent organization, despite its close ties to the parent company. It is classified as a "private foundation" under the Internal Revenue Code and is subject to the same regulations as other private foundations. The foundation receives funds from the parent company based on the company's pre-tax earnings which it then "passes on" to nonprofit organizations in grants, but it also maintains its own endowment, however small. A company-sponsored foundation, therefore, makes it possible for a company to set aside funds for use in future years when company earnings may be reduced and the needs of charitable organizations may be greater.

Many corporations maintain both a company-sponsored foundation and a direct giving program, and these are often coordinated under a general giving policy.

Operating foundations are established to operate research, social welfare, or other charitable programs determined by the donor or the governing body. Some grants may be made outside the foundation, but the majority of the foundation's funds are expended for its own programs. Endowment funds are generally provided by a single source, although many operating foundations also receive some contributions from the general public. New provisions affecting contributions to operating foundations, implemented with the 1984 Tax Reform Act, enable operating foundations to seek funding to support their programs from other foundations and grantmakers.

Community foundations are supported by and operated for a specific community or region. They receive their funds from a variety of donors; in fact,

FIGURE 1. General Characteristics of Four Types of Foundations

Foundation Type	Description	Source of Funds	Decision-Making Body	Grantmaking Activity	Reporting Requirements
Independent Foundation	An independent grantmaking organization established to aid social, educational, religious, or other charitable activities	Endowment generally derived from a single source such as an individual, a family, or a group of individuals. Contributions to endowment limited as to tax deductibility	Decisions may be made by donor or members of donor's family; by an independent board of directors or trustees; or by a bank or trust officer acting on donor's behalf	Broad discretionary giving allowed but may have specific guidelines and give only in a few specific fields. About 70% limit their giving to local area	Annual information returns 990-PF filed with IRS must be made available to public. A small percentage issue separately printed annual reports
Company-sponsored Foundation	Legally an independent grantmaking organization with close ties to the corporation providing funds	Endowment and annual contributions from a profit-making corporation. May maintain small endowment and pay out most of contributions received annually in grants, or may maintain endowment to cover contributions in years when corporate profits are down	Decisions made by board of directors often composed of corporate officials, but which may include individuals with no corporate affiliation. Decisions may also be made by local company officials	Giving tends to be in fields related to corporate activities or in communities where corporation operates. Usually give more grants but in smaller dollar amounts than independent foundations	Same as above
Operating Foundation	An organization which uses its resources to conduct research or provide a direct service	Endowment usually provided from a single source, but eligible for maximum tax deductible contributions from public	Decisions generally made by independent board of directors	Makes few, if any, grants. Grants generally related directly to the foundation's program	Same as above
Community Foundation	A publicly-supported organization which makes grants for social, educational, religious, or other charitable purposes in a specific community or region	Contributions received from many donors. Usually eligible for maximum tax deductible contributions from public	Decisions made by board of directors representing the diversity of the community	Grants generally limited to charitable organizations in local community	IRS 990 return available to public. Many publish full guidelines or annual reports

their endowments are frequently composed of a number of different trust funds, some of which bear their donor's names. Their grantmaking activities are administered by a governing body or distribution committee representative of community interests. Investment funds are managed professionally, usually by trustee banks.

Because of the nature of their support and their other philanthropic activities, nearly all community foundations qualify as "public charities" under the Internal Revenue Code. As such, they are not subject to the excise tax and other regulatory provisions that apply to private foundations, and their donors are able to claim maximum tax deductions for their contributions.

HISTORICAL BACKGROUND

The concept of private philanthropy dates back to ancient times, but legal provision for the creation, control, and protection of charitable funds (the forerunners of today's foundations) was not established until 1601 when England enacted the Statute of Charitable Uses; this granted certain privileges to private citizens or groups of citizens in exchange for their willingness to serve the public good by performing or supporting acts of charity. Since then, legal doctrines in the common law countries have generally preserved this status for all types of charitable organizations, including foundations, churches, hospitals, and colleges, ensuring their right to tax exemption and to existence in perpetuity as long as they meet the test of serving a charitable function.

Most early foundations were established for the benefit of particular institutions or to answer specific social problems, such as feeding or housing the poor. In the late nineteenth and early twentieth centuries, a different approach to foundation philanthropy was introduced in the United States, represented by the establishment of the Carnegie Corporation of New York (1911) and The Rockefeller Foundation (1913). These "modern" foundations were given broad charters enabling their directors to address the causes of and seek solutions to problems affecting the world, rather than to focus solely on alleviating the results of social problems. This approach has led foundations to support, for example, research to determine the causes of disease instead of, or in addition to, providing support for the operation of clinics or hospitals.

The number of foundations established in the U.S. has grown significantly since those early days. In the decade following World War II, there was a large increase in the number of foundations established which has been attributed to the high tax rates resulting from the war, the emergence of company-sponsored foundations, and a new emphasis on family foundations with living donors.

Since the 1950s there has been a gradual decline in the number of new foundations established—a fact which some have attributed to increased regu-

lation and taxation of foundations, questions about the favorability of corporate direct giving programs over company-sponsored foundations, and changes
in the overall economy. According to The Foundation Center's most recent analysis of the establishment dates of foundations currently holding assets of $1
million or more or awarding annual grants totaling at least $100,000, there has
been a significant decline in the establishment of private foundations in the decade following passage of the 1969 Tax Reform Act. These findings were con-
firmed in a recent study released by the General Accounting Office ("Statistical
Analysis of the Operation and Activities of Private Foundations," January 5,
1984), which reported a 59 percent drop in the creation of new grantmaking
foundations between the 1960s and the 1970s.

The community foundation movement in America began in the early twentieth century. The first community trust, The Cleveland Foundation, was established in 1914 by Frederick H. Goff who believed "that better results and greater
efficiency could be secured if the management and control of the property dedicated to charitable use in each community could be centralized in one or at
most a few governing bodies." According to F. Emerson Andrews in *Philanthropic Giving* (Russell Sage, 1950), "the idea of the community trust was ac-
cepted enthusiastically, especially by officers of trust companies, and organizations were set up at the initiative of banks in many towns and cities." Today
there are over 200 community foundations across the country, and they continue to be a significant force in the philanthropic community.

REGULATION OF FOUNDATIONS

Nonprofit organizations that are defined as private foundations by the Internal Revenue Service must be organized and operated under specific regulations, which are primarily derived from the Tax Reform Act of 1969 with some
modifications as a result of the 1976 Tax Reform Act, the Economic Recovery
Tax Act of 1981 (ERTA), and the 1984 Tax Reform Act. The Tax Reform Act of
1969 established the criteria described earlier for distinguishing private foundations from public charities and set up a separate category for operating foundations with a more favorable tax status.

The 1969 Act set forth special rules prohibiting self-dealing between foundations and their donors, restricting foundation ownership and control of private business, limiting the percentage of an individual's annual income that
can be donated to a private foundation as a tax-deductible contribution, and
regulating foundation giving to individuals, other foundations, non-exempt organizations, and activities that influence legislation or political campaigns. To
offset costs incurred by the IRS in regulating tax-exempt organizations, the
1969 Act imposed an excise tax on foundations at the rate of 4 percent of their

net investment income. In 1979, Congress reduced the excise tax to 2 percent, effective for accounting years beginning after September 30, 1977.

The 1969 Act also included specific rules requiring a private foundation to distribute or use for charitable purposes all of their "adjusted net income" or a variable percent of the market value of that year's investment assets. The variable percentage was eliminated by the Tax Reform Act of 1976 and defined as the greater of 5 percent of the market value of assets or all of their net investment income. The Economic Recovery Tax Act of 1981 again amended the payout requirement so that private foundations need pay out only 5 percent of the market value of their investment assets, regardless of how much earned income they received, effective for tax years beginning on or after January 1, 1982.

A reporting requirement was also enacted with the 1969 legislation which called for foundations to file two annual information returns with the IRS (Form 990-AR and 990-PF), to make the forms available for inspection by the public, and to file copies of the forms with state authorities in states where the foundation is incorporated and maintains its principal offices. Beginning in 1982, foundations have been required to file only one form, a revised version of the Form 990-PF which incorporates all information previously required on the separate forms and calls for additional information on the foundation's grant-making policies.

Foundation regulation was the focus of extensive hearings before the House Subcommittee on Oversight of the Ways and Means Committee in the Spring of 1983. These hearings constituted the first full-scale reexamination of private foundations since 1969. Testimony from representatives of the foundation community and a wide variety of nonprofit organizations addressed, among many other topics, the effects of various aspects of current regulations on the birth and termination of foundations, the giving policies of foundations as related to individuals and to voter registration efforts, and the business holdings and investment policies of foundations.

As a result of these hearings, a number of changes in the rules and regulations affecting private foundations were incorporated into the Tax Reform Act of 1984 which was signed into law in July, 1984. This Act reduced the excise tax rate on a foundation's net investment income from 2 percent to 1 percent if the foundation's payout for charitable purposes is increased by an equivalent. The percentage of an individual's annual income which can be donated to a private foundation as a tax-deductible contribution was raised from 20 percent to 30 percent, and contributions in excess of 30 percent of the donor's annual income may be carried over for five years. Administrative expenses incurred in making grants or directly conducting charitable programs may account for no more than 15 percent of the foundation's qualifying distributions. In other words, a foundation is now required to pay out amounts equal to 4.25 percent of its net assets in grants or contributions. Grant administrative expenses can be added to that amount to meet the overall 5 percent qualifying distributions requirement.

HOW MANY FOUNDATIONS ARE THERE?

The Foundation Center's analysis of the Internal Revenue Service transaction files covering the annual information returns (Form 990-PF) filed by private foundations in 1981, 1982, and 1983 shows that there are 23,578 active private grantmaking foundations and 1,309 operating foundations that did not award grants to outside groups in their latest fiscal reporting year.

The combined Internal Revenue Service file for those three years also contains records for 542 foundations that have terminated operations and filed final returns as of 1983, another 904 foundations that are considered inactive because current filing records (1980 or later) are not available, and 4,023 organizations that did not award grants to outside organizations in their latest fiscal year but that are not classified as operating foundations. In general, these 4,023 are organizations that were intended to operate as publicly-supported charities but failed to attract the required public support, and therefore have been classified under the statutory definition of a private foundation under the tax laws. These organizations were not intended to and do not fulfill the philanthropic function commonly ascribed to private foundations and therefore are not included in The Foundation Center's statistical analyses.

In fiscal year 1983, grantmaking foundations held combined assets of $67.8 billion and awarded grants totaling nearly $4.5 billion. Private non-operating foundations, which encompass both independent and company-sponsored foundations, are by far the largest group and account for 94 percent of the total assets and 93 percent of the grants awarded by foundations.

Foundations are located in every state of the union, with a major concentration in the Northeast. New York foundations alone account for 19 percent of all foundation assets. The relatively unequal distribution of foundation assets across the country is rooted in past economic and industrial development patterns and the personal preferences of the founders. This is offset to some extent by the funding policies of the large national foundations that give substantial amounts outside the states in which they are located. Rising economic and industrial growth patterns in the South, Southwest, and Pacific Coast states have stimulated a higher rate of growth in foundation assets in those areas. A recent analysis of the nation's 4,400 largest foundations (*The Foundation Directory*, Edition 10) revealed that although 54 percent of the assets held by these foundations is concentrated in the Middle Atlantic and East North Central states, foundations in these regions have experienced a much slower growth rate in terms of assets than other regions over the last six years.

2

Where Foundations Fit
in the Total Funding Picture

ALTHOUGH THE FOUNDATION STATISTICS presented in the preceding chapter are impressive, it's important to put them in perspective. Private foundation giving represents only a small portion of all private philanthropic contributions, which in turn account for a relatively small percentage of the total support for nonprofit organizations.

According to estimates in *Giving U.S.A.*, published by the American Association of Fund-Raising Counsel, Inc., private philanthropic contributions in 1984 totaled $74.25 billion. The largest portion of these contributions—$66.44 billion or 89.5 percent—came from individual donors through gifts or bequests. Foundations accounted for 5.8 percent of this total, and corporations and corporate foundations were responsible for 4.7 percent of total estimated private giving.

In *Dimensions of the Independent Sector* (Washington, D.C.: Independent Sector, 1984), Virginia Hodgkinson and Murray Weitzman reported that private contributions accounted for only 28 percent of the total support for nonprofit organizations in 1980. While religious organizations and arts and cultural groups are heavily dependent on private contributions for support, receiving respectively 86 percent and 62 percent of their total funding from private gifts, health organizations received a scant 9 percent of their total funding from private donors, and educational institutions and social service agencies received 16 percent and 30 percent of their funding from private gifts, respectively.

FIGURE 2. Private Philanthropic Contributions in 1984 (in billions of dollars)

Source	Amount	Percent
Individuals	$61.55	82.9%
Bequests	$ 4.89	6.6%
Foundations	$ 4.36	5.8%
Corporations	$ 3.45	4.7%

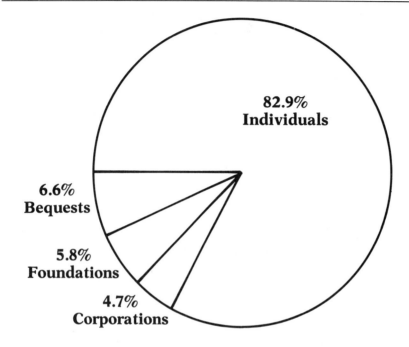

SOURCE: *Giving USA Annual Report 1985: A compilation of facts and trends on American philanthropy for the year 1984*. New York: American Association of Fund-Raising Counsel, Inc. (AAFRC), 1985.

FIGURE 3. Percentage Distribution of Annual Sources of Support for Independent Sector Organizations: 1980

Source of Funds	All Independent Sector Dollars[1]	All Independent Sector Percent	Religious Organizations	Arts/ Culture	Health Services	Education/ Research	Social Services
Government Sector	$40.3	25.2%	—	24.0%	34.3%	16.4%	34.0%
Private contributions	44.7	28.0	86.1%	62.0	8.9	15.5	30.2
Dues, fees, charges	61.7	38.5	—	10.0	48.7	53.1	25.2
Endowments	8.1	5.1	4.4	2.0	1.4	5.5	3.8
Other receipts	5.1	3.2	9.4	2.0	6.7	9.5	6.9

[1]in billions of dollars.

SOURCE: *Dimensions of the Independent Sector*, edition 1, p. 45. Virginia Ann Hodgkinson and Murray S. Weitzman. Washington, DC: Independent Sector, 1984. © Independent Sector, 1984.

The same Independent Sector report shows that nearly 47 percent of the support for nonprofit organizations is drawn from dues, fees, and other charges for services and goods and from income earned on endowments. This is most true for health services organizations and educational institutions, which respectively derive 57 percent and 68 percent of their support from earned income. Social services and arts organizations derive only 36 percent and 14 percent, respectively, of their total support from earned income.

Government is a key source of support for many nonprofit organizations, according to the Independent Sector report. Government funding accounted for 25 percent of the total revenues of nonprofits in 1980, with health organizations and social service agencies each receiving 34 percent of their total support from government sources.

Reductions in federal spending in areas where nonprofit organizations have been active have had a great impact on the funding patterns of many nonprofit organizations. A recent study conducted by the Urban Institute revealed that from 1980 to 1984, "nonprofit social service organizations lost an estimated 37 percent of their federal support; nonprofit community development and advocacy organizations lost 29 percent; and nonprofit arts and culture organizations—which relied least on government support to start with—46 percent.

The changes in federal funding have focused increased attention on private philanthropy. Although there is evidence of significant increases in private giving, it is clear that these increases can only fill a small portion of the gap left by federal cutbacks. The result for grantseekers is an even more competitive fundraising market and a greater need to explore all possible channels of support and revenue.

GOVERNMENT GRANTS

Despite cutbacks in federal spending, government is still a key source of support for nonprofit organizations. Support may come in the form of direct grants or contracts for specific services an organization performs for a government agency. All nonprofits will want to become familiar with the activities and funding programs of the federal, state, and local government agencies with responsibility for their service area.

Information about federal government programs is available through a variety of sources. *The United States Government Manual*, issued by the Office of the Federal Register, describes the broad program responsibilities of all government departments and affiliated agencies, such as the National Endowment for the Arts and Humanities and the National Science Foundation. Although grantmaking and contract programs are not outlined specifically, most agency descriptions include information on publications and brochures available from the agency and how to obtain them. You may want to write to the agencies working in your field to have your name added to their mailing lists for program announcements and other funding information.

The primary resource on federal funding is the *Catalog of Federal Domestic Assistance,* issued annually in June by the Office of Management and Budget with an update in December. The catalog lists all federal funding programs available to state and local governments, for-profit and nonprofit institutions, and individuals. Descriptions of each program provide detailed information on the purpose of the program, eligibility requirements, and application procedures. Indexes by sponsoring agency, subject, functional categories, and eligible applicant groups help users to identify the funding programs most suited to their needs. Copies of the catalog are available in many public libraries or they may be purchased from the Government Printing Office.

In addition to the *Catalog,* the Office of Management and Budget maintains a computer database known as the Federal Assistance Programs Retrieval System (FAPRS) to provide rapid access to federal assistance program information. States have designated access points where computer searches of FAPRS may be requested and grantseekers with their own computer terminals may arrange for direct access to the system through commercial time-sharing companies. For further information on FAPRS, write: Federal Program Information Branch, Room 6001, Budget Review Division, Office of Management and Budget, 726 Jackson Place, NW, Washington, DC 20503.

There are two other key resources for information on federal funding. *The Federal Register* is published weekdays and presents proposed and final rules and regulations developed by all federal agencies as well as information on program deadlines and application procedures. Each issue has a highlights page which can be skimmed for pertinent material. Bid requests for federal contracts are published in *Commerce Business Daily.* Government agencies contract for a wide variety of goods and services, ranging from manufacturing of office supplies to training and education programs. Although it takes some time to learn the acronyms and abbreviations which fill the listings in *Commerce Business Daily,* this is an invaluable resource for anyone interested in marketing their goods and services to the government.

Information about state and local government funding programs is not always so readily available. Most state and large municipal governments issue some type of guidebook or manual listing departments and agencies with their addresses and brief descriptions of their program responsibilities. Check with your local public library to find out about the specific resources available for your area. Sometimes the offices of state senators and congressional representatives can also guide you to appropriate sources of local funding information.

CORPORATE GRANTS

As the federal government cut back its funding for social service, education, and arts programs, the call went out for private sources, notably businesses and corporations, to fill in the gaps in their local communities. The tax deduction limit for charitable contributions was raised from 5 percent to 10 percent of a company's pre-tax earnings in an effort to increase corporate giving levels, and a special Task Force on Private Sector Initiatives was established to explore ways to encourage private giving and greater involvement of corporations in their communities. While it is evident that corporate giving, indeed, private giving, will not be able to fill the gaps left by federal budget cuts, more and more nonprofit organizations are beginning to regard both major corporations and local business as important sources of support.

Corporations may make charitable contributions through a direct giving program administered within the corporation or through a separate company-sponsored foundation. Company-sponsored foundations, as noted in Chapter 1, are classified as private foundations under the Internal Revenue Code and are subject to the same rules and regulations as other private foundations. A corporate foundation is often used by the parent company as a way of setting aside funds to maintain charitable giving in years when profits are lower. Direct giving programs, on the other hand, are subject to fewer regulations, but because funds are drawn directly from a single year's pre-tax earnings, they are more vulnerable to the ups-and-downs of the company's profits and losses.

Many corporations choose to make charitable contributions through both a separate foundation and a direct giving program. There is often little difference in the giving interests and procedures of these two vehicles, and they may even be administered by the same staff and board. There are significant differences, however, in the type and amount of information available about these two funding programs.

By law, company-sponsored foundations must report annually on their activities and grant programs to the IRS on the same Form 990-PF used by all private foundations. Many company foundations also issue annual reports or information brochures detailing their program interests and application procedures. Information on company foundations is included in The Foundation Center's directories and reference publications outlined in Section II of this book.

Corporations are not required to make public information on contributions and grants made directly through the corporation. Although a growing number of corporations are choosing to publicize their giving interests and restrictions and application procedures, it is generally much more difficult to research direct corporate giving programs.

A number of published directories and guides which do provide information on corporate funders are listed in the bibliography in Appendix D. To find out about corporations in your community or in a specific industry, check with the business reference department of your local public library for such sources as *Standard and Poor's Register of Corporations, Dun and Bradstreet Reference Book of Corporate Management*, Chamber of Commerce directories, and corporate annual reports. Other readily available but commonly overlooked resources are the yellow pages of local telephone books.

Corporations often donate goods and services in addition to providing financial support. These "in-kind" contributions can include product overruns or obsolete models manufactured or distributed by the company, office space or furniture and equipment, paper and printing services, and even consulting services from company employees. Again, the information provided in Appendix D outlines some of the approaches and resources nonprofit organizations can use to tap this important funding source.

INDIVIDUAL DONORS

According to the American Association of Fund-Raising Counsel, individuals are by far the largest single source of private philanthropic dollars. Their contributions range from a few pennies to millions of dollars and from used appliances and clothing to priceless art collections. Many individuals also contribute another priceless resource, their time.

There are a number of different approaches nonprofit organizations use to raise money from individual donors, including direct mail appeals, door-to-door solicitation, membership programs, special fundraising events, deferred giving programs—the list could go on and on. Numerous guides and handbooks which detail these approaches have been published, and some of the more heavily-used titles are listed in the fundraising bibliography in Appendix A.

Building a network of individual supporters is an essential component of most fundraising efforts. It demonstrates to other funders, such as corporations and foundations, that the people in your community believe in and support the programs of your organization. It gives your organization a broader, and often more reliable, funding base, and can help your organization stay more closely in touch with the needs and interests of the community you are trying to serve.

EARNED INCOME

A recent analysis conducted by Independent Sector of the annual sources of support for nonprofit organizations revealed that approximately 38 percent of their total support revenues in 1980 were derived from dues, fees, and other earned income receipts. With the retrenchment in federal funding since 1980, more and more nonprofit organizations have turned to income-producing ventures and new dues and fees structures to cover the costs of operating their programs.

For many nonprofit organizations, increasing their earned income has meant simply establishing a fee structure for goods and services they had previously supplied free of charge. Other nonprofits have looked at opportunities to capitalize on their existing resources to make money, renting out unused office or meeting space, computer time or services, and equipment, or selling existing training or information services to businesses and other clients who can afford to pay. Still other organizations have taken a more ambitious approach to raise funds through such ventures as gift shops, publications, travel services, etc.

Much has been written in recent years about the pros and cons of income-producing enterprise for nonprofit organizations as well as about how nonprofit organizations can assess their profit-making potential. A number of these resources are listed in Appendix A for those who wish to explore this channel of support in more depth.

RELIGIOUS ORGANIZATIONS

Churches, temples, and other religious organizations are more often thought of as recipients of charitable contributions than as potential funding sources. Yet a recent study conducted by the Council on Foundations (*The Philanthropy of Organized Religion*, 1985) revealed that religious organizations contribute a minimum of $7.5 billion annually for a wide range of charitable programs.

While many religious institutions operate their own service programs, nearly half of the 485 respondents to the Council on Foundations' survey reported that they make grants or loans to outside organizations engaged in activities they wish to promote. These activities included a range of direct social service programs, community organizing and advocacy programs, and education and research. The final report of the study provides a list of the organizations that reported making grants, loans, or alternative investments.

Relatively little has been written about the best approaches to religious institutions for funding support, and there are few directories or lists of religious bodies that do provide outside support. Still, nonprofit organizations should be aware of this potential source of support for their programs and activities, particularly those who are active in social services or social justice programs, and begin to investigate churches, synagogues, and other religious bodies in their community to learn more about local funding programs.

3

Who Gets Foundation Grants?

THE OVERWHELMING MAJORITY of foundation grants are awarded to non-profit organizations which qualify for "public charity" status under Section 501(c)(3) of the Internal Revenue Code. An organization may qualify for this tax-exempt status if it is organized and operated exclusively for charitable, religious, educational, scientific, or literary purposes, testing for public safety, fostering national or international amateur sports competition (but only if its activities do not involve the provision of athletic facilities or equipment), or the prevention of cruelty to children or animals. These tax-exempt organizations must also certify that no part of their earnings will benefit private shareholders or individuals and that they will not, as a substantial part of their activities, attempt to influence legislation or participate in political campaigns for or against any candidate for public office.

Under federal law, foundations are permitted to make grants to individuals and to organizations that do not qualify for "public charity" status if they follow a set of very specific rules covering "expenditure responsibility." Essentially, these rules for expenditure responsibility involve a number of financial and other reports to certify that the funds were spent solely for the charitable purposes spelled out in the grant agreement and that no part of the funds was spent to influence legislation. Provisions for grants to individuals require advance approval from the IRS and prohibit giving to "disqualified persons"—a broad category covering contributors to the foundation and their relatives, foundation managers, and certain public officials. Although some foundations have instituted such giving programs, they represent a very small portion of foundation dollars.

NONPROFIT ORGANIZATIONS

Foundations award grants to a wide variety of nonprofit organizations, depending on the giving interests and restrictions of the particular foundation. Some may confine their giving to nonprofit organizations that provide services to the foundation's home community. Others may confine their giving to a specific type of institution or to organizations active in a specific subject area, such as medical research, higher education, music, or youth services. Still others focus their giving on major national organizations in a wide variety of fields. The research strategies outlined in Section II of this guide are designed to help nonprofits identify foundations that are likely to fund organizations similar to their own in subject focus, geographic location, and size.

Virtually all foundations you identify through these funding research procedures will want to know that your organization has received official status with the IRS as a 501(c)(3) organization and will ask to see a copy of your IRS exemption letter. Depending on the particular state you are located in, the foundation may also wish to see that your organization has received the appropriate state certification for tax-exempt charitable organizations. If your organization has not yet received tax-exempt status, you will want to read the IRS booklet *How to Apply for and Retain Tax-Exempt Status for Your Organization* (IRS Publication 557). Copies can be obtained by calling the Tax Information number in your phonebook listed under "United States Government, Internal Revenue Service." In some telephone directories, there is a special listing of federal government offices and their phone numbers in the back of the book.

The process of incorporating as a tax-exempt, nonprofit organization is regulated under federal, state, and sometimes local legislation. It is advisable to consult an attorney, preferably one with nonprofit experience, who can guide you through this process. There are also a number of handbooks and texts available that examine the issues you should consider in structuring your organization and explain the application procedures and legal ramifications involved in incorporating as a tax-exempt organization. A number of these publications are listed in the bibliography in Appendix A and are available for free examination at many Foundation Center cooperating libraries.

Nonprofits who do not yet have their official tax-exempt ruling are not entirely closed out of the grantseeking process. Many nonprofits may choose to affiliate with another established organization that is eligible to receive foundation grants and that is willing to exercise administrative and expenditure

FIGURE 4. List of IRS District Offices

Alabama 35233...................................... 500 22d St. S., Birmingham
Alaska 99501... 310 K St., Anchorage
Arizona 85004....................................... 2120 N. Central Ave., Phoenix
Arkansas 77201 .... 700 W. Capitol Ave., Little Rock
California:
    Laguna Niguel 92677 .... 2400 Avila Rd.
    Los Angeles 90012 .... 300 N. Los Angeles St.
    Sacramento 95825........................... 2345 Fair Oaks Blvd.
    San Francisco 94102 .... 450 Golden Gate Ave.
    San Jose 95113 .... Suite 300, 1 N. 1st St.
Colorado 80265 .... 1050 17th St., Denver
Connecticut 06103 .... 135 High St., Hartford
Delaware 19801..................................... 844 King St., Wilmington
District of Columbia (part of Balti-
    more District
Florida 32202 .... 400 W. Bay St., Jacksonville
Georgia 30043 .... 275 Peachtree St. NE, Atlanta
Hawaii 96813 .... 300 Ala Moana Blvd., Honolulu
Idaho 83724.. 550 W. Fort St., Boise
Illinois:
    Chicago 60604................................. 230 S. Dearborn St.
    Springfield 62701 .... 320 W. Washington St.
Indiana 46204....................................... 575 N. Pennsylvania, Indianapolis
Iowa 50309 .... 210 Walnut St., Des Moines
Kansas 67202 .... 412 S. Main, Wichita
Kentucky 40202 .... 601 W. Broadway, Louisville
Louisiana 70130 .... 500 Camp St., New Orleans
Maine 04330 .... 68 Sewall St., Augusta
Maryland 21201 .... 31 Hopkins Plaza, Baltimore
Massachusetts 02203 .... John F. Kennedy Federal Bldg., Boston
Michigan 48226..................................... 477 Michigan Ave., Detroit
Minnesota 55101 .... 316 N. Robert St., St. Paul
Mississippi 39269................................. 100 W. Capitol St., Jackson
Missouri 63101 .... 1114 Market St., St. Louis
Montana 59601...................................... 301 S. Park Ave., Helena
Nebraska 68102..................................... 106 S. 15th St., Omaha
Nevada 89509.. 300 Booth St., Reno
New Hampshire 03801 .... 80 Daniel St., Portsmouth
New Jersey 07102 .... 970 Broad St., Newark
New Mexico 87101................................ 517 Gold Ave. SW, Albuquerque

FIGURE 4 (cont.)

New York:
Albany 12207	Clinton Ave. and N. Pearl St.
Brooklyn 11201	35 Tillary St.
Buffalo 14202	111 W. Huron St.
Manhattan 10007	120 Church St., New York

North Carolina 27401 .... 320 Federal Pt., Greensboro
North Dakota 58102............................. 653 2d Ave. N., Fargo
Ohio:
Cincinnati 45202	550 Main St.
Cleveland 44199	1240 E. 9th St.

Oklahoma 73102 .... 200 NW 4th St., Oklahoma City
Oregon 97204 .... 1220 SW 3d Ave., Portland
Pennsylvania:
Philadelphia 19106	600 Arch St.
Pittsburgh 15222	1000 Liberty Ave.

Puerto Rico (*see* Foreign Operations   Carlos E. Chardon St., Hato Rey
    District)
Rhode Island 02903 .... 380 Westminster Mall, Providence
South Carolina 29201 .... 1835 Assembly St., Columbia
South Dakota 57401............................. 115 4th Ave. SE, Aberdeen
Tennessee 37203.................................. 801 Broadway, Nashville
Texas:
Austin 78701	300 E. 8th St.
Dallas 75242	1100 Commerce St.
Houston 77042	3223 Briorpark

Utah 84111 .... 465 S. 4th East, Salt Lake City
Vermont 05401 .... 11 Elmwood Ave., Burlington
Virgin Islands (*see* Foreign Oper-   22 Crystal Glade, Charlotte Amalie, St.
    ations District)   Thomas
Virginia 23240...................................... 400 N. 8th St., Richmond
Washington 98174 .... 915 2d Ave., Seattle
West Virginia 26101............................. 425 Juliana St., Parkersburg
Wisconsin 53202 .... 517 E. Wisconsin Ave., Milwaukee
Wyoming 82001 .... 308 W. 21st St. Cheyenne
Foreign Operations District   1325 K St., NW, Washington, DC
    20225 ....

responsibility or to take on the new project on a contract basis. Many of the general fundraising and nonprofit management guides listed in Appendix A outline these options in more detail and suggest approaches you might take to securing a sponsor or host for your project.

INDIVIDUALS

Under the provisions of the 1969 Tax Reform Act, private foundations may make grants to individuals for "travel, study, or other similar purposes," if they obtain advance approval from the IRS of their selection criteria and procedures. These procedures must ensure an objective selection process and require extensive follow-up reports that demonstrate adequate performance and appropriate expenditures of the grant funds by the individual receiving the grant.

The Foundation Center's research indicates that only 975 of the approximately 24,000 active private grantmaking foundations currently make grants directly to individuals. These programs are described in the Center's publication, *Foundation Grants to Individuals*. Nearly two-thirds of these funding programs are for educational aid, including scholarships, fellowships, and loans.

Individuals seeking financial aid for education should be sure to consult with the financial aid office at their school. In addition, there are a number of guides and directories which describe grant programs open to individuals through government, corporations, labor unions, educational institutions, and a variety of trade associations and nonprofit agencies. Many public, school, and university libraries maintain collections of these funding information resources that you may consult free of charge.

Individuals seeking funds for research or special projects other than their own education may wish to affiliate with a nonprofit organization in their field that can act as a sponsor for a foundation grant. Universities, hospitals, churches, schools, arts organizations, and theaters are just a few of the many types of nonprofits that have received and administered foundation grants directed to specific individuals.

There are, of course, a wide variety of funding sources beyond foundations that are open to individuals. Several general reference books (such as *The Annual Register of Grant Support*, *The Grants Register*, and *Awards, Honors, and Prizes*) describe grant programs available through government agencies, corporations, associations, and other nonprofit groups in such diverse fields as sports, religion, medicine, and performing arts. There are also a number of special funding guides for individuals in specific subject areas or within specific population groups. A number of the more well-known sources of information about funding for individuals are listed in Appendix C.

PROFIT-MAKING ORGANIZATIONS

It is possible under the 1969 Tax Reform Act for foundations to make grants for specific projects that are clearly charitable in nature to organizations that are not tax-exempt if they exercise "expenditure responsibility." While foundations rarely, if ever, award grants to profit-making groups, they may sometimes offer loans or "program-related investments" (PRIs) if the for-profit organization's program is related to the foundation's funding interests.

A program-related investment is an equity investment, loan, or loan guarantee to a for-profit or nonprofit institution to further the foundation's charitable purposes. PRIs are often made to increase low-income and minority ownership of business and property, to aid businesses that cannot find adequate commercial support but whose existence is an important component of the foundation's program goals, or to provide training or employment opportunities in disadvantaged communities. For example, PRIs can help in the development and strengthening of financial and investment institutions in disadvantaged communities and in persuading other capital sources to invest more of their resources in such communities.

Unlike grants, PRIs must be repaid, sometimes with the addition of a low interest rate, and they are governed by strict regulations that require greater administrative attention than conventional grants. Foundations must prove that the funds are spent only for the designated charitable purpose and that the loan recipient could not have secured funding through normal financial resources. Still, there are a number of foundations that have reported an interest in or have a history of making program-related investments.

Grantseekers interested in program-related investments should contact the Cooperative Assistance Fund (CAF) and the Local Initiatives Support Corporation (LISC) for further information. CAF represents several foundations that pool their funds to make program-related investments primarily for the economic development of low-income urban and rural communities. Their annual report and criteria for investments can be obtained by writing Cooperative Assistance Fund, 2021 K Street, NW, Suite 701, Washington, DC 20006. The Local Initiatives Support Corporation is a nonprofit lending and grantmaking institution that assists experienced community development corporations to improve the physical and economic conditions of their communities. You can obtain their "Statement of Policy and Operating Guidelines" by writing Local Initiatives Support Corporation, 666 Third Avenue, New York, NY 10017.

Two Foundation Center publications, *Source Book Profiles* and *The Foundation Directory, 10th Edition*, provide access to foundations interested in program-related investments in their indexes by "type of support." Further information on how to use these resources is provided in Section II of this book.

Section II

The Search for
Appropriate Funders

4

Planning Precedes
the Proposal

Every year, foundations receive thousands of requests for funding, and competition for scarce foundation resources appears to be growing increasingly intense. It is estimated that less than 7 percent of these requests eventually result in the support they seek. Many proposals fail because there are simply never enough funds to go around, but a large number of requests are denied because the application clearly falls outside the foundation's areas of interest or geographic scope. Some applications are poorly prepared and do not reflect a careful analysis of the applicant organization's needs, its credibility, or its capacity to carry out the project proposed.

The key to successful foundation fundraising—indeed, to any successful fundraising effort—is HOMEWORK. Your homework begins with a careful analysis of your organization, what it is trying to accomplish, and what it needs in order to best fulfill its goals. Once you have completed this essential planning and self-assessment phase, you're ready to begin tracking down those foundations whose giving records or stated objectives are most directly related to your organization's goals and who are most likely to provide the support you need.

In the face of this hard truth, some grantseekers decide to let the law of averages do their work for them. They mail copies of their proposal to some easily targeted groups, such as the largest foundations in the country or in their state or foundations whose names can be readily found in a newspaper article or a book. There is no way to overemphasize the fact that this mass mailing approach just doesn't work. Foundations are only too aware of this technique, and the groups that use it do their cause no good. It's not only a waste of effort and postage; it can damage your reputation as well. So do your homework carefully, and be sure it shows. Explore all of the resources described in this guide, and let the foundations you approach know exactly why you feel your program matches their interests.

KNOWING YOUR ORGANIZATION

The importance of program planning has been stated and restated so often that it has begun to sound trite. Yet far too many nonprofit organizations get so caught up in the press of daily activities and financial crises that they shunt this critical process aside. There is simply no activity that is more important than careful analysis and planning of your organization's program and financial needs. Without it, no amount of foundation research will save the day.

Joseph Breiteneicher, Managing Trustee of the Bird Foundation and President of Pemberton Management Company, states the case clearly in his booklet *Quest for Funds*:

> "I spend some time each day trying to guess which proposals have been generated out of panic and which ones are the results of reasoned approaches to organization's agendas. I can figure out the quality requests and my peers can too. With the increasingly fierce competition for diminishing monies, groups should recognize that fund-raising planning is an essential, not a frill."

Scores of useful guides and handbooks on program planning and nonprofit management are available to help you through this process. We've listed many of these publications in the bibliography in Appendix A, and we won't try to reinvent the wheel here. There are, however, a few basic facts you need to have at your fingertips before you can plot your best approach to find appropriate foundation funding sources.

First of all, you need to know if your organization is structured so that it may receive foundation grants. In Chapter 3, we discussed the different types of groups that are eligible for foundation funding. As we noted, most foundations limit their giving to organizations that have received 501(c)(3) tax-exempt status from the Internal Revenue Service, and therefore the procedures outlined in this section will focus on those groups. Individuals seeking grant support should refer to Appendix C.

As a fundraiser for a nonprofit organization, you need to have a clear picture of the purpose of the program for which you are seeking support, the type of support you need, and the amount of money you will need to raise. The checklist in Figure 5 outlines the specific questions you need to answer before you can plan an effective research strategy for identifying appropriate foundation funding sources.

FIGURE 5. Know Your Organization

An effective funding research strategy must be based on a realistic appraisal of the types of foundations that are most likely to be interested in your project. Your first step, then, is to get all relevant aspects of your program clearly in focus.

1. Is your organization structured to receive foundation support? Note date of IRS ruling or agreement with qualified sponsoring organization.

2. What is the central purpose of the activity for which your are seeking funding?_____

   _____

   _____

   _____

   (a) What is the *subject* focus of the activity? _____

   _____

   _____

   (b) What *geographical* area will be served by the activity? _____

   _____

   (c) What *population groups* will benefit from the activity? _____

   _____

   _____

3. How does this activity fit into the central purpose of your organization? _____

   _____

   _____

   _____

FIGURE 5 (cont.)

4. Will this project have impact beyond the immediate geographical area served?

   How? _____

   _____

   _____

   _____

5. What are the unique qualifications of your organization and its staff to accomplish

   the proposed activity?_____

   _____

   _____

   _____

6. What is the total budget for the project? _____

   (a) What *type of support* (building funds, equipment, operating support, etc.) are you

       seeking? _____

   (b) How much foundation support are you seeking? _____

   (c) What other sources of support will be used to meet the project costs? _____

       _____

7. Who has supported or expressed an interest in your organization's programs? (Note

   past and current funders, members of the board of directors, volunteers, etc.) _____

   _____

   _____

   _____

RESEARCH STRATEGIES

Once you have analyzed your organization thoroughly and identified your funding needs, you can begin to develop your strategy for identifying foundations that might be interested in your proposal. You can use a variety of approaches to identify appropriate funding sources, but all of them boil down to three basic steps:

1. Develop a broad list of prospects—that is, foundations that have shown an interest in funding some aspect of your program.

2. Refine your list of prospects to eliminate foundations that are unable or unlikely to fund projects in your subject field or geographic area or that do not provide the type of support you need.

3. Investigate thoroughly the foundations remaining on your list to determine those that are most likely to consider your proposal favorably.

The key to success, once again, is HOMEWORK. The process requires serious, time-consuming research, but it is not difficult or beyond the reach of any nonprofit organization.

Recordkeeping

Throughout the research process, you should gather as many pertinent facts about your funding prospects as possible. Develop careful records on each potential foundation contributor, noting their address, telephone, trustees, staff, financial data, funding patterns, sample grants, prior contacts with the organization, etc. These records should be updated on a regular basis to provide a dynamic, centralized base of funding information for the organization. Developing such a system helps to compensate for one of the biggest problems nonprofits face—the lack of continuity in fundraising efforts resulting from high staff turnover.

It is also important to document your research at every step. As you gather facts about a foundation, note the source and date of the information so that when you discover conflicting information you can quickly determine which is the more current and accurate. Recordkeeping at the outset may seem painfully time-consuming, but is ultimately guaranteed to save you and your organization time and money.

Step One: Developing a Broad Prospect List

The first step in foundation fundraising is to identify foundations that have indicated in their purpose statements or grantmaking activities an interest in funding some aspect of your program. In analyzing your organization and its funding needs, you looked at the subject fields you are active in, the geographic area and the population groups you are serving or want to serve, and the type and amount of grant support you need. The information you outlined on the checklist "Know Your Organization" will help you determine the best research approach for your funding needs.

Our experience at The Foundation Center has led us to recommend three basic strategies you can use to develop a broad list of funding prospects:

1. **The Subject Approach** identifies foundations that have expressed an interest in funding programs in your specific subject field.

2. **The Geographic Approach** identifies foundations that fund programs in a specific city, state, or region.

3. **The Types of Support Approach** identifies foundations that provide specific types of support to nonprofit organizations, such as building construction or renovation, research, endowments, program-related investments, etc.

We'll examine each of these strategies in more depth in subsequent chapters. We recommend that all grantseekers conduct both a subject search to identify foundations with an interest in their field and a geographic search to pinpoint local foundations that might fund them because of the service they provide to the foundation's home community. If your fundraising campaign is geared to a specific type of support, you should also follow that strategy to identify the broadest possible list of foundation prospects.

During this initial phase of your research you will want to focus on certain basic facts about the foundations you discover, including their name, state location, the subject and geographic focus of their grantmaking activities, any stated restrictions on their giving program, and the size and type of grants they typically award. The Initial Prospect Worksheet (Figure 6) is one of the formats most commonly used by grantseekers at The Foundation Center. Many grantseekers will want to develop their own recordkeeping forms, but they should still focus on the same essential facts about each prospect.

FIGURE 6. Initial Prospect List

The Initial Prospect List is used to record basic facts about foundations that have indicated some interest in the subject field or geographic focus of your project or the type of support you are seeking. Be sure to note any restrictions on the foundation's giving program which would prevent it from funding your program. When you have completed your initial prospect list, you will want to complete a Final Prospect Worksheet for each foundation which seems most likely to be interested in funding your project.

Search Approach Used: _____

Resources Consulted: _____

Foundation Name, Address, and E.I. Number:	Subject Interests:	Geographic Focus:	Types of Support Awarded:	Type of Organization Funded:
Listed in:	Limitations:	Limitations:	Limitations:	Limitations:

Foundation Name, Address, and E.I. Number:	Subject Interests:	Geographic Focus:	Types of Support Awarded:	Type of Organization Funded:
Listed in:	Limitations:	Limitations:	Limitations:	Limitations:

FIGURE 6 (cont.)

Foundation Name, Address, and E.I. Number: **Subject Interests:** **Geographic Focus:** **Types of Support Awarded:** **Type of Organization Funded:**

Listed in: **Limitations:** **Limitations:** **Limitations:** **Limitations:**

Foundation Name, Address, and E.I. Number: **Subject Interests:** **Geographic Focus:** **Types of Support Awarded:** **Type of Organization Funded:**

Listed in: **Limitations:** **Limitations:** **Limitations:** **Limitations:**

Foundation Name, Address, and E.I. Number: **Subject Interests:** **Geographic Focus:** **Types of Support Awarded:** **Type of Organization Funded:**

Listed in: **Limitations:** **Limitations:** **Limitations:** **Limitations:**

Step Two: Refining Your List

Once you have developed a broad list of foundation prospects using one or more of the research strategies we will outline, you need to narrow your list to those foundations which are of the most interest and therefore merit further research. You will want to eliminate foundations on your list that:

1. cannot fund projects in your geographic location, even though they may have an interest in your subject field;

2. do not fund projects in your subject area, even though they are located in your community or they provide the type of support you need;

3. cannot provide the type of support you need, e.g., they do not fund endowments or building campaigns, etc.

If you follow the research strategies we outline, you will compile a more manageable list of foundations that merit in-depth investigation without overlooking any potential prospects.

Step Three: Finding Your Most Likely Prospects

The final phase of your research will focus on identifying which of your foundation prospects seem most likely to consider your proposal favorably. During this final research process, which is outlined in depth in Chapter 9, you will be gathering information on the foundation's staff and trustees, its current financial status, its application procedures, and its most recent grantmaking activities. Background information on the foundation's donor or sponsoring company, financial and institutional history, and future plans will not only help you to eliminate prospects that are unlikely to provide funding for your proposal but will also help you to present a more convincing proposal to your final prospects.

LARGE AND SMALL FOUNDATIONS

When we described the world of foundations in Chapter 1, we noted that out of the roughly 24,000 active grantmaking foundations only about 4,400 have assets of over $1 million or annual giving totaling at least $100,000. Even among these 4,400 foundations, there are a relatively small number of large, staffed foundations which operate quite differently from the vast majority of foundations which are far smaller in size and scope.

Though it's always dangerous to make generalizations, there are some differences between these two categories of grantmakers which will be useful to keep in mind as you research and approach particular foundations.

Obviously, larger foundations have more money to give away. Their individual grants also tend to be larger. In many cases, they have paid staff to review and investigate proposals, develop programs, deal with the public, and carry out the directives of the board of trustees. They usually have well-developed statements of program interests and make information on these interests and their application requirements publicly available through annual reports or brochures. The existence of staff generally allows them to participate in seminars, address conferences, and respond to requests from the public for more information about the foundation field and their particular foundation. All of these factors lead to greater visibility for the larger, staffed foundations. This visibility and ease of access also means greater numbers of proposals and increased competition for their grants. Because of the great range of proposals they receive, large foundations can be highly selective even within their own narrowly defined areas of interest. Wishing to maximize their investments, they tend to be particularly interested in funding model or prototype projects with national impact in particular fields.

Smaller foundations are generally more oriented toward giving in their own geographic area, which they may define as their city, county, or state. Within their geographic boundaries, however, they often support a wide range of activities. Though their grants are smaller, they are more likely to give general budgetary support and may also be inclined to continue their support for a longer period of time. With these foundations, geographic location will generally be a more significant factor than the subject focus of a proposal. The lack of staff and the nature of operating a philanthropic organization within a specific community combine to make personal contact with foundation board members more significant in dealing with small foundations.

It is easier to learn about larger foundations for a variety of reasons. Most larger foundations publish materials describing their interests and activities. More than 600 foundations issue annual reports, usually the most complete source of information on a foundation. Most of the foundations currently publishing such reports can be considered large foundations, with assets of more than $1 million or annual grants totaling over $100,000.

Published directories also focus on the larger foundations, describing anywhere from 100 to 4,400 of the top foundations, depending on the publication's criteria. Newspaper articles and journals which discuss foundation-related subjects generally focus on the largest foundations. It is usually best to begin researching large foundations by the subject areas in which they have made grants or stated an interest. Your research strategy will be to identify all large foundations with a demonstrated interest in your subject area and then thoroughly investigate each of them to be sure the particular project fits their general funding pattern in terms of the: (1) size of grant; (2) geographic location of project; (3) type of support needed; and (4) type of recipient organization.

If your project seems more likely to fit the interests of a smaller foundation because of the size of the grant request or the local focus of the project, your research strategy will begin with the development of a complete list of all foundations that are located or make grants in your geographic area. The next step will be to investigate each foundation in your area to find those that: (1) make grants of a size that fits your need: (2) make grants for the type of support you are seeking; (3) are not restricted to funding particular organizations; and (4) are not restricted to subject areas of giving other than your own.

5

Resources
for Researching
Private Foundations

A WIDE RANGE OF MATERIALS is available to help you identify sources of support for your agency or project. The types and number of resources you will use will depend upon the type of foundation support you are seeking and the search strategy you choose to identify appropriate funding sources. Before you can plan the most effective search strategy for your needs, you should become familiar with the basic resources available to you.

Materials that describe private foundations fall under four general categories: indexes to foundation grants awarded in the recent past; directories of foundations; specialized funding directories or guides; and materials generated or published directly by foundations, such as annual reports, brochures, and the information returns (Form 990 or 990-PF) filed annually by foundations with the Internal Revenue Service.

Indexes to foundation grants provide listings of actual grants awarded and enable you to determine the specific subject interests of a foundation, the types and locations of organizations it has funded, the size of the grants it has generally made, and the types of support it has awarded.

Directories of foundations may be national or local in focus, and they vary widely in the amount of information provided. In this publication, we are focusing on the national directories published by The Foundation Center and the state and local foundation directories available through our library network. You should also be aware of the many other foundation directories available from both commercial and nonprofit publishers, many of which are listed in the bibliographies in Appendices A and B. When possible, your research should encompass all pertinent reference books available.

Specialized funding directories or guides enable you to focus on a particular aspect of your fundraising needs, such as a particular field (e.g., the arts, health programs, etc.), population group served (e.g., women, minorities, etc.), or type of grantmaker (e.g., corporations, community foundations, etc.). Some of the most well-known of these directories are listed in the bibliography in Appendix A, but you should also check with your colleagues or local library to learn about others related to your field. A number of journals, periodicals, and newsletters, particularly those issued by professional associations, include regular features or columns on funding possibilities in their fields, so be sure to check for such listings in your professional literature as well.

The annual information returns filed by private foundations (Form 990-PF) are often the only source of information on the grantmaking activities and interests of small foundations. Most other materials generated or published directly by foundations will be used to get detailed information about those foundations you have identified through other resources as potential funding sources for your agency or project.

SOME IMPORTANT CONSIDERATIONS

Once you've gotten a general overview of the available resources, we'll explore the ways you can put these resources to work for you. Most, if not all, of the materials described here can be consulted at the four Center-operated libraries or the nearly 160 cooperating collections around the country listed in Appendix G. Some of the publications described may be useful additions to your organization's library, but we recommend that initially grantseekers invest their time rather than their money. Visit one of our library collections and examine all of the available materials in the field before making any decisions as to what publications to purchase. Use the tools available in the libraries for your initial research, and then decide which publications, if any, you will need immediately at hand on a continuing basis.

When you are examining any publication, you need to be discerning about the quality of the individual resource and its relevance to your funding search. It is especially important to:

- Note the date the book was published and how frequently new editions are issued. You want to be sure you are using the most current edition available.

- Read carefully the introduction and any instructions on how to use the book. You want to know how the information was obtained, how current the information is, and what verification procedures have been used to determine how reliable the information will be.

- Familiarize yourself with the book's format and indexes to analyze how useful it will be in your funding search. What kinds of information about funding sources does it contain?

Taking the time to evaluate the resources prior to using them can save countless hours of time which would be wasted if the information were out-of-date, incomplete, or inaccurate.

INDEXES TO FOUNDATION GRANTS

Indexes to foundation grants help you to identify funders who have demonstrated an interest in your subject or geographic area by examining the actual grants they have awarded. Studying listings of grants a foundation has awarded in the recent past helps grantseekers to understand that foundation's giving priorities in terms of the types of programs or organizations it has funded, the amount of money it has awarded for specific programs, the geographic locations of grant recipients, any special population groups served through its grants, and the types of grant support it has offered.

The Foundation Center maintains a computer database of grants information based on reports of grants of $5,000 and over awarded by about 500 major foundations, including the nation's 100 largest foundations. The database was begun in 1972 and currently contains over 150,000 grant records. Approximately 2,000 new records are added to the database every two months and an additional 20,000 records are added at the end of the year. The information included in the database is made available to grantseekers in a wide variety of formats designed to facilitate their individual funding searches.

Each grant record includes the name and state location of the grantmaker and the organization receiving the grant, the amount of money awarded and the duration of the grant (in other words, how long the grant funds are expected to last), and a brief description of the purpose for which the grant was made. When applicable, a statement of any geographic, subject, or other restrictions on the grantmaker's giving program is also provided (see Figure 7). Foundation

FIGURE 7. Sample Grants Index Database Record

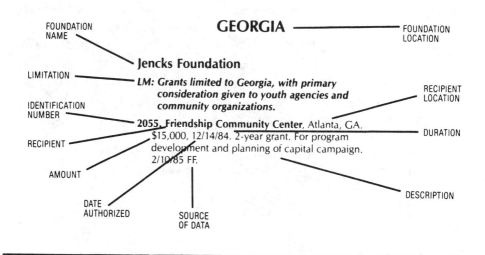

Center editors analyze and index each grant by subject focus, type of organization receiving the grant, special population group served, and the type of support awarded (e.g., endowment, research, building and equipment, etc.).

There are three types of publications produced from the Grants Index Database: *The Foundation Grants Index Annual, COMSEARCH Printouts,* and *The Foundation Grants Index Bimonthly.* Each Grants Index database publication is designed to offer a different mode of access to the information in the database. As you become more skilled at foundation research, you will be able to decide immediately which of the resources will be most useful for you, but in the beginning it's a good idea to use all of them and to become familiar with their contents and formats.

The Foundation Grants Index Annual

During the course of a year, The Foundation Center receives information about thousands of grants. These are entered into the database and cumulated for inclusion in *The Foundation Grants Index Annual.* To date, the *Annual* is the most comprehensive subject index to the actual grants of major U.S. foundations.

The Foundation Grants Index Annual offers access to information on more than 43 percent of all grant dollars awarded annually by private foundations. The volume is arranged by state, then alphabetically by foundation name.

Grants are listed alphabetically under the appropriate foundation by the name of the recipient organization. Several indexes are provided which enable you to customize your foundation search depending upon your needs.

- The Subject Index identifies grants by specific key words and phrases in education, health services, counseling and welfare, the humanities and performing arts, library systems, medical research, environmental improvement, youth programs, and scores of other subjects. This allows you to identify your project or program by a multitude of subject terms and then to use the index to gain access to the grants listed in the main body of the book.

- The Recipient Name Index helps you to locate records of grants that have been awarded to specific organizations. This makes it possible for you to identify foundations that have funded organizations that have goals or service programs similar to yours.

- The Recipient Category Index cross-indexes types of recipient organizations with the type of support received. Since many foundations are unable to provide certain types of support (general, operating, building funds, etc.), this index will speed your search for foundations interested in providing agencies similar to yours with the type of support you need.

- The Subject/Geographic Index lists grant record numbers under approximately 50 broad subject areas by the state location of the recipient. Because of the geographic and subject restrictions of many foundations, this cross-indexing of fields of interest and state locations enables you to quickly determine potential funders by focusing on two important aspects of a foundation's giving in one step.

The Foundation Grants Index Annual is useful to get a broad overview of a specific foundations's giving, to compare foundation giving within a state, and to survey giving to a particular recipient or recipient type and to gain insight into the subject areas that have traditionally been most attractive to private foundations.

COMSEARCH Printouts

Since many grantseekers want to focus their funding search on a particular subject or geographic area, The Foundation Center issues a series of computer printouts that list grants from the *Grants Index Annual* in a more convenient format. *COMSEARCH Printouts* are available as *Broad Topics*, and *Subject* and *Geographic* printouts.

COMSEARCH: *Broad Topics* are fully-indexed listings of foundation grants in 24 broad areas of grantmaking. Each *Broad Topic* is a "mini" *Grants Index Annual*, listing grants of $5,000 and over arranged by foundation state and name. Grant listings are indexed by recipient name and state and by subject key words. *COMSEARCH: Broad Topics* are currently available in the following areas:

Arts & Cultural Programs
Business & Employment
Children & Youth
Higher Education
Hospitals & Medical Care
   Programs
Museums
Science Programs
Social Science Programs
Women & Girls
International & Foreign
   Programs
Minorities
Religion & Religious Education
Public Health

Public Policy & Political Science
Recreation
Community & Urban Development
Elementary & Secondary
   Education (Public & Private
   Schools)
Matching & Challenge Grants
Film, Media, & Communications
Crime & Law Enforcement
Environmental Law, Protection &
   Education
Family Services
Medical & Professional Health
   Education
Physically & Mentally Disabled

COMSEARCH: *Subjects* are smaller printouts of grants awarded in specific subject fields, such as adult and continuing education, dance, chemistry, child abuse, etc. (see Figure 8). The grant listings are arranged by foundation state and name, and a list of foundations covered with their addresses and general giving restrictions is provided in the back of each booklet. The title page of each booklet includes a "scope note" which provides a brief description of the number and type of grants included in that particular printout and recommendations about other subject listings that might be relevant to your search.

COMSEARCH: *Geographics* list grants from the annual database that have been awarded to organizations in a specific geographic area. Currently, geographic printouts are available for two cities, eleven individual states, and seven broad regions (see Figure 9). Grant listings are arranged alphabetically by foundation name and indexed by the names of grant recipients, enabling you to identify foundations that have funded organizations in your area with goals and activities similar to your own. Like the other *COMSEARCH Printouts*, a list of foundations included with their addresses and giving restrictions is provided in the back of each booklet.

FIGURE 8. List of COMSEARCH: SUBJECTS

Order Number/Title
Communications
  3. Language, Literature &
     Journalism
  4. Publications
Education
  15. Adult & Continuing Education
  17. Student & Professional
      Internships
  18. Higher Education—Capital
      Support
  19. Higher Education—
      Endowments
  20. Higher Education—Faculty and
      Professorships
  21. Higher Education—Fellowships
  22. Scholarships, Student Aid
      & Loans
  23. Library & Information Services
  24. Educational Research
  25. Vocational Education, Career
      Development & Employment
  26. International Studies, Education
      & Exchange
  27. Teacher Training
Health
  30. Health & Medical Care—Cost
      Containment
  32. Medical Research &
      Advancement
  33. Dentistry
  34. Nursing
  37. Mental Health
  39. Alcohol & Drug Abuse
  40. Cancer Care & Research
  41. Hospices
  42. Abortion, Birth Control &
      Family Planning
  43. Children & Youth—Health
      Programs
  44. Children & Youth—Medical
      Research
Cultural Activities
  46. Humanities Programs
  47. Theater
  48. Music Schools & Music
      Education
  49. Orchestras & Musical
      Performances

  50. Architecture, Historical
      Preservation & Historical
      Societies
  51. Dance
Population Groups
  64. Boys
  65. Blacks
  66. Hispanics
  67. Blind & Visually Impaired
  68. Deaf & Hearing Impaired
Science & Technology
  74. Mathematics
  75. Biology & Genetics
  76. Agriculture & Farming
  77. Chemistry
  79. Computer Science & Systems
  80. Energy
  81. Engineering
Social Sciences
  85. Business Education
  86. Economics
  88. Law Schools & Legal Education
  89. Psychology & Behavioral
      Sciences
Welfare
  90. Peace Initiatives & Arms Control
  91. Legal Services
  92. Housing & Transportation
  93. Community Funds
  95. Child Abuse
  97. Community Centers
  98. Young Men's & Women's
      Associations
  99. Food & Nutrition
  101. Animal Welfare & Wildlife
  102. Rural Development
  104. Camps & Camperships
  105. Parks, Gardens & Zoos
  106. Refugee & Relief Services
  107. Volunteer Programs
  108. Homeless
  109. Human Rights
Other
  110. Nonprofit Management
  111. Philanthropy & Nonprofit Sector
       Research
  112. Governmental Agencies
  114. Conferences & Seminars

FIGURE 9. List of COMSEARCH: GEOGRAPHICS

Cities

Washington, D.C.
New York

States

California
Illinois
Massachusetts
Michigan
Minnesota
New Jersey
New York (excluding NYC)
North Carolina
Ohio
Pennsylvania
Texas

Regions

Northeast (Maine, New Hampshire, Rhode Island, Vermont, Connecticut)
Southeast (Florida, Georgia, Alabama, Mississippi, Louisiana, South Carolina, Tennessee)
Northwest (Alaska, Washington, Oregon)
Rocky Mountains (Arizona, New Mexico, Colorado, Utah, Nevada, Idaho, Montana, Wyoming)
South Atlantic (Delaware, Maryland, Virginia)
Central Midwest (Indiana, Iowa, Kansas, Kentucky, Missouri)
Upper Midwest (Nebraska, North Dakota, South Dakota, Wisconsin)

The Foundation Grants Index Bimonthly

Foundation grants are reported to the Center and entered into the Grants Index Database throughout the year. Every two months that information is gathered and published in the Center's magazine, *The Foundation Grants Index Bimonthly*. Approximately 2,000 recent grants are listed in each edition of the *Bimonthly*, with indexes to the names of organizations receiving grants as well as the subject focus of each grant. Because the *Bimonthly* focuses on the most recent grants data reported, it is an ideal way for grantseekers to keep abreast of the current giving interests of major foundations.

The Foundation Grants Index Bimonthly also includes two other features that have relevance to your search for funding:

- "Updates on Grantmakers" which notes changes in name, staff, address, giving interests, and application procedures at the nation's major foundations (see Figure 10).

- "Grantmakers' Publications" which lists brochures, newsletters, and annual reports issued by grantmakers. Many of these are available to any organization on request and would be useful additions to your files (see Figure 11).

FIGURE 10. "Updates on Grantmakers" from the FOUNDATION GRANTS INDEX BIMONTHLY

Chatlos Foundation, Inc., The, NY
  Officers and Trustees: William J. Chatlos is now the Treasurer as well as the
  President, leaving Alice E. Chatlos with the duties of Chairman and
  Vice-President. Carol J. Williams is the Assistant Secretary.

Chiles Foundation, OR
  Address: 111 S. W. Fifth Ave., Suite 4050, Portland, OR 97204.

Cole (Quincy) Trust, VA
  Correction: The Quincy Cole Trust has not changed its name. All of its grants
  are administered by the Windsor Foundation
  Address: c/o Sovran Bank, P.O. Box 26903, Richmond, VA 23261
  Grant application address: Clinton Webb, President, Windsor Foundation, P.O.
  Box 1377, Richmond, VA 23211.

Cummins Engine Foundation, IN
  Officers and Directors: William K. Hall is now a member of the board.

Davis (The Leonard and Sophie) Foundation, Inc., NY
  Address: 601 Clearwater Park Road, West Palm Beach, FL 33041.

Dresser Foundation, Inc., TX
  Telephone: (214)740-6744
  Officers: J. J. Corboy has replaced Edward R. Luter as the President and
  Director.

FIGURE 11. "Grantmakers' Publications" from the FOUNDATION GRANTS INDEX BIMONTHLY

ANNUAL REPORTS

Alden (George I.) Trust. *Annual Report 1984,* 20p. 370 Main St., Worcester, MA
01608.

Amarillo Area Foundation. *1984 Annual Report,* 20p. 1000 Polk, P.O. Box 2569,
Amarillo, TX 79105-2569.

Bingham (The William) Foundation. *1984 Annual Report,* 12p. 1250 Leader Bldg.,
Cleveland, OH 44114.

Buffalo Foundation. *Report 1985,* 33p. 237 Main St., Buffalo, NY 14203.

Carlsbad Foundation. *Annual Report 1985,* 36p. 405 W. Greene, Carlsbad, NM
88220.

Carolinas, Foundation for the. (Formerly the Greater Charlotte Foundation). *1984
Annual Report,* 32p. 301 S. Brevard St., Charlotte, NC 28202. (n)

Coonley (Queene Ferry) Foundation. *Report on Grants 1984,* 6p. 3415 36th St., NW,
Washington, DC 20016.

Corning Glass Works Foundation. *1984 Annual Report,* 23p. Corning, NY 14831.
National.

Cowell (S.H.) Foundation. *Annual Report for the year ending September 30, 1984,*
24p. 260 California St., Suite 1501, San Francisco, CA 94111.

Cummins Engine Foundation and Cummins Engine Company. *1984 Contributions
Report,* 35p. Mail Code 60814, Box 3005, Columbus, IN 47202-3005.

DIRECTORIES OF FOUNDATIONS

Directories of foundations vary widely in terms of the number of foundations they cover, the geographic focus of the directory, and the type and amount of information they provide about each foundation listed. They range from simple listings of foundations to detailed descriptions of the activities and interests of particular grantmakers. Some directories are national in focus, defining the criteria for inclusion by size or type of foundation, while others focus on foundations in a particular geographic area or foundations active in a particular subject area. As you undertake your search for funding sources, you will probably use a number of different types of directories to identify potential funding sources and to find out more detailed information about particular funders before you send in your grant request.

The National Data Book

The National Data Book is the only directory published which lists all currently active grantmaking foundations in the United States. Published each January, the *Data Book* lists over 24,000 foundations that awarded at least $1 in grants in their most recent fiscal year, as well as over 200 active community foundations.

The listings in the *Data Book* are derived from the Internal Revenue Service's computer files of the information returns (Form 990-PF) filed by private foundations during the preceding year. The Center verifies address and fiscal data for each foundation awarding grants of $5,000 or more to ensure keyboarding accuracy and eliminates records for organizations that are classified as private foundations by the IRS but do not conduct grantmaking programs.

Community foundations have a different tax status than private foundations and do not file the same type of information return with the IRS. Therefore, The Foundation Center surveys community foundations separately and adds this information to the computer file. The information is then made available to the public in the published volume and as an online computer file with DIALOG Information Service.

The published book is divided into two volumes. Volume One includes separate listings of private grantmaking foundations (including company-sponsored foundations), community foundations, and operating foundations (most of which do not award grants). The listings of private and community foundations are arranged alphabetically by state and then in descending order within each state by the amount of grants paid. Since operating foundations generally don't award grants, this list is arranged by state and then in descending order by asset amount.

FIGURE 12. Sample Entry from the NATIONAL DATA BOOK

DATA BOOK ENTRY

SEQ. NO.	ST	FOUNDATION NAME/ PRINCIPAL OFFICER	CARE OF/ADDRESS CITY	ZIP	FISCAL DATE	GRANTS PAID	ASSETS	EXPENDITURES/ GIFTS RECD	IRS NO.
18682	PA	MYRIN TR. MABEL PEW THE GLENMEDE TR CO., TTEE	229 S 18TH ST PHILADELPHIA	19103	12/83	5658101	154179063	6268517	236234666
18683	PA	ANNENBERG FUND INC	100 MATSONFORD RD PO BOX 750 RADNOR	19088	12/83	5079166	41790071	5200003	236286756
18684	PA	WALTER H ANNENBERG, PRES BENEDUM FDN OKLAUD EXWORTHINGTON V-P	1400 BENEDUM-TREES BLDG PITTSBURGH	15222	12/83	5077119	107511454	6434211	251086799 R
18685	PA	GULF OIL FDN PHILO A HUTCHESON, EXEC DIR	PO BOX 1166 PITTSBURGH	15230	12/83	4977242	1007008	5012442 2897330	237164363
18686	PA	HEINZ END. HOWARD ALFRED W WISHART, JR., EXEC DIR	301 FIFTH AVE. STE 1417 PITTSBURGH	15222	12/83	4637323	191404941	5361723	251064784 R
18687	PA	WHITAKER FDN MILES J GIBBONS JR, EX DIR	% CHEMICAL BANK TTEE 875 POPLAR CHURCH RD CAMP HILL	17011	02/84	4580667	157893494	6282290	222096948 R

1. **Sequence Number**—A unique consecutive number assigned to each entry providing access to each foundation through the alphabetical foundation name *Index*.

2. **State**—Postal service abbreviation for the state in which the foundation is located.

3. **Foundation Name**

4. **Principal Officer**—Found directly below the foundation name and indented is the name of the person designated by the foundation on the IRS return as the chief executive.

5. **Care of Name**—Included only if necessary for mailing.

6. **Address, City, and Zip Code**—If no "Care of" is necessary for mailing, the street address is on the top line of each entry, with the city and zip code on the line below.

7. **Fiscal Date**—Closing date for the foundation's fiscal or calendar year used for the financial figures listed.

8. **Grants Paid**—Total dollar amount of annual grants for the year noted.

9. **Assets**—Value of the foundation's holdings at market value at the end of the year indicated.

10. **Expenditures**—Total annual expenses for the year indicated, including expenses of earned income, excise tax, administrative expenses, and total grants paid.

11. **Gifts Received**—Found directly below the foundation's expenditures is the amount of new funding received by the foundation in the year noted.

12. **IRS Number**—A unique nine-digit number assigned to each organization, also known as the Employer Identification Number (EIN).

13. **Annual Report Code**—An "R" indicates that a foundation publishes a report periodically, usually on an annual basis.

FIGURE 13. Sample Entry from the NATIONAL DATA BOOK INDEX

SEQ. NO.	FOUNDATION NAME	ST.
11905	ATLANTIC FDN	NJ
433	ATLANTIC RICHFIELD FDN OF CALIFORNIA	CA
19777	ATLAS FDN	PA
3279	ATLAS FDN	DC
2711	ATLAS FOUNDERS EDUC TR	CT
6736	ATLAS FDN INC	NY
2025	ATMORE-PEYTON FDN	CA
24867	ATOMIC RESEARCH INC	NY
12957	ATRAN FDN INC	NY
23438	ATTLEBORO FDN	MA
9125	ATTMAN FAMILY FDN INC	MD
15530	ATTUCKS FDN, CRISPUS	NY

1. **Sequence Number**—A consecutive number assigned to each foundation in the *Data Book* providing alphabetical access through the *Index*.

2. **Foundation Name**

3. **State**—Code for state where foundation is located.

SEQ. NO.	FOUNDATION NAME	ST.
19325	AVNER MEM FDN, MICHAEL BILL	PA
8248	AVNET TR, CHARLES	MA
16155	AVON FAMILY FDN INC	NY
12746	AVON PRODUCTS FDN INC	NY
18017	AVONDALE EDUC & CHAR FDN INC	AL
18032	AVONDALE EDUC & CHAR FDN INC	OH
9532	AVRIL FAMILY FUND, GEORGE A	MI
13564	AWREY FDN	NY
13289	AXE-HOUGHTON FDN	NY
7788	AYER FDN INC, N W	NY
11837	AYER HOME, TTEES OF THE	MA
25164	AYER TR, WALDO & ALICE	NH
	AYERS HOME FOR NURSES INC, LUCY C	RI

Each foundation listing includes the mailing address, principal officer, IRS identification number (or "EI number"), the fiscal year covered, and the foundation's assets at market value, gifts received, and total grants paid during that year. Foundations that publish annual reports are coded "R" at the end of the entry (see Figure 12).

Volume Two is an index to the listings in Volume One by foundation name. Each index entry notes the name of the foundation, the state it is located in, and the Volume One entry number so you can check back to the full entry for information (see Figure 13).

The National Data Book is most helpful in preliminary research on funding sources, particularly for smaller foundations which may not be covered in any other published source. The columnar format enables users to identify foundations within a given city or zip code or to identify foundations in their state within a certain giving range. Although *Data Book* listings provide only brief information about a foundation, they do provide the Employer Identification Number for each foundation. This number identifies the foundation with the Internal Revenue Service and is necessary for ordering copies of the foundation's public information returns (Form 990-PF).

The Foundation Directory

The Foundation Directory is the oldest and one of the most widely used directories of private foundations. It includes descriptions of all grantmaking foundations in the U.S. that have assets of $1 million or more or that award grants totaling at least $100,000 annually. The Tenth Edition of the *Directory*, published in October 1985, includes approximately 4,400 foundations which together account for approximately 93 percent of the total assets and 85 percent of the total grant dollars awarded annually by private foundations. The *Directory* is published every two years, with a *Supplement* updating information on foundation addresses, personnel, program interests, etc., published in the intervening year.

Each *Directory* entry includes the foundation's name, address, and telephone number; current financial data including assets, expenditures, and total grants, scholarships, matching gifts, loans, and program amounts; officers and trustees; purpose and activities; and application procedures (see Figure 14). The volume is arranged by state, then alphabetically by foundation name. The Tenth Edition includes five indexes to help the user identify foundations of interest:

1. an index by foundation name;

2. an index of donors, trustees, and officers;

FIGURE 14. Sample Entry from THE FOUNDATION DIRECTORY

Sample Entry

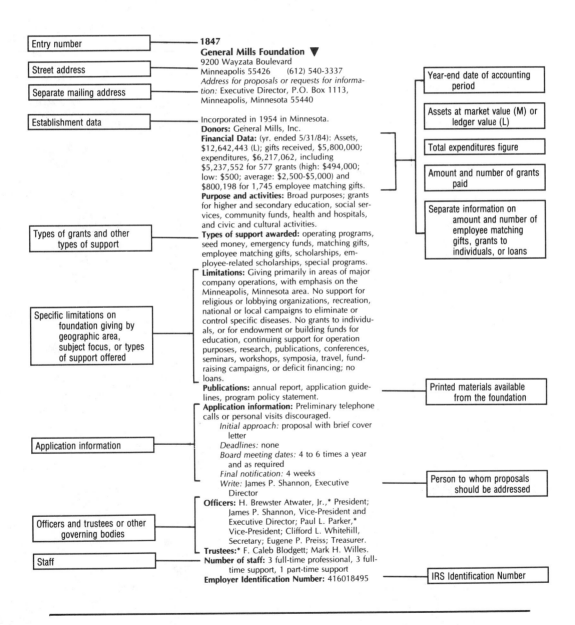

3. a geographic index to foundation locations by city and state which includes references to foundations located in one state but which also focus their giving in another state;

4. an index to giving interests by over 150 subject categories, each of which is also broken down by the states where the foundations are located;

5. an index to types of support offered by foundations, broken down by the states where the foundations are headquartered.

In the geographic, subject, and types of support indexes, foundations with national or regional giving patterns are indicated in bold type, while foundations restricted to local giving are listed in regular type. As you define the limits of your search for funding, these indexes can help you to focus on locally-oriented foundations in your community or on national foundations that have an interest in your field of activity.

Source Book Profiles

Source Book Profiles is a quarterly information service which provides detailed descriptions of the nation's 1,000 largest grantmakers during a two-year publishing cycle (500 foundations are analyzed each year). *Source Book Profiles* provides a more extensive description of each foundation's giving program, history, and application procedures than *The Foundation Directory*, but it covers a smaller universe.

Each profile notes the foundation's name, address, and telephone number; officers, trustees, and principal staff; background history of the foundation or sponsoring company; financial data; publications issued by the foundation; grant application procedures and deadlines; a detailed analysis of the foundation's giving patterns by subject, type of support awarded, types of organizations receiving grants, and geographic distribution of grant awards; and a listing of sample grants (see Figure 15).

There are four indexes to *Profiles* to facilitate funding research. The indexes, which are cumulated quarterly, include:

• an index by foundation name,

• an index by types of support,

• an index by subject giving interests, and

• a geographic index of foundation locations by city and state, with references to foundations which focus giving in states other than their own.

FIGURE 15. Sample Entry from SOURCE BOOK PROFILES

LYNDHURST FOUNDATION

Address: 701 Tallan Building
Chattanooga, Tennessee 37402

Telephone: 615-756-0767
Contact: Deaderick C. Montague, President

Limitations: Giving limited to the southeastern region of the United States. Generally no support for capital funds (including building or equipment), deficit financing, endowment funds, medical or university-based research, newsletters, workshops, seminars, or short-term courses or conferences; no loans. No grants for general support of hospitals, colleges or universities, religious organizations, or arts and social service organizations in metropolitan areas. Lyndhurst Prizes for individuals are awarded only upon the initiative of the foundation.

Officers:
John T. Lupton, Chairman and Trustee
Deaderick C. Montague, President and Trustee
Rodolph B. Davenport III, Vice-President and Trustee
Joel W. Richardson, Jr., Secretary
Charles B. Chitty, Treasurer

Trustee:
Robert Coles

Staff:
Jack E. Murrah, Associate
Catherine Cox, Administrative Director
Susan Barclift, President's Assistant

Financial Data: (Year ended 12/31/83)

Assets (market value):	$	80,105,833
Gifts Received:		0
Expenditures Including Grants:	$	5,346,943
Total Giving:	$	4,105,744
Grants Paid:	$	3,873,234
Number of Grants:		41
High:	$	984,850
Low:	$	4,000
General Range:	$30,000-150,000	
Grants to Individuals:	$	232,510
Number of Grants to Individuals:		18
Loans:	$	500,000
Number of Loans:		1

Number of Staff: Four full-time professional, three full-time support

Foundation Publications: Annual Report

Purpose: Grants generally are limited to the Southeast with emphasis on health, education, and the arts. Health-related grants mainly support activities surrounding primary care, particularly for areas which are poorly served. Grants to arts organizations are usually directed at secondary schools. Grants for education are to help increase or diversify audiences, improve management, or strengthen potential for earnings.

Background: The Lyndhurst Foundation, prior to 1978 called the Memorial Welfare Foundation, was established in 1938 in Delaware by the late Thomas Cartter Lupton, who was a pioneer in the development of the Coca-Cola bottling industry. Gifts to the foundation were made by Cartter Lupton and by the Central Shares Corporation. The market value of the foundation's assets has increased steadily in recent years, from $70.5 million in 1981 to $80 million in 1983; while annual grant payments remained at more than $4 million during the same period. The foundation is governed by a board of four trustees and five officers.

Grant Analysis: In 1983, contributions remained at the same level ($4.1 million) as in recent years, and were in line with the foundation's stated interest in education, health, and the arts. Giving in these areas represented over one-half of the year's contributions. In 1983, community development projects received the largest share of funds (42%), including the high grant of the year, $984,850 to the City of Chattanooga for the Miller Park Board of Directors. Significant funding also went to the Local Initiatives Support Corporation-Southeastern Office in Chattanooga ($375,000 in two grants). The foundation stresses its regional emphasis.

Education received 27% of the total grant dollar: 22% to colleges, universities, schools, and projects; 5% for the Lyndhurst Prizes to individuals; and less than 1% for the Lyndhurst Teachers' Awards. The Baylor School received $224,230, the largest grant in the category, and $208,000 went to the University of North Carolina at Chapel Hill. Remaining grants in the category ranged from $4,000 to $146,946.

Eighteen percent of total giving supported the arts, with the bulk of funds disbursed to Allied Arts of Greater Chattanooga ($350,000) and Friends of the Festival (two grants totaling $310,000). Other grants in the category were in the $30,000 range. Health grants accounted for 9% of funding, with the largest awards disbursed to the Tennessee Association of Primary Health Care Centers ($69,600) and the Georgia Student Health Association ($45,000). Remaining funds were disbursed to four miscellaneous organizations (4%) in grants ranging from $5,000 to $75,000. About one-half of the 1983 grantees had received support from the foundation the previous year.

	No. of grants	Amount	Percent of grant dollars
Community Development	9	$1,717,508	42
Education	12	894,876	22
Arts	6	759,500	18
Health	10	357,000	9
Lyndhurst Prizes	8	200,000	5
Other	4	144,350	4
Lyndhurst Teachers Awards	10	32,510	Less than 1%
Totals	59	$4,105,744	100%

Types of Support: In 1983, the foundation reported that their priorities continue to be health, education, and the arts.

Grants in education have been and will continue to focus on secondary education, specifically the enhancement of the quality of teachers and teaching in high schools. Arts organizations have received grants to increase and diversify their audiences, to improve management, and to strengthen income. Health-related grants are currently aimed at improving primary care, especially through the work of "student health coalitions" in the region; the foundation is currently reviewing its giving policy for health.

Grants to enhance the vitality of Chattanooga are given for urban design, amenities, neighborhoods, and improvement of local leadership opportunities. Occasionally, funds are contributed for economic development throughout the region, although this area of giving is also under review. Most community development grants are for rural areas in the region.

The foundation made a $500,000 program-related investment loan to the Mountain Association for Community Economic Development, Inc. for a low-interest housing consortium among banks in the Berea, Kentucky area.

The foundation tries to support unconventional, narrowly focused, or very old ideas. In general, support for operating budgets, seed money, general support, program support, scholarships, matching gifts, program-related investments, and foundation-managed projects. The foundation awards both single- and multiple-year grants. **Ordinarily, no support for capital funds (including building or equipment), deficit financing, endowment funds, newsletters, workshops, seminars, or short-term courses and conferences. Medical or university-based research is not a priority. No loans.**

Lyn

FIGURE 15 (cont.)

Recipient Type: Recipients in 1983 included the City of Chattanooga and community development, planning, and revitalization organizations; colleges, universities, schools, and special educational programs; fine and performing arts associations; health service agencies; a youth services organization and a philanthropic association. **No grants for general support of hospitals, colleges or universities, religious organizations, or arts and social service organizations in metropolitan areas.**

Awards to individuals include the Lyndhurst Prizes, annual grants of $25,000, distributed generally for a three-year period to those doing unusual or interesting work but really found their stride to continue their interests as they see fit. Lyndhurst Teachers' Awards, presented to ten secondary school teachers in grades seven through twelve representing public and accredited private schools in Hamilton County, Tennessee, are intended to enable teachers to pursue further academic instruction, travel, or individual study during the summer months.

Geographic Distribution: **Giving limited to the southeastern region of the United States.** In 1983, two-thirds of funding went to organizations located or working in Tennessee, largely in the Chattanooga area. The largest part of the foundation's regional work is designed to be done in rural areas. Grants rarely made for work in metropolitan areas outside of Chattanooga.

Grants: The following is a partial list of grants paid by the foundation in 1983. The foundation's grants of $5,000 or more are recorded in the annual and bimonthly Foundation Grants Index. Unless otherwise noted, recipients were located in Tennessee.

Community Development
City of Chattanooga, Miller Park Board of Directors $984,850
  To purchase land for park expansion
Local Initiatives Support Corporation-Southern Office, Chattanooga 375,000
  For loans and grants to community groups, $250,000
  Operating support, $125,000
Delta Foundation, Greenville, MS 150,000
  For administrative budget for organization that works to create
  jobs, income, and assets for poor blacks and their communities
  in the Mississippi Delta Region.
Mississippi Action for Community Education, Greenville, MS 55,000
  For leadership program
Partners for Livable Places, Washington, DC 35,000
  For enhancing the quality of life in Chattanooga

Education
Baylor School 224,230
  For faculty salaries and scholarships for minority students
University of North Carolina, School of Education, Chapel Hill 208,000
  Fellowships for graduate students to obtain master's degrees
  in academic fields and teaching certificates
Vanderbilt Institute for Public Policy Studies, Nashville 146,946
  For project to determine results of financial incentives upon
  elementary schools' efforts to improve instructional effectiveness
Program for Rural Services and Research, University, AL 53,200
  Rural education project
Chattanooga Nature Center, Yellowstone Workshop 4,000
  For eight teachers from Hamilton County to participate in workshop

Arts
Allied Arts of Greater Chattanooga 350,000
  For fund raising campaign

Friends of the Festival 310,000
  Administrative expenses for 1983 Riverbend Festival, $165,000
  Operating support for 1984 festival, $145,000
Appalshop, Whitesburg, KY 30,000
  For marketing efforts of Roadside Theater

Health
Tennessee Association of Primary Health Care Centers, Nashville 69,600
  To develop "primary care network" for Medicaid clients
Georgia Student Health Association, Atlanta, GA 45,000
North Carolina Action for Farmworkers, Durham, NC 20,000
Siskin Memorial Foundation 18,000
  For feasibility study for establishing an in-patient facility for
  handicapped children and physical and occupational therapy
  for those in need of rehabilitation

Other
Boys Club of Chattanooga 75,000
  Operating support, and to help members acquire skills needed
  to seek and hold a job
Southeastern Council on Foundations, Atlanta, GA 5,000

Policies and Application Guidelines:

Grants to Organizations: The foundation issues guidelines for submitting a grant application. A grant request should be initiated by a two- or three-page letter describing the organization and the project for which support is sought. An estimated project budget, proof of IRS tax-exempt status, and names of directors and staff members should be included. Further information and an interview or site visit may be requested by the foundation. A formal proposal (one copy) will be solicited if it appears that the project is compatible with the foundation's philosophy and current priorities. The foundation acknowledges receipt of proposals. It is the staff's responsibility to research, recommend, and monitor proposals. Each grant recipient must submit periodic reports and accounting of expenditures.

Grants to Individuals: For Lyndhurst Teachers' Awards, the foundation sends applications and announcements in the fall and winter to teachers and principals at all public and accredited private secondary schools in Hamilton County, Tennessee. Recipients are selected by March 31, and the funds are disbursed in April for use during the summer months. **Lyndhurst Prizes are awarded only at the initiative of the foundation; applications or appeals are not considered.**

Funding Cycle:
Board meeting dates – February, May, August, and November
Application deadlines – Generally, four weeks before board meetings; by February 1 for
  Lyndhurst Teachers' Awards
Final notification – Three months

Sources: 990-PF, Information provided by the foundation.

3/85
fv

Like *The Foundation Directory* indexes, *Profiles* indexes indicate foundations with national or regional focus in bold type, while locally-oriented foundations are listed in regular type.

Source Book Profiles is useful in both preliminary research for identifying potential funding sources among the nation's 1,000 largest foundations, as well as in the final stages of your research when you will be gathering as much information as you can about the few foundations you want to submit proposals to.

State and Regional Directories

Directories of foundations located in a particular city, state, or region can be extremely useful in identifying foundations interested in supporting a variety of programs on their own turf. There are currently approximately 80 directories available covering foundations and corporate giving programs in 47 states and 14 cities or metropolitan areas. These directories are compiled by a wide variety of organizations, including commercial publishers, state government agencies, libraries, foundations or associations of foundations, and university development offices. They vary a great deal in both the amount and quality of the information they provide. The examples in Figures 16, 17, and 18 illustrate how varied these directories can be.

Relatively few of the area foundation directories contain subject indexes. Where subject indexing or subject coding is included, be sure to read the instructions carefully so you understand the basis on which subject classifications were made. The use and meaning of certain terms may vary.

Most local foundation directories are a very good supplemental source of information, particularly for the smaller foundations not covered in the major foundation reference works. Those local directories that do include a subject index provide the only subject access to the interests of smaller foundations. The availability of such a resource will greatly simplify your research if you are focusing on smaller, locally-oriented foundations as a more likely source of funds. Be aware, however, of the varying quality and currency of these resources before you use them.

Many of the state directories provide listings of sample grants which give some indication of the foundation's interests; some local directories are now including information on corporations that have giving programs in their areas which can be a useful complement to the foundation information provided.

A bibliography of all available area foundation directories can be found in Appendix B. The Center monitors this field carefully and updates the bibliography whenever it learns about new directories or editions. Copies of all state and city foundation directories are available for public use in The Foundation Center's New York and Washington, D.C. libraries, and the Center's cooperating library collections (Appendix G) generally have directories for their state or region.

FIGURE 16. Sample Entry from GUIDE TO CALIFORNIA FOUNDATIONS

Hewlett, William and Flora Foundation ★

525 Middlefield Road
Menlo Park, CA 94025
(415) 329-1070

1/85
941655673

Contact person	Roger Heyns, President
Purpose	To promote the well being of mankind by supporting selected activities of a charitable, religious, scientific, literary or educational nature, as well as organizations or institutions engaged in such activities
Fields of interest	Conflict resolution, education, environment, performing arts, population, regional grants
Program limitations	In education: no grants for student aid, construction, equipment purchases, basic scientific research, health research or health education programs. In performing arts: no grants for capital improvements, general fund drives, visual arts, elementary or secondary school performing arts programs, community arts classes, community outreach, ethnic arts, recreational, therapeutic, and social service arts programs, including those for senior citizens and the handicapped, and independent radio, television, and film projects, except as they address one of the arts program emphases as stated in the guidelines. In population: no support for biomedical research on reproduction or the development of contraceptives, no population education programs directed toward the general public. In Regional Grants: no physical or mental health programs, law and related fields, criminal justice or juvenile delinquency, public school education, drug and alcohol addiction, or the problems of the elderly and the handicapped
Geographic limits	Conflict resolution, education, and environment: National; Performing arts: primarily San Francisco Bay Area; Population: international; Regional: exclusively San Francisco Bay Area
Contact procedure	Letter of inquiry
Funding cycle	Quarterly; January, April, July, October
Application deadlines	For performing arts only, see guidelines
Total assets	$475,415,250
Total grants	$35,838,069
Future payment	$27,691,076
Number of grants	225
First time recipients	116
Grant range	$2,000 - $750,000
Information available	Annual report, application guidelines
Sample grants	$25,000 to Cornell University, Ithaca. NY $40,000 to American Land Forum, Bethesda, Maryland $50,000 to Center for Negotiation and Public Policy, Boston, Massachusetts $75,000 to Student Conservation Association, Inc., Charlestown, N.H. $100,000 to American Conservatory Theatre, San Francisco, CA
Officers & Directors	Roger W. Heyns, President; Marianne Pallotti, Vice President and Corporate Secretary; William F. Nichols, Treasurer; William R. Hewlett, Chairman; Walter B. Hewlett, Vice Chairman; Robert Minge Brown, Robert F. Erburu, Eleanor H. Gimon, Arjay Miller, Lyle M. Nelson, William D. Ruckelshaus

Reprinted with permission from *Guide to California Foundations*, 6th edition. ©1985, Northern California Grantmakers, 334 Kearny St., San Francisco, CA 94108.

**EUGENE and AGNES E. *MEYER*
FOUNDATION**

1200 15th Street, N. W., Suite 500
Washington, D. C. 20005
(202) 659-2435

Officers and Directors:
  Mallory Walker, Chairman
  Delano Lewis, Vice Chairman
  Newman T. Halvorson, Jr., Secretary/Treasurer
  Monsignor Geno Baroni (deceased)
  Dr. Lucy M. Cohen
  Charles C. Glover III, Esquire
  Mary Graham
  Honorable John W. Hechinger, Jr.
  Theodore C. Lutz
  Honorable Aubrey E. Robinson, Jr.
  Dr. Pearl L. Rosser
  James O. Gibson, President
  Kathy L. Dwyer, Program Officer
  Edith J. Beauchamp, Administrative Assistant
  James L. Kunen, Consultant
Contact: Kathy Dwyer

Financial and Grant Data for 1983

Total Assets	$	28,843,029
Total Grants	$	700,944
High: $ 25,000	Low: $	100
Number of Grants: 85		

Five Largest Grants:

1. Washington School of Psychiatry	$	33,750
2. Greater Washington Research Center	$	30,000
3. National Symphony	$	25,000
4. Associates for Renewal in Education, Inc.	$	25,000
5. Capital Children's Museum	$	25,000

Areas of Interest:
  "...concerned with local affairs...does not normally contribute to programs of national or international scope. ...makes grants for a wide variety of projects principally in the fields of community service, education, health and mental health, law and justice, and arts and humanities." Publishes annual report.

FIGURE 18. Sample Entry from THE HOOPER DIRECTORY OF TEXAS FOUNDATIONS

```
1)   1  Abell-Hanger Foundation
2)      EMPHASIS: Culture, Elementary/Secondary, Medical Care
        and Treatment, Medical/Health Education/Research,
        Protestant Religious Support and Welfare/Community
        Development
3)      GEOGRAPHIC FOCUS: Local giving (Midland)
4)      POPULATION GROUPS: Handicapped, women and youth
5)      RESTRICTIONS: No grants to individuals or for
        scholarships and fellowships; no loans.
6)      TAX YEAR: 06/30/83
7)&8)   ASSETS: $49,224,386        INCOME: $10,396,614
9)      TOTAL GRANTS: $4,476,797 (88)
10)     RANGE: $600 - $250,000 / Typical $10,000
11)     APPLICATION PROCESS: Guidelines available, initial
        approach by letter, application form required; submit
        3 copies of proposal by April 15 or November 15; board
        meets semiannually in June and December.
12)     TRUSTEES: Abell, Gladys H. - Pres. / Trott, James I.
        - V.P. / Leibrock, Robert M. / Butler, John P. /
        Younger, John F.
13)     CONTACT: David L. Smith, Fdn. Manager
        P.O. Box 430
        Midland, TX 79702
        915-684-6655
```

1) **ENTRY NUMBER AND FOUNDATION NAME** - Entry numbers are assigned by the order of appearance in the directory. Four-digit numbers denote smaller or excluded foundations.

2) **EMPHASIS** - Lists types of programs the foundation has supported in the past. Grants are assigned to categories and subcategories listed in **"Explanation of Program Categories"**. Only categories are listed in the entries unless the foundation has focused its support in one or two subcategories. Subcategories will be listed in the **"Foundation Program Area"** index.

3) **GEOGRAPHIC FOCUS** - Lists the geographic area that is the focus of the foundation's grantmaking. **"Local Giving"** indicates that the foundation prefers to support projects in the city or county where the foundation is located. **"Local Giving Only"** indicates the foundation's grants are restricted to that area.

4) **POPULATION GROUPS** - Indicates if the foundation's programs have helped any of the following groups: Aged, Handicapped, Minorities, Women, and Youth.

5) **RESTRICTIONS** - Lists any kind of stated limitations on giving.

6) **TAX YEAR** - Ending date of latest available tax return.

7) **ASSETS** - Total market value of the foundation's investments at the end of the tax year.

8) **INCOME** - Total income for the tax year.

9) **TOTAL GRANTS** - Lists the total dollar amount and number of the foundation's grants.

10) **RANGE** - Shows the largest and smallest grants and the size of a typical grant.

11) **APPLICATION PROCESS** - Lists information about the foundation's application process.

12) **TRUSTEES** - Lists all trustees and officers when that information is available.

13) **CONTACT** - Lists name, address, and telephone number for all communications.

Reprinted with permission from *The Hooper Directory of Texas Foundations*, 8th edition. ©1984, Funding Information Center of Texas, 507 Brooklyn, San Antonio, TX 78215.

SPECIAL FUNDING GUIDES

There are a vast number of subject areas in which organizations seek special funding, and there are a growing number of special funding directories available to meet these needs. Special funding directories generally detail a wide range of funding sources within a given subject field, including federal and local government agencies, foundations, corporations, individuals, etc.

A bibliography in Appendix A lists a large number of special funding guides in such diverse areas as the arts, youth programs, religion, services to the handicapped, and education. You should also check with colleagues and local libraries to see if a directory or guide exists in a field related to your interests. A list of philanthropic service organizations that focus on specific subject areas or population groups is provided in Appendix E, and you may find it useful to contact one of these organizations for further information about resources.

The Foundation Center does not make recommendations as to specific resources, publications, or services grantseekers might use in their search for funds. The four Center-operated libraries collect virtually everything that is published about foundations and foundation grants, however, and many of our cooperating collections across the country also purchase a great deal of what is published. We recommend that you examine all of the available materials in the field before deciding which items you will purchase or use in your funding search.

GENERAL FUNDING GUIDES

There are a variety of other reference works available from commercial and nonprofit publishers, and their number continues to grow. Again, The Foundation Center makes no recommendations as to specific resources beyond our own publications that you should use, but a thorough funding search should encompass all pertinent reference sources.

The bibliography in Appendix A lists most of the major funding directories available, and copies of the listed publications can be examined at the four Center-operated libraries as well as at many of our cooperating collections. These resources vary widely in scope and format. They generally focus on the largest foundations, but some also include information on giving from corporations and government agencies. Take a few minutes to examine the bibliography and check with your colleagues and local library to determine if any of these materials might be of use to you.

FOUNDATION INFORMATION RETURNS

One of the best sources of information about private foundations is the information return (Form 990-PF) they are required to file annually with the Internal Revenue Service. Federal law requires that these documents, unlike personal or corporate tax returns, be made available to the public by both the IRS and the foundations themselves. This means that for all foundations, regardless of size, a public record is available with basic facts about their operations and grants. For many smaller foundations, the information return is the only full record of their operations and grantmaking activities. For larger foundations, the Form 990-PF supplies important information about the foundation's assets and investments, as well as a complete list of grants awarded, that supplements the descriptions provided in published sources. Unless there is a complete published annual report available from the foundation, it is always wise to examine the most current IRS information returns for your final foundation prospects.

Community foundations are generally not classified as private foundations under current tax law and therefore they are not required to file a Form 990-PF. Most community foundations, however, publish annual reports or otherwise make information about their activities available in their local areas.

On the following pages Figure 19 details the key facts about a foundation you should be able to find on its Form 990-PF including:

1. **Name and address.** Note that some foundations have a different address for grant applications (see item 9 of this list).

2. **Assets at market value.** A more detailed listing of assets at market and book value is provided on page 2 of the 990-PF. Foundations are also required to provide a separate schedule or attachment listing all securities or stock investments and any land, buildings, or major equipment they own.

3. **Telephone number.** This may be the number of an accountant or other fiscal agent, such as a bank, that maintains the books of the foundation and therefore it may not be possible to reach the foundation directly by phone.

4. **Gross contributions, gifts, grants, etc. received by the foundation** (page 1, line 1). A listing of all gifts of $5,000 or more received by the foundation during the year must be provided in a separate schedule or attachment with the name and address of the donor and the amount contributed to the foundation.

5. **Total contributions, gifts, grants paid by the foundation** (page 1, line 25). A full list of grants and contributions paid during the year or approved for future payment is provided on page 8 of the 990-PF or, because of space limitations, in a separate schedule or attachment. This list should include the name and address of the grant recipient, the purpose of the grant or contribution, and the amount of the grant.

6. **Officers, directors, trustees, foundation managers** (page 4, Part VI). Often the names and addresses of foundation managers will be provided on a separate schedule or attachment.

7. **Staff** (page 4, Part VI). If the foundation employs staff members who are paid more than $30,000, their names, addresses, and titles will be listed here or on a separate schedule.

8. **Qualifying distributions** (page 6, Part X). If the foundation has made any program-related investments (low-interest loans for activities related to the foundation's charitable interests) or set-asides (relatively large grants that have been "set aside" for future payment), the amounts will be indicated here rather than as part of total contributions and grants paid.

9. **Grant restrictions and application information** (page 7). The most recently revised Form 990-PF asks foundations to indicate the name, address, and telephone number of the person to whom applications should be addressed, the form in which applications should be submitted, any submission deadlines, and any restrictions or limitations on awards. Again, some foundations may include this information on a separate schedule or attachment.

Where to Find Copies of Foundation IRS Returns

As we mentioned earlier, federal law requires that foundation information returns be made available to the public by both foundations and the IRS. Foundations make copies of their 990-PFs available in their principal office for public inspection for 180 days after filing. The foundation must announce in a newspaper of general circulation that the form is available for inspection; generally these are found in "public notices" sections.

Free inspection of any foundation return can be arranged in any IRS district office by writing to the District Director (Attention: Taxpayer Service) and requesting the specific returns. You can also order complete sets of foundation returns or copies of individual returns from the IRS for a nominal fee. Further information on this process is provided in Appendix F.

FIGURE 19. Key Facts Found on IRS FORM 990-PF

Form **990-PF**	**Return of Private Foundation**	OMB No. 1545-0052
Department of the Treasury Internal Revenue Service	**or Section 4947(a)(1) Trust Treated as a Private Foundation**	**1984**
	Note: *You may be able to use a copy of this return to satisfy State reporting requirements.*	

For the calendar year 1984, or tax year beginning _____ , 1984, and ending _____ , 19 ___

Please type, print, or attach label. See Specific Instructions.	Name of organization **1**	Employer identification number
	Address (number and street)	State registration number (see instructions)
	City or town, State, and ZIP code	Fair market value of assets at end of year **2**

If application pending, check here ▶ ☐   If address changed, check here ▶ ☐   Foreign organizations, check here . ▶ ☐

Check type of organization
☐ Exempt private foundation   ☐ 4947(a)(1) trust   ☐ Other taxable private foundation

Section 4947(a)(1) trusts filing this form in lieu of Form 1041, check here and see General Instructions. ▶ ☐

If the foundation is in a 60-month termination under section 507(b)(1)(B) check here . . . ▶ ☐

The books are in care of ▶ --
Located at ▶   Telephone no. ▶ **3** ----------

Check this box if your private foundation status terminated under section 507(b)(1)(A) . . . . ▶ ☐

Part I **Analysis of Revenue and Expenses**
(See Instructions for Part I)

		(A) Revenue and expenses per books **4**	(B) Net investment income	(C) Adjusted net income	(D) Disbursements for charitable purpose
Revenue	1 Contributions, gifts, grants, etc. received (attach schedule)				
	2 Contributions from split-interest trusts				
	3 Interest on savings and temporary cash investments				
	4 Dividends and interest from securities				
	5 Gross rents				
	6 Net gain or (loss) from sale of assets not on line 10				
	7 Capital gain net income				
	8 Net short-term capital gain				
	9 Income modifications				
	10 Gross profit from any business activities: (Gross receipts ▶ $ _____ minus cost of sales ▶ $ _____)				
	11 Other income (attach schedule)				
	12 Total (add lines 1 through 11)				
Operating and Administrative Expenses	13 Compensation of officers, directors, trustees, etc .				
	14 Other employee salaries and wages				
	15 Pension plans, employee benefits				
	16 (a) Legal fees				
	(b) Accounting fees				
	(c) Other professional fees.				
	17 Interest				
	18 Taxes (attach schedule)				
	19 Depreciation and depletion				
	20 Occupancy				
	21 Travel, conferences, and meetings				
	22 Printing and publications.				
	23 Other expenses (attach schedule)				
	24 Total operating and administrative expenses (add lines 13 through 23)				
	25 Contributions, gifts, grants paid (from Part XIII) **5**				
	26 Total expenses and disbursements (add lines 24 and 25)				
	27 (a) Excess of revenue over expenses and disbursements (line 12 minus line 26)				
	(b) Net investment income (if negative enter -0-) .				
	(c) Adjusted net income (if negative enter -0-) . .				

For Paperwork Reduction Act Notice, see page 1 of the instructions.   Form **990-PF** (1984)

Part V	Statements Regarding Activities (continued)	Yes	No

12 Taxes on excess business holdings (section 4943):

(a) Did you hold more than 2% direct or indirect interest in any business enterprise at any time during the year? . .

(b) If "Yes" did you have excess business holdings in 1984 as a result of any purchase by you or disqualified persons after May 26, 1969; after the lapse of the 5-year period to dispose of holdings acquired by gift or bequest; after the lapse of the 10-year first phase holding period, or after the 15-year first phase holding period? . . . . . .

Note: *You may use Schedule C, Form 4720, to determine if you had excess business holdings in 1984.*

13 Taxes on investments which jeopardize charitable purposes (section 4944):

(a) Did you invest during the year any amount in a manner that would jeopardize the carrying out of your charitable purposes? . . . .

(b) Did you make any investment in a prior year (but after December 31, 1969) that could jeopardize your charitable purpose that you had not removed from jeopardy on the first day of your tax year beginning in 1984? . . . .

14 Taxes on taxable expenditures (section 4945):

(a) During the year did you pay or incur any amount to:

(1) Carry on propaganda, or otherwise attempt to influence legislation by attempting to affect the opinion of the general public or any segment thereof, or by communicating with any member or employee of a legislative body, or by communicating with any other government official or employee who may participate in the formulation of legislation?

(2) Influence the outcome of any specific public election, or to carry on, directly or indirectly, any voter registration drive? . . . .

(3) Provide a grant to an individual for travel, study, or other similar purposes? . . . .

(4) Provide a grant to an organization, other than a charitable, etc., organization described in section *509(a) (1), (2), or (3)?* · · · · · ·

(5) Provide for any purpose other than religious, charitable, scientific, literary, or educational purposes, or for the prevention of cruelty to children or animals? . . . .

(b) If you answered "Yes" to any of questions 14 (a)(1) through (a)(5), were all such transactions excepted transactions as described in regulations section 53.4945? . . . .

(c) If you answered "Yes" to question 14(a)(4), do you claim exemption from the tax because you maintained expenditure responsibility for the grant? . . . .

If "Yes" attach the statement required.

15 Did any persons become substantial contributors during the tax year? . . . .
If "Yes" attach a schedule listing their names and addresses.

16 During this tax year did you maintain any part of your accounting/tax records on a computerized system? . . . .

Part VI	Information About Officers, Directors, Trustees, Foundation Managers, Highly Paid Employees and Contractors

1 List all officers, directors, trustees, foundation managers and, if paid, their compensation for 1984 (see instructions):

Name and address	Title, and average hours per week devoted to position	Contributions to employee benefit plans	Expense account, other allowances	Compensation
6				

Total . . . . ▶

2 Compensation of five highest paid employees for 1984 (other than included in 1 above—see instructions):

Name and address of employees paid more than $30,000	Title, and time devoted to position	Contributions to employee benefit plans	Expense account, other allowances	Compensation
7				

Total number of other employees paid over $30,000 ▶

Part X Qualifying Distributions (see Instructions)

1 Amounts paid (including administrative expenses) to accomplish charitable, etc., purposes:

   (a) Expenses, contributions, gifts, etc.—total from Part I, column (D), line 26 . . . .

   (b) Program-related investments . . . .

2 Amounts paid to acquire assets used (or held for use) directly in carrying out charitable, etc., purposes . . .

3 Amounts set aside for specific charitable projects that satisfy the:

   (a) Suitability test (prior IRS approval required) . . . .

   (b) Cash distribution test (attach the required schedule) . . . .

4 Total qualifying distributions made in 1984 (add lines 1, 2, and 3)—also enter in Part XI, line 4 . . . .

8

Part XI Computation of Undistributed Income (see instructions)	(a) Corpus	(b) Years prior to 1983	(c) 1983	(d) 1984
1 Distributable amount for 1984 from Part IX . .				
2 Undistributed income, if any, as of the end of 1983:				
(a) Enter amount for 1983				
(b) Total for prior years: ____ , ____ , ____ .				
3 Excess distributions carryover, if any, to 1984:				
(a) From 1979				
(b) From 1980				
(c) From 1981				
(d) From 1982				
(e) From 1983				
(f) Total of 3(a) through (e)				
4 Qualifying distributions for 1984 _____				
(a) Applied to 1983, but not more than line 2(a)				
(b) Applied to undistributed income of prior years (Election required)				
(c) Treated as distributions out of corpus (Election required)				
(d) Applied to 1984 distributable amount . .				
(e) Remaining amount distributed out of corpus				
5 Excess distributions carryover applied to 1984 . (If an amount appears in column (d), the same amount must be shown in column (a))				
6 Enter the net total of each column as indicated below:				
(a) Corpus. Add lines 3(f), 4(c), and 4(e). Subtract line 5				
(b) Prior years' undistributed income. Line 2(b) minus line 4(b)	(b)			
(c) Enter the amount of prior years' undistributed income for which a notice of deficiency has been issued, or on which the section 4942(a) tax has been previously assessed . . .	(c)			
(d) Subtract line 6(c) from line 6(b). Taxable amount— see instructions.	(d)			
(e) Undistributed income for 1983. Line 2(a) minus line 4(a). Taxable amount—see instructions. .				
(f) Undistributed income for 1984. Line 1 minus lines 4(d) and 5. This amount must be distributed in 1985				
7 Amounts treated as distributions out of corpus to satisfy requirements imposed by section 170(b)(1)(D) or 4942(g)(3) (see instructions) . .				
8 Excess distributions carryover from 1979 not applied on line 5 or line 7 (see instructions) . . .				
9 Excess distributions carryover to 1985. (Line 6(a) minus lines 7 and 8)				
10 Analysis of line 9:				
(a) Excess from 1980 . . .				
(b) Excess from 1981 . . .				
(c) Excess from 1982 . . .				
(d) Excess from 1983 . . .				
(e) Excess from 1984 . . .				

Part XII	Private Operating Foundations (See Instructions and Part V, question 9)

1 (a) If the foundation has received a ruling or determination letter that it is an operating foundation, and the ruling is effective for 1984, enter the date of the ruling . . . . ▶

(b) Check box to indicate whether you are an operating foundation described in section ☐ 4942(j)(3) or ☐ 4942(j)(5).

		Tax year		Prior 3 Years						
2 (a) For 1984, 1983 and 1982, enter the lesser of the adjusted net income from Part I or the minimum investment return from Part VIII of the return for each correct year. For 1981, enter the adjusted net income from that return		**(a)** 1984	**(b)** 1983		**(c)** 1982		**(d)** 1981		**(e)** Total	
(b) 85% of line (a)										
(c) Qualifying distributions from Part X, line 4, for 1984 (enter corresponding amount for prior years)										
(d) Amounts included in (c) not used directly for active conduct of exempt activities .										
(e) Qualifying distributions made directly for active conduct of exempt purposes (line (c) minus line (d))										
3 Complete the alternative test in (a), (b), or (c) on which you rely:										
(a) "Assets" alternative test—enter:										
(1) Value of all assets										
(2) Value of assets qualifying under section 4942(j)(3)(B)(i)										
(b) "Endowment" alternative test—Enter ⅔ of minimum investment return shown in Part VIII, line 6, for 1984 (enter ⅔ of comparable amount for prior years)										
(c) "Support" alternative test—enter:										
(1) Total support other than gross investment income (interest, dividends, rents, payments on securities loans (section 512(a)(5)), or royalties) . .										
(2) Support from general public and 5 or more exempt organizations as provided in section 4942(j)(3)(B)(iii) . .										
(3) Largest amount of support from an exempt organization										
(4) Gross investment income. . . .										

Part XIII	Supplementary Information (see Instructions)

1   Information Regarding Foundation Managers

(a) List here any managers of the foundation who have contributed more than 2% of the total contributions received by the foundation before the close of any tax year (but only if they have contributed more than $5,000). (See section 507(d)(2).)

(b) List here any managers of the foundation who own 10% or more of the stock of a corporation (or an equally large portion of the ownership of a partnership or other entity) of which the foundation has a 10% or greater interest.

2   Information Regarding Contribution, Grant, Gift, Loan, Scholarship, etc., Programs

If you make gifts, grants, awards, (see instructions) etc., to individuals or organizations, check here ☐ and complete these items:

(a)   The name, address, and telephone number of the person to whom applications should be addressed

9

(b)   The form in which applications should be submitted and information and materials they should include

(c)   Any submission deadlines

(d)   Any restrictions or limitations on awards, such as by geographical areas, charitable fields, kinds of institutions, or other factors

The Foundation Center makes microfilmed copies of foundation returns available for free public use at most of its cooperating libraries. Complete sets of IRS records for all foundations are available in the Center's New York and Washington, D.C., libraries. The Center's Cleveland and San Francisco offices contain IRS records for foundations in the midwestern and western states, respectively. Cooperating libraries which maintain collections of IRS records for foundations in their own states are indicated in Appendix G.

OTHER RESOURCES

In addition to the resources we've described here, Foundation Center libraries maintain collections of annual reports, information brochures, and newsletters published by foundations and corporate grantmakers, as well as files of news clippings, releases, and historical materials about foundations. These resources will be particularly helpful in the final stages of your funding search when you try to gather as much information as possible about those few foundations you have identified as the most likely funding sources for your program or organization.

6

Finding the Right Foundation: The Subject Approach

THE SUBJECT APPROACH to foundation funding research will help any non-profit organization identify foundations that have shown an interest in funding programs in their field of activity, programs that serve the same population groups, or organizations that are similar in function and purpose to the grantseeker's own agency.

Foundation subject interests are expressed in two broad ways: what a foundation says it does and what it actually did. Foundations describe their giving priorities in their annual reports, newsletters, program pamphlets, and brochures. Publishers in the field describe the giving interests of specific foundations in their directories, indexes, computer printouts, pamphlets, and books. These statements of giving interests provide useful guidelines to the grants a foundation is likely to make, but be sure to check the descriptions of foundation interests and priorities against actual giving records to get the full picture. Often foundation program statements are left purposely broad in order to allow for future shifts in emphasis. Statements of program interests are developed to last for substantial time periods, but actual grantmaking priorities may change subtly as the needs or problems shift in a field. Many foundations have such broad statements of purpose it will be impossible for you to know whether to approach them without examining their full giving record. Statements like "general charitable giving" and "to promote human welfare" don't really mean that a foundation will make grants for any purpose at all. Examining descriptions of recent foundation grants generally provides more specific and current information about funding priorities.

STEP ONE: DEVELOPING A SUBJECT PROSPECT LIST

Before you begin to develop your subject prospect list, you need to take a few minutes to think about all the subject fields related to your organization's activities or to your specific project. For example, if you are working for a day care center which is planning a special program for parents on nutrition for children, your list of subject terms might include day care, children, food, nutrition, boys, girls, parent education, health, etc. If you are seeking funding for a museum which wants to produce a slide show on women artists that can be shown in local schools, your list of subject terms might include art education, museums, audiovisual materials, children, women, elementary education, etc. Scanning the subject indexes of published references such as *The Foundation Directory* and *The Foundation Grants Index Annual* may help you to think of terms applicable to your project. Define your list of terms as broadly as possible.

As you develop your prospect list, you will be looking for foundations that have indicated an interest in any one of your areas of activity. It would be rare—and probably not desirable—to find a foundation that has funded a program exactly like yours, so rather than search for an exact match, you will want to investigate programs that are similar or related to your own. At this stage of your research, keep your focus as wide as possible and err on the side of inclusion.

As you uncover each potential funding source, you will want to focus on the basic facts outlined in the Initial Prospect Worksheet (Figure 6). You may discover many foundations interested in your subject field whose giving is limited to a different location or that are restricted from providing the type of support you need. Noting these facts when you find them will save you from retracing your steps later or wasting time preparing a proposal for a foundation that must ultimately reject your application.

You will be using three types of reference books to develop your subject prospect list: indexes of foundation grants, directories describing foundation giving interests, and specialized subject guides to funding sources. Although all fundraisers eventually develop their own research styles, experience has led Foundation Center staff to recommend the sequence of investigation outlined in Figure 20.

FIGURE 20. Finding the Right Foundation: The Subject Approach

The Subject Approach helps you identify potential funding sources that have expressed an interest in your subject field, the population groups you serve, and the type of organization you represent. Most of the resources listed below cover both national and local funding sources. As you complete your Initial Prospect List using these resources, be sure to check for any stated restrictions on the foundations' giving programs to eliminate those which do not fund in your geographic area, do not provide the type or amount of support you need, or do not fund your type of organization.

STEP 1. INDEXES OF FOUNDATION GRANTS list grants of $5,000 or more awarded by about 450 major foundations. By reviewing actual grants, you can identify funders with a demonstrated interest in your subject area.

- **COMSEARCH: SUBJECTS** list grants within over 60 specific subject categories. Check the list of foundations at the back to eliminate funders with specific limitations, then review the grant records of the remaining funders to identify potential funding sources.

- **COMSEARCH: BROAD TOPICS** list grants in over 20 broad fields. Use if there is no specific subject printout for your area or if you are active in the broader field. Scan grant lists of foundations located in your state. Use Index by Recipient Location and list of Foundation Addresses and Limitations to identify foundations in other states who have funded or might fund organizations in your area.

- **FOUNDATION GRANTS INDEX ANNUAL** lists all grants reported in previous year. Use if there is no COMSEARCH for your area, if you are active in a variety of fields, and to review the broad grant activities of a foundation. Check the Subject Keyword Index under all applicable terms, the Subject-Geographic Index under your category and state, and the Recipient Category Index under your type of institution, type of support needed, and state.

- **FOUNDATION GRANTS INDEX BIMONTHLY** lists grants reported during preceding 2 months. Use to investigate the most current giving interests of major foundations. Check Subject Keyword Index under all applicable terms and Recipient Name Index for organizations similar to your own. Scan grant lists of foundations in your state, as well as foundations in other state which are not restricted from giving in your geographic area.

STEP 2. SOURCE BOOK PROFILES analyzes the 1,000 largest foundations in depth. Check Subject Index under all relevant terms for foundations in your own state or national foundations (listed in bold type) in other states.

STEP 3. THE FOUNDATION DIRECTORY describes foundations with assets of $1 million or more or annual giving of at least $100,000 (approx. 4500). Check Subject Index under appropriate terms for foundations in your own state or national foundations (listed in bold type) in other states.

STEP 4. STATE AND LOCAL FOUNDATION DIRECTORIES. Coverage and content varies. Check bibliography and your local library to find directories that cover your state. Use subject index, if available, or scan entries to identify possible prospects.

STEP 5. SPECIAL FUNDING GUIDES. Coverage and content varies. Check bibliography and your local library to identify relevant guides.

STEP 6. REVIEW YOUR INITIAL PROSPECT LIST to eliminate foundations that are unable or unlikely to provide funding in your geographic area, to provide the type or amount of support you need, or to fund your type of organization. Research remaining prospects (Figures 36 and 37) to determine those most likely to consider your request favorably.

Indexes to Foundation Grants

Indexes to foundation grants provide listings of actual grants awarded and enable you to determine the specific subject interests of a foundation, the types and locations of organizations it has funded, the size of the grants it has typically given, and the types of support it has awarded. The three indexes we will focus on are all derived from The Foundation Center's Grants Index Database which was described more fully in Chapter 5. As you may remember, this database covers grants of $5,000 or more awarded by about 460 major foundations. As many of these foundations make relatively large grants for programs that have a national focus, these tools will be most useful for grantseekers whose projects are of a size and scope to attract the interest of those foundations.

You should begin your research by checking the list of COMSEARCH: Subjects (Figure 8) to see if there are any subject printouts in your fields of interest. These printouts are currently available in 65 different areas of foundation giving. Grant listings are arranged alphabetically by the foundation's state location and name. Because of their specificity, these printouts are short and relatively easy to scan.

Begin with the alphabetical list of foundations provided in the back of each printout. This listing includes the foundation's address and a brief statement of any restrictions on their giving program. This will help you to quickly eliminate foundations that do not award grants in your geographic area. Then scan the grants listed under foundations whose restrictions do not seem to prohibit funding your proposal to complete the other facts on your prospect worksheet, i.e., types of grant recipients, types of support awarded, etc.

If there is no COMSEARCH: Subjects printout in your field of interest or if the focus of your project falls under many related subject fields, you will want to look at the COMSEARCH: Broad Topic that is most applicable to your program. There are 24 COMSEARCH: Broad Topics, and they are also arranged alphabetically by foundation state and name. Each Broad Topic includes a list of foundations with their address and brief giving limitations, a specific subject index, a geographic index by the states where grant recipients are located, and an index by the names of recipient organizations.

We recommend again that you begin with the list of foundations at the back of the book to eliminate foundations that would clearly be restricted from providing support to your organization (see Figure 21). Then scan the lists of grants under the remaining foundations to complete your broad prospect worksheet.

Many grantseekers will find they need to consult both a COMSEARCH: Subjects printout and a COMSEARCH: Broad Topic to identify the greatest number of foundation prospects. For example, a fundraiser for a university which is seeking support for chemistry research will want to consult the COMSEARCH: Subjects printout on "Chemistry," as well as the Broad Topic, Grants for Higher

FIGURE 21. Sample List of Foundations in COMSEARCH: BROAD TOPICS

FOUNDATIONS

The following is an alphabetical list of foundations appearing in this volume. The list is meant to serve as a quick reference tool and not as a mailing list. Descriptions of the limitations on giving under which many of the foundations award grants are included in a limitations statement (LM) following the foundation's address. Foundations usually will not consider proposals which fall outside their limitations or their areas of interest. Careful research to determine your eligibility for consideration and the foundation's possible interest in your proposal is essential before applying to any of the foundations listed below. IF YOU DO NOT QUALIFY, DO NOT APPLY. (See the introduction to this volume for further information.) Additional information identifying foundations meeting certain criteria is coded as follows:

R--publishes an annual or periodic report;
CS--company-sponsored foundation;
CM--community foundation; and
*--100 largest foundations.

Abell (The A. S.) Company Foundation, Inc.
1116 Fidelity Bldg.
210 N. Charles St.
Baltimore, MD 21201-4013
LM: Grants primarily in the Baltimore, MD area

Achelis Foundation, The
c/o Morris & McVeigh
767 Third Avenue
New York, NY 10017
LM: Grants primarily in the New York City, NY area

Aeroquip Foundation
300 South East Avenue
Jackson, MI 49203-1972
LM: Grants in areas of Aeroquip Corporation operations
CS R

Arizona Community Foundation
4350 E. Camelback Rd., Suite 216C
Phoenix, AZ 85018
LM: Grants limited to AZ
CM R

*Astor (The Vincent) Foundation
405 Park Avenue
New York, NY 10022
LM: General limitation to programs in or of primary benefit to New York City, NY. Generally, no grants to the performing arts
R

Athwin Foundation
901 Midwest Plaza East
Minneapolis, MN 55402
R

Bat Hanadiv Foundation, No. 3
c/o Carter, Ledyard & Milburn
2 Wall Street
New York, NY 10005
Application address outside Israel:
Mr. M. Rowe, Trustee
5 Rue Pedro Mevlan
Geneva, Switzerland
Application address in Israel:
Mr. A. Fried
16 Ibn Gvirol Street
Jerusalem 92430 Israel
LM: Grants primarily in Israel

Bay (Charles Ulrick and Josephine) Foundation, Inc.
14 Wall Street, Suite 1600
New York, NY 10005

Education, to identify foundations with a more general interest in higher education institutions.

Once you have developed an initial list of prospects using *COMSEARCH Printouts,* you may want to expand your list by checking the references in *The Foundation Grants Index Annual.* The *Index* lists all grants of $5,000 or more reported by foundations in the preceding year, regardless of subject focus. It is particularly useful if your program or agency falls under a variety of subject fields or if there is no appropriate *COMSEARCH Printout* for your subject area.

The *Index* is also arranged by foundation name and state and includes indexes to the grant listings by recipient name, specific subject focus, broad subject categories subdivided by the state location of the grant recipient, and type of recipient organization subdivided by the type of support awarded. To add to your prospect list, you can:

1. Scan the grant lists of foundations located in your state.

2. Check grants in your specific subject field in the Subject Keyword Index and the Subject/Geographic Index (see Figures 22 and 23).

3. Check grants to organizations similar to your own in the Recipient Name Index and the Recipient Category Index (see Figures 24 and 25).

FIGURE 22. Keyword Index in THE FOUNDATION GRANTS INDEX ANNUAL

Abortion, education 14903
Abortion, information service 5729
Abortion, opposition 36090, 36110, 36113, 36120
Abortion, prevention 20341, 34572, 36157
Abortion, public affairs 16009
Abortion, rights 1744, 1865, 18851, 18874, 20059, 20385, 20708, 20770, 26331, 27458, 27474, 28103, 29024, 29136, 29172
Accounting (public interest) 8477, 16122
Accounting, association 5913, 5946, 8570, 13986, 16526, 16564, 23794
Accounting, education 14324, 28572, 28643
Accounting, minorities 8540
Accounting, nonprofit agencies 771, 1823, 3534, 12856, 16703, 17243, 21051, 31195, 31873, 32431, 32710
Accounting, research 31572
Accounting, student aid 14324
Accounting, university 4653, 28672, 35350, 35351, 35461, 35542, 35588
Administration (arts) 20984
Administration (business) 20425, 21110, 22110

Administration (college) 610, 3686, 11083, 12532, 12542, 12543, 12553, 12568, 12590, 12599, 12626, 12642, 12653, 12672, 12681, 12684, 12686, 12687, 12730, 13043, 15827, 16899, 19453, 19459, 19493, 19494, 19561, 19638, 19710, 19711, 22354, 23757, 23957, 30678, 33415, 33524, 35111
Administration (college) conference 18709
Administration (education) 999, 15619, 15620, 15639, 25028
Administration (educational) 5679, 20321, 20402, 20884, 21125, 31625, 35880
Administration (health) 6058, 8412, 10625, 12531, 12551, 16421, 26003, 27833, 31720, 31737, 33868
Administration (hospital) 19224, 28563, 31707, 32587
Administration (law) 20702
Administration (public) 5299, 5328, 8603, 9835, 18712, 20357, 20425, 20875, 22689, 23422, 23833, 25165, 29988, 30919, 35513
Administration (school) 1187, 2558, 3200-3202, 6476, 9658, 10692, 12970, 12971, 13410, 13668, 15376, 15567, 15648, 16032, 20140, 21289, 27046, 29055, 29206, 31352, 31363, 31464, 31465, 33875, 33888, 34304, 34738

FIGURE 23. Subject/Geographic Index in THE FOUNDATION GRANTS INDEX ANNUAL

Adult or continuing education

Alabama 12526
Argentina 20411
Arizona 19480, 21590
Arkansas 2839, 2862, 7208
Australia 12713, 20333
Bangladesh 20340, 20349
Brazil 20577, 20696
California 394, 487, 502, 1105, 1559, 1565, 1900, 2214, 2417, 2437, 2474, 2479, 2558, 2568, 2616, 2840, 2868, 2992, 3036, 3048, 3131, 3200-3202, 3404, 3454, 3461, 3468, 3506, 3546, 3566, 3614, 3615, 3619, 3628, 3785, 3822, 3850, 3852, 3864, 3891, 3905, 4337, 4478, 5108, 5738, 11018, 12569, 12674, 13095, 13793, 17380, 19816, 19817, 19854, 20270, 20571, 20825, 21078, 21188, 21917, 23124, 25329, 26491, 26552, 26560, 27298, 32260, 34745
Canada 13132
Chile 20805
Colombia 7264, 20722
Colorado 532, 4875, 5039, 5082, 5083, 5269, 5284, 5328, 6846, 6989, 8697, 12132, 17718, 19445, 24113
Connecticut 5679, 6295, 6342, 6355, 6366, 6374, 6438, 6476, 15912, 21083, 21319, 21323, 21720

District of Columbia 910, 999, 2256, 2576, 2705, 3257, 6013, 6758, 6825, 6826, 6830, 6969, 7181, 7396, 9883, 10984, 12527, 12948, 12949, 13088, 13769, 15985, 16638, 16690, 18414, 18640, 18665, 19484, 19642, 19717, 20226, 20308, 20402, 20686, 20823, 21180, 23448, 23534, 25299, 25301, 25343, 25453, 25639,
England 13024, 20372, 20713
Florida 17416, 19701, 25146
Georgia 7880, 13772, 21121, 21693, 32280, 33896
Guam 21638
Hawaii 2188, 8145, 12586, 21648
Honduras 20489
Illinois 1350, 1572, 5866, 8643, 9282, 9521, 9763, 9827, 9829, 9917, 9961, 10013, 10480, 12577, 13947, 15653, 17385, 20240, 20272, 21091, 21200, 21846
India 20433, 20663, 20665, 20667, 20830, 20831, 20870, 21103, 21157
Indiana 10873, 11048, 11055, 11068, 11070, 15418, 22051, 29188
Indonesia 20294, 20597, 21208
Iowa 18933
Israel 20316, 20719, 20775
Ivory Coast 21182
Jordan 20361

FIGURE 24. Recipient Name Index in THE FOUNDATION GRANTS INDEX ANNUAL

A Better Chance, MA, 523, 5795, 9216, 11317, 11695, 15948, 16497, 16702, 19026, 22786, 23738, 26208, 26770, 30643, 32358, 33014, 33388, 35079

A Better Chance, NJ, 17242

A Better Chance, NY, 24688, 25065

A Better Chance, OH, 29272

A Better Chance Counseling Service, MA, 17387

A Chance to Change, OK, 30250

A Contemporary Theater, WA, 26372, 35854

A Non Smoking Generation-United States, NY, 14319

A Womans Place, PA, 32359, 32659

A. L. Castle Memorial, HI, 8188

A. Philip Randolph Educational Fund, NY, 23678

A. Philip Randolph Institute, NY, 6507

A.A. and Hattie Mae Bush Scholarship, TX, 34058

A.G. Rhodes Home, GA, 7925

A-Center, WI, 36282

Abandoned Properties Action Group of Germantown, PA, 32660

Abbott House, NY, 24689

Abbott-Northwestern Hospital, MN, 15532

ABC Learning Centre, IN, 10843, 10947

Abernethy Memorial United Methodist Church, NC, 27554

Abilene Boys Ranch, TX, 33963

Abilene Christian University, TX, 524, 34080, 34385

Abilene Intercollegiate School of Nursing, TX, 33964

Abington Art Center, PA, 31861

Abington Memorial Hospital, PA, 14604, 16498, 21365

Abortion Education and Referral Service, MN, 14903

Abraxas Foundation, PA, 22787, 30644, 31474, 31599

Abuse Counseling and Treatment, FL, 21461

Abuser Treatment Program, NC, 7199

Academic Development Institute, IL, 9820

Academic Library Management Intern Program, DC, 6825, 6826

Academy at Charlemont, MA, 11318

Academy for Educational Development, NY, 20207, 20208

Academy for State and Local Government, DC, 16296, 20209, 32360

Academy of American Poets, NY, 17379

Academy of Basic Education, WI, 36188

Academy of Independent Scholars, CO, 19446

Academy of Media and Theater Arts, CA, 4393

Academy of Music of Philadelphia, PA, 525, 31994, 32661

Academy of Natural Sciences, PA, 526, 7763, 7764, 23922, 29273, 31374, 32155, 32361, 34637, 35689

FIGURE 25. Recipient Category Index in THE FOUNDATION GRANTS INDEX ANNUAL

AGENCY (DIRECT SERVICE)

Capital support

Alabama 33640

Arizona 482, 3213, 12778, 21465, 21484, 21529, 21590, 21630, 21670, 21812, 30046, 36122

Arkansas 30240

California 253, 259, 260, 263, 266, 267, 292, 297, 300, 323, 327, 334, 343, 355, 399, 402, 423, 427, 453, 458, 470, 479, 481, 485, 489, 494, 496, 498, 548, 594, 670, 729, 805, 951, 1340, 1425, 1438, 1442, 1629, 1873, 1911, 1948, 1952, 1953, 1956-1966, 1975, 1978, 1979, 1982, 1985-1990, 1992, 1994-1998, 2001, 2002, 2007, 2008, 2010, 2011, 2015, 2017-2019, 2023, 2025, 2028, 2032, 2033, 2036, 2039, 2041, 2043-2048, 2054, 2056, 2058-2060, 2062, 2099, 2108, 2132, 2192, 2196, 2276, 2394, 2415, 2416, 2419, 2422-2430, 2437, 2441, 2448, 2454, 2459, 2461, 2464, 2469, 2470, 2475, 2482, 2484, 2501, 2513-2517, 2520, 2525, 2527, 2531, 2534, 2538, 2546, 2549-2551, 2586, 2707, 2709, 2718, 2731, 2736, 2745, 2748, 2762, 2776, 2777, 2814, 2837, 2894, 2941, 2955, 2962, 2987, 3023, 3037, 3049, 3087, 3088, 3097, 3122, 3152, 3156, 3160-3162, 3199, 3209, 3210, 3242, 3253, 3256, 3265, 3302, 3317, 3318, 3325, 3342-3344, 3351, 3358, 3361-3365, 3367, 3368, 3370, 3372, 3374, 3381, 3386, 3391, 3392, 3394-3397, 3409, 3410, 3416, 3437, 3441, 3453, 3457, 3462, 3493, 3525, 3538, 3573, 3574, 3587, 3594, 3625, 3627, 3645, 3717, 3720, 3727, 3732, 3753, 3763, 3828, 3831, 3863, 3900, 3909, 3911, 3918, 3920-3922, 3926, 3927, 3929, 3930, 3933, 3938-3942, 3946, 3947, 3951, 3954, 3955, 3957, 3958, 3963, 3964, 3968, 3975, 3977, 3979, 3981, 3987, 3988, 3990, 3991, 3997, 4020, 4033, 4040, 4063, 4064, 4072, 4076, 4083, 4089, 4090, 4135-4139, 4171, 4176, 4247, 4395, 4404, 4405, 4407, 4417, 4439, 4448, 4474, 4477, 4496, 4502, 4511, 4512, 4516, 4554, 4558, 4560, 4584, 4615, 4616, 4662, 4663, 4672, 4680, 4682, 4683, 4685, 4689, 4690, 4696, 4698, 4702-4706, 4708-4712, 4720, 4730, 4731, 4733, 4736, 4747, 4748, 7215, 12741, 12784, 12816, 12829, 13240, 13298, 13783, 13891, 21477, 21496, 21519, 21619, 21629, 21658, 21662, 21726, 21732, 21798, 21861, 21895, 22000, 22039, 22808, 22922, 27220, 27268, 28846, 28994, 29882, 30061, 33421

Cameroon 7016

Canada 21511, 32204

Colorado 618, 4774, 4775, 4777, 4780, 4790, 4792, 4809, 4821, 4822, 4825, 4826, 4830, 4831, 4842, 4861, 4873, 4890, 4910, 4940, 4956, 4977, 4990, 5000, 5025, 5026, 5029, 5031, 5033, 5045, 5052, 5056-5058, 5068, 5072, 5073, 5076, 5078, 5080, 5085, 5086, 5107, 5113, 5119, 5122, 5134, 5174, 5315, 21729, 21740, 21782, 27216

Again, you will want to look at the size and type of awards the foundation has funded generally, as well as the types and locations of organizations it supports. Note any giving limitation statement provided immediately under the foundation's name.

To get the most current information on foundation funding interests and to add to your prospect list the names of foundations newly active in your field, you will want to check the listings in *The Foundation Grants Index Bimonthly*. Each *Bimonthly* lists 2,000 recently reported foundation grants with indexes by subject and recipient organization names.

Directories of Foundations

You may have developed a fairly long list of prospects by now, but because all of the *Index* publications cover only about 450 of the nation's foundations, you have only examined a small portion of the foundation community. To expand your prospect list, you should turn to the directories of foundations available to you. Include local foundation directories as well as national ones, and be especially alert for special subject directories published in your field. In general, you will find that indexes to foundation grants provide far more specific subject references because they classify actual grants. Directories of foundations usually use very general terminology to describe foundation program interests, and therefore the terms provided in any subject indexes are equally general.

We generally recommend that you begin with The Foundation Center's *Source Book Profiles*, a quarterly information service which provides detailed analyses of the nation's 1,000 largest foundations. Each volume includes a subject index, which lists foundations under the subject fields where they have made grants (see Figure 26). Once you have noted foundation names from the appropriate index categories, you should examine the actual profiles of the foundations to complete your prospect worksheet. Note especially the giving restrictions which are printed in bold type for easy reference.

Your next stop should be *The Foundation Directory*. It covers over 4,400 foundations that have at least $1 million in assets or award total grants of $100,000 or more annually and includes the "Subject Index" to help you quickly identify foundations which have expressed an interest in your subject field (see Figure 27). This index includes over 100 broad subject categories which are subdivided by foundation state locations. Foundations with national or regional giving patterns appear in bold type under the state where they are located; foundations that are restricted to local giving appear in regular type. As you check the references in your subject category, add to your prospect list foundations in your own state as well as the names of foundations in other states that are indicated in bold type. Make a note of the foundation's state and entry number so that you can easily check back to the full entry. Again, the full entry will

FIGURE 26. Subject Index in SOURCE BOOK PROFILES

Accounting
New York: **Deloitte 85, Price Waterhouse 84**
Ohio: **Ernst 84, 86U**

Adult education
Michigan: **Kellogg (W.K.) 86, Mott (Charles) 85, 86U**
New Jersey: **Newcombe 85**

Africa
Wisconsin: **DeRance 85, Young 84**

Aged
California: California 85, 86U, Factor 85, Haas (Evelyn) 86, Hancock 86, **Levi 84, 85U, 86U,** Lytel 85, **Parsons 86,** Peninsula 86
Colorado: Anschutz 86, Hill 86, Hunter 85
Connecticut: **Educational 85, 86U,** Hartford Public 85, 86U, List 84
Florida: Bush (Edyth) 85, Selby 85
Georgia: Callaway Foundation 86, Pitts 84, 86U, Whitehead (Lettie) 84
Hawaii: Cooke 85, Wilcox 85
Illinois: **Abbott (Clara) 86,** Crown (Arie) 86, Field Foundation (IL) 85, **Retirement 85**
Michigan: Gerstacker 86, Kalamazoo 85, 86U, Strosacker 85
Minnesota: Bremer 85, Gamble 85, Mardag 85, **Medtronic 84, 85U**

Missouri: Hall Family 86, Speas (John) 85, Speas (Victor) 85
New Jersey: **Allied 86,** Rippel 86
New York: Astor 86, **Burden 85, Commonwealth 85,** Cummings 85, 86U, **Dreyfus (Max) 85, General Foods 86,** Gifford 85, Greenwall 85, 86U, **Hartford (John) 86,** Jones (Daisy) 85, Kaufman 84, 86U, **McDonald 84,** Moses 85, 86U, New York Foundation 84, 86U, Nias 85, Ramapo 85, Spingold 84
North Carolina: Foundation for the Carolinas 86, Winston-Salem 85
Ohio: McGregor (A.M.) 86, Moores 85, Richland 86
Oregon: Chiles 85, Meyer (Fred) 84, 86U
Pennsylvania: Grundy 85, Medical 86, Smith (W.W.) 85, **Westinghouse Electric 84**
Rhode Island: Champlin 85, Rhode 85
South Carolina: Self 85
Tennessee: Church 84
Washington: Norcliffe 85
Wisconsin: **Johnson Controls 84,** McBeath 85, 86U, Milwaukee 85, Schroeder 86, Siebert 86

Agriculture
Arkansas: Rockefeller (Winthrop) 85
California: Lytel 85
Illinois: **Moorman 84**
Michigan: **Kellogg (W.K.) 86**
Minnesota: Bremer 85

FIGURE 27. Subject Index in THE FOUNDATION DIRECTORY

Accounting
New York: **Deloitte 2395, Price 2840**
Ohio: Ernst 3207

Adult education
California: **American 69**
Michigan: Faigle 1695, **Kellogg 1732, Mott 1752**
New Jersey: **Newcombe 2162**
Rhode Island: **Genesis 3777**

Africa
Rhode Island: **Genesis 3777**
Wisconsin: **DeRance 4314, Young 4391**

Aged
California: Arakelian 70, California 114, Callison 118, East Bay 159, Factor 162, Garland 182, Goldman 195, Haas 202, Hancock 209, Joslyn 241, Kirchgessner 245, **Levi 258,** Lytel 269, **Parsons 311,** Pasadena 314, Peninsula 318, San Diego 336, Smith 371
Colorado: Anschutz 435, Hill 452, Hunter 455, Joslyn 460, Rabb 474
Connecticut: **Bissell 500, Educational 516,** EIS 517, Hartford 533, List 551, Robinson 568

District of Columbia: Lehrman 668, **Villers 684**
Florida: Bush 701, **du Pont 713, Eagles 717,** Falk 720, Howell 729, Selby 766
Georgia: Callaway 810, Courts 820, English 830, Pitts 866, **Whitehead 885**
Hawaii: Cooke 895, King's 902, Wilcox 908
Illinois: **Abbott 917,** Alton 924, Beidler 941, Camp 962, Eisenberg 996, Field 1001, **Retirement 1132,** Siragusa 1153, Stern 1167, Willett 1191
Indiana: Smock 1253
Iowa: Van Buren 1285
Maryland: Warfield 1461
Massachusetts: Bacon 1472, Boynton 1484, Campbell 1492, Chase 1498, Farnsworth 1526, Home 1552, Old 1589, Sailors' 1616
Michigan: Gerstacker 1712, Kalamazoo 1728, Strosacker 1780, Whiting 1796
Minnesota: Gamble 1845, Mardag 1879, **Medtronic 1884,** Rivers 1909
Missouri: Hall 1968, Oppenstein 2003, Speas 2018, St. Louis 2020
New Jersey: **Allied 2098,** Duke 2118, Elizabeth 2120, **Rippel 2171**
New York: Albany's 2226, Astor 2248, Brookdale 2305, **Brooklyn 2307,** Bruner 2309, **Burden 2315, Commonwealth 2362,** Cummings 2376, de Kay 2389, **Dorr 2408, Dreyfus 2413,** Faith 2427,

provide the additional information you need to complete your prospect worksheet, that is, grant range, program interests, and limitations on the giving program.

State and local foundation directories, as we noted in Chapter 5, are available for many locations, but they vary a great deal in content and quality. Check the bibliography in Appendix B to find out which directories include your area. You should examine the most current edition of each relevant directory and identify potential funding sources through the subject index, when provided, or by scanning the entries themselves.

Special Funding Guides

The final step in developing your broad prospect list is to examine any special funding guides devoted to your field, i.e., performing arts, higher education, women's programs, etc. A listing of the major guides available in many Foundation Center libraries is provided in Appendix A, and professional journals in your field may include information about other guides. While these guides vary tremendously in currency and content, many may be helpful in identifying additional prospects.

STEP TWO: REFINING YOUR LIST

Your initial prospect list should now be fairly long, and you are ready to begin to narrow your list to those foundations that appear to be your most likely funding resources. If you have taken the time to fill out your prospect worksheets, you should now be able to quickly eliminate foundations:

1. that do not award grants in your geographic area;

2. that do not provide the type of support you need;

3. whose average grant range is too large or too small for your funding needs; or

4. that have a different geographic scope (i.e., national, regional, or local) than the focus of your project.

Now you are ready to investigate thoroughly the remaining foundations on your list to find our whether their funding interests truly match your organization's needs and, if so, how to proceed with your grant application. We'll tell you exactly how to do that in Chapters 9 and 10, but first let's look at the other approaches you might take to identify potential funding sources.

7

Finding the
Right Foundation:
The Geographic Approach

ALL NONPROFITS INTERESTED in attracting foundation funding should learn as much as possible about the foundations in their own backyard, both big and small. It is particularly important if you are seeking relatively small grants or funds for projects with purely local impact. When the grantmaking interests of the larger foundations in your community coincide with the program of your organization, you will want to develop a good relationship with appropriate foundation staff members. It might be possible to build a funding structure using a variety of components. For example, you could cultivate small grants of $100 to $5,000 from local foundations for continuing general support and approach large local foundations working in your field of interest when introducing a special project.

Smaller local foundations should be investigated for grants according to their interests and giving range. You will probably find that many of these small foundations give to the same local organizations year after year and rarely make grants to new recipients. However, this should not discourage you from investigating all local sources. Some of your work with potential grantors is education. You must make them aware of the service you are providing and the ways in which you enhance life in their home community.

FIGURE 28. Finding the Right Foundation: The Geographic Approach

The Geographic Approach helps you identify potential funding sources in your state or local community or that have provided funding to organizations in your geographic area. As you complete your Initial Prospect List using these resources, be sure to check for any stated restrictions on the foundations' giving interests as well as their subject interests and types of support offered to determine whether they would be unable or unlikely to support your type of organization or activities in your subject area or to provide the type and amount of support you need.

STEP 1. **STATE AND LOCAL DIRECTORIES.** Coverage and content varies, but generally are useful in identifying local funders. Check bibliography and your local library to find current editions of any relevant directories.

STEP 2. **SOURCE BOOK PROFILES** analyzes the 1,000 largest foundations in depth and includes both national and local funders. Check Geographic Index for foundations located in your state and foundations with a specific interest in your state (indicated with "see also" references).

STEP 3. **THE FOUNDATION DIRECTORY** describes foundations with assets of $1 million or more or annual giving of at least $100,000 (approx. 4500). Arranged alphabetically by state so you can scan all entries for foundations in your area. Also check Geographic Index to identify foundations located elsewhere that have a specific interest in your state or community.

STEP 4. **THE NATIONAL DATA BOOK** lists all active grantmaking foundations in the U.S. alphabetically by state, then in descending order by grant amount. Check for smaller foundations in your state that do not meet criteria for larger directories. Also check the separate section on community foundations to identify those in your community or region.

STEP 5. **INDEXES OF FOUNDATION GRANTS** list grants of $5,000 or more awarded by about 450 major foundations. Useful to identify national foundations that have awarded grants in your area.

- **COMSEARCH: GEOGRAPHICS** lists grants awarded to organizations in specific cities, states or regions. Check the list of foundations at the back to eliminate funders with specific giving limitations, then review the grant records for the remaining funders to determine possible prospects.

- **FOUNDATION GRANTS INDEX ANNUAL** lists all grants reported in previous year. Arranged alphabetically by state where foundation is located. Check Subject/Geographic Index for grants in your subject areas to organizations in your state; Recipient Category Index for grants to similar types of organizations in your state that have received to type of support you need; and Recipient Name Index for grants to organizations in your area or state.

- **FOUNDATION GRANTS INDEX BIMONTHLY** lists grants reported during preceding two months. Use to investigate the most current giving interests of major foundations in your state or check Recipient Name Index for grants to organizations in your area.

STEP 6. **REVIEW YOUR INITIAL PROSPECT LIST** to eliminate foundations that are unable or unlikely to provide funding in your subject area or to your type of organization or the type and amount of support you need. Research remaining prospects (Figures 36 and 37) to determine those most likely to consider your request favorably.

STEP ONE: DEVELOPING A GEOGRAPHIC PROSPECT LIST

Developing a list of foundations that are located in or that fund projects in your city or state is relatively easy. The resources available include both directories of foundations and indexes of foundation grants. Remember, however, that simply matching locations is an inadequate rationale for requesting funds. Once identified, each foundation must be fully researched to see if their grantmaking activities correlate in any way to your proposal.

Figure 28 outlines the sequence of investigation recommended by Foundation Center staff to identify foundation prospects using the geographic approach. Whether you are focusing on large or small foundations, you will want to begin your search with any local or state directories that cover your area. The bibliography in Appendix B lists all area directories the Center is currently aware of. New directories and editions are published frequently, however, so check with the Center or your local library to be sure no more current information has been published. If there is more than one directory for your area, use them all until you are able to verify through your own research which are most accurate and comprehensive.

As you add foundation names to your prospect list from an area directory, be sure to read the entire entry to complete the items on your prospect worksheet. Note any restrictions on the foundation's giving program that would prevent them from funding your project. Some of the smaller foundations are restricted by will or charter to giving to only a few designated organizations. Others may not fund projects in your subject area or they may not be able to offer the type of support you need.

Once you have investigated any relevant local directories, you'll want to examine *Source Book Profiles,* The Foundation Center's quarterly information service which analyzes the nation's 1,000 largest foundations. Each volume includes a geographic index that lists foundations under the state and city where they are located (see Figure 29). At the end of each state listing, a "see also" reference cites foundations located elsewhere that have a history of substantial grantmaking in that state. Once you have gathered the names of foundations from this index, you will want to examine the actual profile of each foundation to complete the additional items on your prospect worksheet. Again, you should take special note of any limitations on the foundation's giving program; these are printed in bold type for easy reference.

To expand your list of funding prospects, you should now consult *The Foundation Directory* which covers the approximately 4,400 foundations that hold assets of at least $1 million or whose annual giving totals $100,000 or more. It is arranged alphabetically by state and includes a geographic index of foundations by state and city to help you identify foundations in your specific community (see Figure 30). Like *Source Book Profiles,* additional references are made at

FIGURE 29. Geographic Index in SOURCE BOOK PROFILES

ALABAMA
Birmingham Meyer (Robert) 84, **Sonat 85**
see also Campbell (J. Bulow) 84, 85U, Steelcase 84

ALASKA
see Murdock 84, 85U

ARIZONA
Phoenix First Interstate Arizona 85, Flinn 84, 85U, Webb 85
Prescott **Kieckhefer 85**
Tucson **Research 85**
see also Boswell 84, Bush (Edyth) 85, Frost 85, Goldsmith 84, Motorola 85, Stocker 85

ARKANSAS
Little Rock **Inglewood 84,** Rockefeller (Winthrop) 85
Malvern Sturgis 84
see also Frost 85, Kerr Foundation 84, Mabee 85

CALIFORNIA
Beverly Hills Factor 85, **Litton 85,** Lloyd 85, Mayer (Louis) 84
Burbank Disney 84
Burlingame Peninsula 84
Corona del Mar Beckman 84
Daly City Gellert (Fred) 84
Ferndale Lytel 85
Hollywood Gospel 85
Irvine **Fluor 84, 85U**
La Canada **Atkinson (Myrtle) 85**
La Jolla Copley 85, Gildred 84, Parker 84, 85U
Livermore **Hertz 84**
Long Beach Norris 85
Los Altos Packard 84, 85U
Los Angeles Ahmanson 85, **Atlantic Richfield 85,** Boswell 84, Braun (Carl) 85, Braun Foundation 85, Burns 84, California 85, Crocker 85, Doheny 85, First Interstate California 85, Goldwyn 84, 85U, Haynes 84, 85U, **Hilton 84,** Hoag 85, Jones Foundation 85, **Keck 84, 85U,** Leavey 85, **Leonhardt 85,** McAlister 84, Murphy (Dan) 85, **Parsons 84,** Pfaffinger 85, Seaver 85, Security 84,

FIGURE 30. Geographic Index in THE FOUNDATION DIRECTORY

ALABAMA
Alexander City Russell 18
Birmingham Birmingham 3, Daniel 7, Linn-Henley 10, McWane 13, Meyer 14, **Sonat 21,** Stockham 22, Webb 24
Brewton McMillan 12
Daphne **Malbis 11,** Smith 20
Enterprise Gibson 9
Mobile Bedsole 2, Chandler 5, Middleton 15, Mitchell 16, Mobile 17
Montgomery Blount 4, **Christian 6,** Flack 8
Mountain Brook Shook 19
Sylacauga Avondale 1
Tuscaloosa Warner 23

see also 775, 813, 865, 1775

ALASKA
Anchorage Alaska 25, Atwood 26

see also 1853, 4241, 4245, 4252, 4262

ARIZONA
Dragoon **Amerind 27**
Flagstaff Raymond 43, Wilson 50
Paradise Valley Waddell 48

Phoenix Arizona 28, Arizona 29, Circle K 31, Dougherty 32, du Bois 33, First 34, Flinn 35, Hervey 38, **Tell 45, Van Schaik 46,** VNB 47, Webb 49
Prescott Butz 30, **Kieckhefer 39,** Morris 41
Scottsdale Goppert 37
Sierra Vista Fry 36
Tucson Marshall 40, Mulcahy 42, **Research 44**

see also 98, 290, 377, 449, 701, 1104, 1204, 1813, 1989, 2483, 3375, 4357

ARKANSAS
Arkadelphia Ross 59
El Dorado Murphy 54
Fort Smith **Reynolds 56**
Little Rock **Inglewood 51,** Lyon 53, Rebsamen 55, Riggs 57, Rockefeller 58, **Wrape 62**
Malvern Sturgis 60
Pine Bluff Trinity 61
Springdale Jones 52

see also 326, 449, 1369, 1374, 3434, 3439, 3443, 3831, 4305, 4360

the end of each state's listing to foundations located elsewhere that have a history of grantmaking in the state. Foundations that make grants on a regional or national basis are indicated in bold type, while local foundations are listed in regular type. You should thoroughly familiarize yourself with the programs of all foundations in your area that are large enough to be included in *The Foundation Directory* or *Source Book Profiles*. If yours is a large state, you may want to limit yourself to foundations in nearby cities.

If your search is focusing on small foundations in your local area, your next stop should be *The National Data Book*, the only directory that offers access to the over 23,500 active grantmaking foundations in the U.S. (Even most state and local directories set some minimum asset or grant criteria to eliminate the very smallest foundations.)

The National Data Book is arranged alphabetically by state, and within states, in descending order by annual grant totals. Because of the columnar format of the *Data Book*, it's easy to go down the list of foundations in your state and identify foundations in your city or broader zip code area (see Figure 31). Although the information presented in the *Data Book* is brief, it does allow you to make some preliminary observations about each foundation based on its size, location, and principal officer. For example, if you are seeking a $1,500 grant, thee is no point in investigating a foundation with assets of $200 and grants of $50. Further, if a bank or trust department is listed as the principal officer, you know that making contact with the foundation could be more difficult.

When you identify foundation prospects from the *Data Book*, be sure to note the employer identification number. This number will help you to locate or order the foundation's annual IRS information return (Form 990-PF), which is generally the best and sometimes the only source of information about the giving programs of smaller foundations.

The *Data Book* also includes a separate listing of all currently active community foundations, which are invaluable local resources. In addition to financial support, many community foundations provide assistance to nonprofit organizations in budgeting, public relations, fundraising strategies, and management. This listing is also arranged alphabetically by state so it will be easy to find out if there is an active community foundation serving your area.

Indexes to Foundation Grants

By now, you have undoubtedly uncovered a large number of foundation prospects from your geographic search. Before you complete this first phase of your research, you should also check indexes of foundation grants to identify foundations that have actually awarded grants to organizations in your area.

The Foundation Grants Index Annual is arranged alphabetically by the states in which the foundations are located. It includes a Subject/Geographic

FIGURE 31. Sample Entry from the NATIONAL DATA BOOK

SEQ NO.	ST	FOUNDATION NAME/ PRINCIPAL OFFICER	CARE OF/ADDRESS CITY	ZIP	FISCAL DATE	GRANTS PAID	ASSETS	EXPENDITURES/ GIFTS RECD	IRS NO.
661	CA	PACIFIC WESTERN FDN / CHAS. F. BANNAN, PRES	8344 E FLORENCE STE E / DOWNEY	90240	11/83	236360	3185997	275671	956097360
662	CA	WILSEY FDN / A. S. WILSEY, PRES	BOX 3532 / SAN FRANCISCO	94119	03/84	236129	265926	238274	946098720
663	CA	PEPPERS FDN, ANN / W PAUL COLWELL, PRES	35 S RAYMOND AVE FOURTH FL / PASADENA	91105	12/83	232505	3289163	135000 / 266928	952114455
664	CA	MCCALLUM DESERT FDN / BANK OF AMERICA NT & SA, TTEE	801 E TAHQUITZ / PALM SPRINGS	92262	02/84	231800	2334403	280488	953175567
665	CA	DOE FDN, MARGUERITE / ANTONIO ROMASANTA, DIR	308 E CARPRILLO ST / SANTA BARBARA	93101	12/83	231500	364317	237521 / 156347	956226536
666	CA	KECK TR FOR POMONA COLLEGE, W M / HOWARD B. KECK, TTEE	% HANNA & MORTON / 600 WILSHIRE BLVD, 17TH FL / LOS ANGELES	90017	06/84	231223	7072759	69145	956482774
667	CA	KECK TR FOR OCCIDENTAL COLLEGE, W M / HOWARD B. KECK, TTEE	% HANNA & MORTON / 600 WILSHIRE BLVD 17TH FL / LOS ANGELES	90017	06/84	231065	7072760	69152 / 0	956484977
668	CA	GALLO FDN, ERNEST / ERNEST GALLO, PRES	PO BOX 1130 / MODESTO	95353	10/83	230485	3071327	235128 / 350000	946061537
669	CA	SIGNAL COMPANIES FDN / JOHN R SPENCER, CHM	11255 N TORREY PINES RD / LA JOLLA	92037	11/83	229170	4510273	295261	237002892
670	CA	YORKIN FDN / BUD YORKIN, PRES	132 S RODEO DR, STE 600 / BEVERLY HILLS	90212	11/83	227552	50439	228445	953454331
671	CA	FUSENOT CHARITY FDN, GEORGES & GERMAINE / ELIZABETH HERLIHY, TTEE	7061 HOLLYWOOD BLVD STE 912 / LOS ANGELES	90028	07/83	226000	3558393	305177	956207831
672	CA	WALKER FDN, T B / BROOKS WALKER, PRES	1280 COLUMBUS AVE / SAN FRANCISCO	94133	09/83	225000	4403491	253212	521078287
673	CA	CHARIS FUND / PAUL FRANCIS D'ANNEO, PRES	% RAYMOND HANSON / 246 E BAYSHORE EMBARCADERO STE 301	94303	12/83	223500	1643702	300834	946077619
674	CA	MERRY MARY CHAR FDN INC / STEPHEN MEADOW, PRES	13003 S FIGUEROA ST / LOS ANGELES	90061	03/84	223313	940304	235288 / 572976	953263582
675	CA	STEINER TR, LIONEL / BANK OF AMERICA, TTEE	PO BOX 37121 / SAN FRANCISCO	94137	06/84	222008	2656584	248670	946445242
676	CA	ASSOCIATED FOUNDATIONS INC / GEORGE HERLIHY, CHM	600 S COMMONWEALTH AVE, STE 1300 / LOS ANGELES	90005	08/83	220500	3130429	276150	237324126
677	CA	SATURNO FDN	% BANK OF AMERICA N T & S A TTEE / PO BOX 37121 / SAN FRANCISCO	94137	10/83	210510	3524647	223369	946073765
678	CA	PEERY FDN, RICHARD T / RICHARD T PEERY, DIR	2560 MISSION COLLEGE BLVD STE 101 / SANTA CLARA	95050	09/83	208368	2935983	221992 / 854600	942460894
679	CA	CARNATION CO SCHOL FDN / STAN KVAMME, MEMBER BOARD OF ADVISORS	5045 WILSHIRE BLVD / LOS ANGELES	90036	12/83	206500	2435099	235409	956118622
680	CA	STANS FDN / MAURICE H STANS, PRES	301 COLORADO BLVD / PASADENA	91101	12/83	205356	2203756	234031	366008663
681	CA	HOUSELS FDN, HUBERT / E AND M TR FOR LONG BEACH, TTEE	PO BOX 991 / LONG BEACH	90801	12/83	205204	2964515	232267 / 0	956381605
682	CA	DE FUIGNE MEM TR FOR CHRISTIAN / FRANCIS DE SUGNY BARK	% ODONNELL WAISS WALL & MESCHKE / 100 BROADWAY THIRD FL / SAN FRANCISCO	94111	12/83	205024	2979411	223298	946076503
683	CA	WEILER FDN, RALPH J / BARTLETT, BUNAP J PRES	9465 WILSHIRE BLVD STE 203 / BEVERLY HILLS	90212	04/84	202855	5252283	302678	237418821
684	CA	BROTMAN FDN OF CALIFORNIA / MICHAEL B SHERMAN, PRES	433 N CAMDEN DR 600 / BEVERLY HILLS	90210	12/83	202535	5479821	353170	956094639
685	CA	GHIDOTTI FDN / WILLIAM & MARIAN / MARY BOUMA, TTEE	% BANK OF AMERICA TR DP / 900 4TH ST / SACRAMENTO	95814	12/83	202040	4248466	237502 / 1673081	946181833
686	CA	SCRIPPS FDN, ELLEN BROWNING / DORINE D SCHAMENS, PRINCIPAL OFF	% CALIFORNIA FIRST BANK TR DEPT / 530 B ST / SAN DIEGO	92101	06/83	201000	2177963	213238	951644633
687	CA	LEVY FDN, ACHILLE / A A MULLIGAN, PRES	% BANK OF A LEVY / 143 W FIFTH ST PO BOX 272 / OXNARD	93032	11/83	199735	83487	200658 / 100000	956264755
688	CA	CARVER FDN / MARGARET CARVER, PRES	3232 PACIFIC AVE / SAN FRANCISCO	94118	05/84	197803	57659	199072 / 222157	942825557
689	CA	MUNGER FDN, ALFRED C / CHARLES T. MUNGER, PRES	% R D ESBENSHADE / 612 S FLOWER ST 5TH FL / LOS ANGELES	90017	11/83	197383	4333521	198789 / 16280	952462103

Index that helps you to identify grants to organizations in your state by the broad subject focus of the grant and a Recipient Category Index that enables you to identify grants to similar types of organizations (e.g., hospitals, private universities, museums, etc.) in your state.

To help you in identifying foundation prospects by geographic focus, The Foundation Center also publishes the grant records from the *Grants Index Annual* in convenient computer printouts titled *COMSEARCH: Geographics*. These printouts list grants awarded to organizations located in each of two cities, eleven states, and seven regions. In each geographic printout, grants are listed alphabetically by the name of the foundation awarding the grant so that you can easily scan the types of programs the foundation has funded in your area. A list of foundations with a brief statement outlining any limitations on their giving program is also included.

As you scan the listing of grants, eliminate foundations that have awarded grants to organizations in your state solely on the basis of their subject focus or because of an affiliation with a specific institution. Note the types of organizations receiving grants, the subject focus of the project, and the size and type of support offered by a particular foundation. Even if a foundation has not provided a limitation statement, you will find some foundations that limit their giving to specific subject areas or to specific types of institutions, such as hospitals or museums. If the foundation's giving pattern does not match your funding needs, it doesn't belong on your prospect list.

STEP TWO: REFINING YOUR LIST

At this point you could have a fairly long list of potential funding sources based on their geographic location or interest. As you completed your prospect worksheets, however, you should have gathered other relevant facts about your prospects that will enable you to quickly eliminate foundations:

1. that do not award grants in your subject field;

2. that do not provide the type of support you need;

3. whose giving is restricted to a city or county other than your own; or

4. whose average grant range is too large or too small for your funding needs.

Now you are ready to examine more carefully the remaining foundations on your list. In Chapter 9, we'll explain the resources and procedures you can use to find out if your organization's needs really fit with a particular foundation's funding interests; but there is one other approach to foundation funding research—the types of support search—that we should examine first.

8

Finding the Right Foundation: The Types of Support Approach

DURING THE PLANNING STAGES that precede a search for funding, you should clarify the specific types of support your organization needs. These might include:

1. **Capital support** for construction or renovation of buildings or for purchase of major equipment, land, or buildings;

2. **Endowment funds** which can be invested to provide future support for your organization;

3. **General operating support** to cover the daily costs involved in running your program;

4. **Seed money** to help start a new project or organization;

5. **Special project funds** to finance a specific service project as opposed to general operation of the organization;

6. **Matching or challenge grants** to help stimulate giving from other potential donors;

7. **Emergency funds** to cover short-term funding needs; or

8. **Loans or program-related investments** to support a project which traditional financial institutions would be unwilling to invest in or would charge prohibitive interest rates for.

The list of types of support available to nonprofit organizations could go on and on and should include resources other than the traditional dollar grant. For example, an organization that needs a new photocopier might look for a local company willing to donate a "demonstration" model instead of seeking a dollar grant to buy the needed equipment. These "in-kind" contributions can include such diverse items as office supplies, computer services, office space, or management assistance from various specialists in the corporate world.

Within the foundation community, you will find that some foundations limit their giving to one or a few specific types of grant support, such as research, special projects, or capital campaigns. Other foundations may offer a variety of types of support but are specifically restricted from providing the specific type of support you need. It is extremely important, therefore, to examine this aspect of a foundation's grantmaking program before submitting a grant request.

When the Types of Support Approach Is Most Useful

There are essentially two types of resources available to help you identify foundations that provide a specific type of support: indexes of foundation grants and *Source Book Profiles*, The Foundation Center's quarterly guide to the nation's 1,000 largest foundations. Since both of these resources focus on the larger foundations, grantseekers who are looking for relatively large grants for institutions that have a national focus or impact will find this approach most useful. Nonetheless, many large foundations do focus their giving on a specific state or local community and provide many smaller grants to local organizations. In short, the types of support approach will be useful to any grantseeker focusing on a specific funding need.

STEP ONE: DEVELOPING A BROAD PROSPECT LIST

Your research will begin with the indexes to foundation grants described more fully in Chapter 5. As you'll recall, *The Foundation Grants Index Annual* lists grants of $5,000 or more reported to The Foundation Center during the previous year by about 460 major foundations. Each annual volume includes a Recipient Category Index which references grants awarded to 15 different types of institutions (e.g., church or temple, community fund, museum, library, private university or college, etc.) by the specific type of support provided to those institutions (see Figure 33). There are ten basic categories of support under which grants are referenced, including capital support, endowment, fellowship or scholarship funds, general or operating support, matching or challenge grants, program development, and research. To ease your research, the references are then subdivided by the states in which grant recipients are located.

FIGURE 32. Finding the Right Foundation: The Types of Support Approach

The Types of Support Approach helps you identify foundations that have expressed an interest in providing the specific type of support your organization needs. It is most useful for fundraising campaigns that focus on endowment funds, capital support for buildings or equipment, matching or challenge grants, conferences or seminars, and other specific types of support. It is important to supplement this approach to identifying potential funders with a subject and geographic search. As you complete your Initial Prospect List using the resources listed below, be sure to check for any stated restrictions on the foundations' giving programs to eliminate those that do not fund in your geographic area, do not fund your type of organization, or do not fund activities in your subject area.

STEP 1. **INDEXES OF FOUNDATION GRANTS** list grants of $5,000 or more awarded by about 450 major foundations. By reviewing actual grants, you can identify foundations that have previously provided the type of support you are seeking.

- **COMSEARCH: SUBJECTS** includes printouts of grants awarded for specific types of support, e.g., Conferences and Seminars, Higher Education—Capital Support, etc. Check the list of foundations at the back to eliminate funders with specific giving limitations, then review the grant records of remaining funders to identify potential funding sources.

- **COMSEARCH: BROAD TOPICS** list grants in over 20 broad fields, including "Matching and Challenge Support." Check the list of foundations at the back to eliminate funders with specific giving limitations, then review the grant records of remaining funders to determine the types of institutions and subject fields they support.

- **FOUNDATION GRANTS INDEX ANNUAL** lists all grants reported in previous year. Unless there is a COMSEARCH printout for your type of institution or type of support, this volume is most useful for the support search. Check the Recipient Category Index under your type of institution, type of support needed, and state.

- **FOUNDATION GRANTS INDEX BIMONTHLY** lists grants reported during preceding 2 months. Use to investigate the most current giving interests of major foundations.

STEP 2. **SOURCE BOOK PROFILES** analyzes the 1,000 largest foundations in depth and includes both national and local funders. Use the Index of Types of Support for foundations in your own state or national foundations (listed in bold type) in other states that provide the type of support you need.

STEP 3. **THE FOUNDATION DIRECTORY** describes foundations with assets of $1 million or more or annual giving of at least $100,000 (approx. 4500). Check Index of Types of Support for foundations in your own state or national foundations (listed in bold type) in other states that provide the type of support you need.

STEP 4. **STATE AND LOCAL FOUNDATION DIRECTORIES.** Coverage and content varies, but some do include information on types of support provided. Check bibliography and your local library to find directories that cover your state.

STEP 5. **SPECIAL FUNDING GUIDES.** A few special guides focus on specific types of support or fundraising campaigns. Check bibliography or your local library for relevant guides.

STEP 6. **REVIEW YOUR INITIAL PROSPECT LIST** to eliminate foundations that are unable or unlikely to provide funding in your geographic area, to provide the type or amount of support you need, or to fund your type of organization. Research remaining prospects carefully (Figures 36 and 37) to determine those most likely to consider your request favorably.

FIGURE 33. Recipient Category Index in THE FOUNDATION GRANTS INDEX ANNUAL

AGENCY (DIRECT SERVICE)

Capital support

Alabama 33640
Arizona 482, 3213, 12778, 21465, 21484, 21529, 21590, 21630, 21670, 21812, 30046, 36122
Arkansas 30240
California 253, 259, 260, 263, 266, 267, 292, 297, 300, 323, 327, 334, 343, 355, 399, 402, 423, 427, 453, 458, 470, 479, 481, 485, 489, 494, 496, 498, 548, 594, 670, 729, 805, 951, 1340, 1425, 1438, 1442, 1629, 1873, 1911, 1948, 1952, 1953, 1956-1966, 1975, 1978, 1979, 1982, 1985-1990, 1992, 1994-1998, 2001, 2002, 2007, 2008, 2010, 2011, 2015, 2017-2019, 2023, 2025, 2028, 2032, 2033, 2036, 2039, 2041, 2043-2048, 2054, 2056, 2058-2060, 2062, 2099, 2108, 2132, 2192, 2196, 2276, 2394, 2415, 2416, 2419, 2422-2430, 2437, 2441, 2448, 2454, 2459, 2461, 2464, 2469, 2470, 2475, 2482, 2484, 2501, 2513-2517, 2520, 2525, 2527, 2531, 2534, 2538, 2546, 2549-2551, 2586, 2707, 2709, 2718, 2731, 2736, 2745, 2748, 2762, 2776, 2777, 2814, 2837, 2894, 2941, 2955, 2962, 2987, 3023, 3037, 3049, 3087, 3088, 3097, 3122, 3152, 3156, 3160-3162, 3199, 3209, 3210, 3242, 3253, 3256, 3265, 3302, 3317, 3318, 3325, 3342-3344, 3351, 3358, 3361-3365, 3367, 3368, 3370, 3372, 3374, 3381, 3386, 3391, 3392, 3394-3397, 3409, 3410, 3416, 3437, 3441, 3453, 3457, 3462, 3493, 3525, 3538, 3573, 3574, 3587, 3594, 3625, 3627, 3645, 3717, 3720, 3727, 3732, 3753, 3763, 3828, 3831, 3863, 3900, 3909, 3911, 3918, 3920-3922, 3926, 3927, 3929, 3930, 3933, 3938-3942, 3946, 3947, 3951, 3954, 3955, 3957, 3958, 3963, 3964, 3968, 3975, 3977, 3979, 3981, 3987, 3988, 3990, 3991, 3997, 4020, 4033, 4040, 4063, 4064, 4072, 4076, 4083, 4089, 4090, 4135-4139, 4171, 4176, 4247, 4395, 4404, 4405, 4407, 4417, 4439, 4448, 4474, 4477, 4496, 4502, 4508, 4511, 4512, 4516, 4554, 4558, 4560, 4584, 4615, 4616, 4662, 4663, 4672, 4680, 4682, 4683, 4685,

4689, 4690, 4696, 4698, 4702-4706, 4708-4712, 4720, 4730, 4731, 4733, 4736, 4747, 4748, 7215, 12741, 12784, 12816, 12829, 13240, 13298, 13783, 13891, 21477, 21496, 21519, 21619, 21629, 21658, 21662, 21726, 21732, 21798, 21861, 21895, 22000, 22039, 22808, 22922, 27220, 27268, 28846, 28994, 29882, 30061, 33421
Cameroon 7016
Canada 21511, 32204
Colorado 618, 4774, 4775, 4777, 4780, 4790, 4792, 4809, 4821, 4822, 4825, 4826, 4830, 4831, 4842, 4861, 4873, 4890, 4910, 4940, 4956, 4977, 4990, 5000, 5025, 5026, 5029, 5031, 5033, 5045, 5052, 5056-5058, 5068, 5072, 5073, 5076, 5078, 5080, 5085, 5086, 5107, 5113, 5119, 5122, 5134, 5174, 5315, 21729, 21740, 21782, 27216
Connecticut 6281, 6284, 6287, 6297, 6310, 6311, 6313, 6322, 6327, 6331, 6339, 6353, 6360, 6371, 6377, 6390, 6408, 6428, 6429, 6431, 6433, 6455, 6481, 6497, 6499, 6918, 12758, 12770, 12780, 19326, 19333, 19334, 19370, 21817, 21834, 22041
Delaware 6599, 6603, 6611, 6612, 6614, 6621, 6622, 6627, 6628, 6633, 6635, 6638-6641, 6654, 6656-6659, 7606, 7683, 21504, 21575, 21703, 21744
District of Columbia 701, 1506, 2881, 6738, 6740, 6792, 6795, 6925, 6927, 6942, 6943, 6959, 7153, 7377, 11257, 11273, 11281, 11290, 11852, 11853, 17529, 21486, 21690, 29210, 29900, 32220, 34934, 36159
Florida 7493-7495, 7500-7504, 7513, 7517, 7526, 7533, 16875, 20542, 21461, 21474, 21508, 21521, 21641, 21712, 21876, 21884, 22003, 22036, 22544, 29356, 29363, 29377, 29378, 31137, 35733
Georgia 2815, 7811, 7816, 7862, 7872, 7890, 7892-7894, 7897, 7903, 7904, 7908, 7910, 7911, 7914, 7920, 7922, 7924, 8124, 8125, 12752, 12828, 28847, 28891, 28958, 28994, 32073, 33417
Guam 21678, 21936
Hawaii 8132, 8136, 8140-8143, 8147, 8152, 8166, 8171, 8176, 8184, 8186, 8188, 8191, 8198, 8199, 8205, 8217, 8228, 8229, 8235, 8257, 8261, 8263, 8266, 8286,

8291, 8317, 8335, 8338, 8349, 8363, 8374, 8375, 21512
Idaho 21606, 21866
Illinois 623, 735, 804, 1435, 6410, 9207, 9338, 9351, 9362, 9387, 9396, 9402, 9429, 9438, 9445, 9458, 9462, 9493, 9516, 9529, 9548, 9742, 9743, 9745, 9757, 9759, 9770, 9771, 9775, 10192, 10635, 12406, 12789, 14514, 14711, 21691, 21700, 21999, 22025, 22037, 22055, 27211
India 21104
Indiana 917, 1660, 10926-10929, 10932, 10934, 10940, 10974, 11007, 11024, 12242, 12402, 21869, 22050, 29888, 30694, 31075
Iowa 14399, 14566, 15796, 15800, 15812, 21642, 30834, 31148, 31177
Kansas 9665, 30191, 30197, 30221, 30229
Kentucky 1032, 1710, 2878, 2928, 29295, 29376
Louisiana 649, 8687, 11203, 11204, 11206, 11209, 11210, 11212, 11213, 11215, 21551, 21785, 21796, 21851, 21889, 21890
Maine 19434
Maryland 7292, 7317, 7656, 11258, 22784
Massachusetts 10956, 11191, 11324, 11373, 11382, 11423, 11433, 11446, 11455-11457, 11461, 11481, 11483, 11492, 11498, 11500, 11504, 11523, 11529, 11531, 11536, 11538, 11542, 11560, 11562-11567, 11585, 11597, 11601, 14699, 15926, 22422, 22426, 22431-22433, 22445, 22452, 22457, 22458, 22466, 22469, 22470, 22480, 22494, 22510, 22511, 22514, 22517, 22518, 28857, 28925, 33750
Michigan 6924, 11825, 11827, 11843, 11846, 11856, 11860, 11863, 11864, 11885, 11893, 12006, 12054, 12082, 12224, 12408, 12457, 12458, 12464, 12469, 12484-12486, 12488, 12505, 12506, 12510, 12516, 12524, 12525, 12530, 12545, 12731, 12777, 12779, 12823, 12837, 12860, 12861, 12865, 12879, 12918, 13191, 13198, 13202, 13210, 13212, 13217, 13230, 13232, 13238, 13242, 13247, 13276, 13296, 21494, 21509, 21627, 22725

Once you have identified the type of agency that most closely resembles your own and the specific type of support you are seeking, make a note of the grant records for organizations in your state and turn to the full grant listings. You will want to note on your prospect worksheet the name of the foundation awarding the grant, its state location, and any limitations on its giving program. You should also scan the full listing of grants reported by that foundation to determine its general subject focus, the types of organizations receiving grants, and the typical size of its grants.

There are five *COMSEARCH Printouts* listing grants included in *The Foundation Grants Index Annual* that have been awarded for specific types of support. These are:

- Higher Education—Capital Support

- Higher Education—Endowments

- Scholarships, Fellowships, Student Aid, Loans

- Conferences and Seminars

- Matching and Challenge Grants.

COMSEARCH Printouts are computer-produced guides designed to save you time flipping from an index to the actual grant records. Like the *Grants Index Annual*, they are arranged alphabetically by state, then by the names of the foundations located in that state. At the back of each *COMSEARCH Printout* is a list of foundations that includes their addresses and a brief statement of any restrictions on their giving programs.

If you are looking for one of the types of grants covered by a *COMSEARCH Printout*, we recommend that you begin with the list of foundations at the back of the book to eliminate foundations that clearly do not award grants in your subject field or geographic area. Then look over the grants listed under the remaining foundations to complete your prospect worksheet.

You should now turn to *Source Book Profiles* and the Index of Types of Support provided in the back of each volume (see Figure 34). This index identifies the top 1,000 foundations by the types of support they have typically provided based on Foundation Center staff's in-depth analysis of each foundation's grantmaking patterns. Beginning with the 1985 *Source Book Profiles* volumes, this index indicates foundations with a national or regional focus in bold type and foundations with a clearly local focus in regular type. This should speed your research process by allowing you to zero in on those foundations whose geographic focus matches the focus of your organization.

As you note the names of foundations listed under the type of support you are seeking, be sure to note the year (e.g., 83, 84, 85, etc.) in which the foundation was profiled. (As you'll recall, *Profiles* operates on a two-year publishing cycle with 500 foundations profiled during each calendar year.) Then turn to the actual profile to find the basic facts you need to complete your prospect worksheet.

To expand your list of prospects, turn to the Types of Support Index provided with *The Foundation Directory, 10th Edition*. This index covers the types of support typically provided by the nation's 4,400 largest foundations based on questionnaires completed by the foundations. Like the index in *Source Book Profiles*, foundations are listed under each type of support by the state they are located in, and foundations with national giving programs are indicated in bold type.

When you have listed the names of foundations in your own state and, when appropriate, national foundations in other states that provide the type of support you are seeking, be sure to check their full entries in the *Directory* to ascertain their program interests and any limitations of their giving programs.

There are also a number of special guides available that discuss fundraising techniques geared to a specific type of support, many of which are listed in the bibliography in Appendix A. You should also check with your local library to find out about new publications or guides that have been developed specifically for your local area.

FIGURE 34. Index of Types of Support in SOURCE BOOK PROFILES

Annual campaigns

Arizona: First Interstate Arizona 85, **Kieckhefer 85**

California: A.I.D. 84, **BankAmerica 85,** Beckman 84, Copley 85, Crocker 85, Disney 84, Fireman's 85, First Interstate California 85, **Fluor 84, 85U,** Gellert (Carl) 85, Gildred 84, Goldwyn 84, 85U, Haas (Walter) 85, Koret 85, Lear 84, **Litton 85,** Lurie 85, Orleton 84, Parker 84, 85U, Security 84, Stern (Sidney) 85, Ticor 85, Times 85, **Union Oil 84**

Colorado: Anschutz 84, El Pomar 85, Hunter 85, Johnson (Helen) 85

Connecticut: **General Electric 84, 85U,** Hartford Courant 85, Hartford Insurance 85, **Olin Corporation 84, 85U, Xerox 84, 85U**

Delaware: **Beneficial 84,** Laffey-McHugh 84, Longwood 85, Welfare 85

District of Columbia: Cafritz 84, **Freed 84,** Kiplinger 85

Florida: **duPont 85, Koch 85, Winn-Dixie 84**

Georgia: Callaway (Fuller) 85, Callaway Foundation 84, **Day 85,** Rich 85

Hawaii: Castle (Harold) 84, Cooke 85

Illinois: **Abbott 84, Amoco 84, Amsted 84, 85U,** Coleman 84, Crown (Arie) 84, **Deere 85,** Dillon Foundation 84, First National Chicago 85, **Gould Inc. 85, Harris 84, McGraw Foundation 84, Nalco 84,** Northern 85, **Northwest Industries 84, Quaker 84,** Sara Lee 85, **Sears-Roebuck 85, United Air 84,** USG 85, **Walgreen 84**

Indiana: Cummins 84, Indianapolis 85, Krannert 85, **Lilly Endowment 84, 85U**

Iowa: Hall Foundation 85, Maytag 85, Pella 85

Kansas: Powell 84, 85U, Wiedemann 85

Kentucky: Bingham Enterprises 84

Maryland: Hoffberger 84, Meyerhoff 84, 85U

Massachusetts: **Alden 84,** Bank of Boston 85, **Cabot Corporation 85,** Cabot Family 84, **Eastern 84,** Fuller 85, Hyams 85, Norton 85, Pappas 84, 85U, Stoddard 85, **Webster 85**

Michigan: **Chrysler 84, 85U,** Dow (Herbert) 85, **Ford Motor 84, 85U, General Motors 85,** Gerstacker 84, Holden 85, Hudson-Webber 84, McGregor Fund 85, **Mott (Charles) 85,** Skillman 84, Towsley 84, **Whirlpool 84**

Minnesota: **Bemis 84,** Bremer 85, **Davis (Edwin) 84, Dayton 84, 85U,** First Bank System 85, First National Minneapolis 85, Groves 85, Honeywell 85, **Medtronic 84, 85U, Minnesota 84,** O'Shaughnessy 84, **Pillsbury Company 84, 85U**

Missouri: **Anheuser-Busch 84,** Brown Group 84, Centerre 85, Edison 84, **Monsanto 84,** Olin (Spencer) 84, Reynolds (J.B.) 84, Union Electric 84

Nebraska: Hitchcock 84, **InterNorth 85**

New Jersey: **Allied 84, 85U, Crum 85, Huber 84, Johnson & Johnson 85,** Prudential 85, **Schering-Plough 84, Union Camp 85, Vollmer 84, Warner-Lambert 84**

New York: Abrons 84, **American-Standard 85,** Barker 85, **Bristol-Myers 84, Chatlos 85,** Clark Foundation (NY) 85, **Coles 84, Compton 84, Dillon Fund 84, Dun 84,** Emerson (Fred) 85,

STEP TWO: REFINING YOUR LIST

As we discussed in the subject and geographic approach chapters, you now need to look over your prospect list to eliminate foundations that would clearly be unable to fund your project because their subject or geographic focus or their typical grant range does not fit your organization's needs.

If you have followed through each research approach we've described, you should now have a reasonable number of foundation prospects you wish to investigate further to find out which are most likely to consider your proposal favorably. In the next chapter, we'll examine the specific facts you need to know about each prospect and how to find them.

9

Learning All You Can About Your Foundation Prospects

As you worked through each of the three approaches for identifying potential funding sources, you gathered names of foundations that, on the basis of partial evidence, appear to have an interest in some aspect of your project or field. Now you must take a hard look at each foundation and eliminate those that on closer examination seem unlikely to consider your proposal favorably.

First of all, you need to gather the most current information on the foundation's address, staff, officers and trustees, assets, gifts received by the foundation, application procedures, and, most important, its actual grants. As you uncover these facts, you will be looking for answers to the following questions:

- **Has the foundation demonstrated a real commitment to funding in your subject field?** You may have noted one or more grants by a particular foundation in your subject field. Upon examining their full grants list, however, you may find that these few grants were made for reasons other than a commitment to the field. For example, the grants may have been made because of a special relationship with a particular recipient. Some foundations have historic and continuing relationships with particular universities or institutions because of ties to the donor's family or some specified interest of the donor, and they may fund activities at those institutions that do not fall within their normal giving interests. In other cases, grants may have been made because the foundation is interested in the recipient's location rather than its field of endeavor.

- **Does it seem likely that the foundation will make grants to recipients in your geographic location?** It isn't necessary for the foundation to have actually made grants in your state or city, but you should examine grant records carefully for explicit or implied geographic restrictions. Be on the lookout for local or regional giving patterns or concentrations in rural or urban areas.

- **Does the amount of money you are requesting fit within the foundation's grant range?** Obviously you would not request $25,000 from a foundation that has never made a grant larger than $10,000, but look for more subtle distinctions. If a foundation's arts grants range from $10,000 to $20,000 and its social welfare grants are in the $3,000 to $5,000 category, consider the policy emphasis implied by those figures. It's unlikely you'll get a $15,000 grant for a social welfare project from that foundation.

- **Does the foundation have any policy prohibiting grants for the type of support you are requesting?** Many foundations will not make grants for operating budgets. Others will not provide funds for building, equipment, etc. Be sure the foundation is willing to award the type of support you need.

- **Does the foundation like to make grants to cover the full cost of a project or do they favor projects where other foundations or funding sources share the cost?**

- **For what period of time does the foundation generally make grants?** Some foundations favor one-time grants, while others will continue their support over a number of years. It is rare to find foundations that will continue to support an organization indefinitely, however, so be sure you are aware of avenues of support for the future before approaching foundations. They will expect you to have thought through a long-term funding plan for any project in which they might participate.

- **What types of organizations does the foundation tend to support?** Does it favor large, well-established groups like symphonies, universities, and museums or does it seem to lean toward grass-roots community organizations? A foundation's past recipients will give you a feeling for its focus. Look carefully at the mix of its recipients.

- **Does the foundation have application deadlines or does it review proposals continuously?** Note carefully any information you find about board meeting dates so you can plan to submit your proposals at an appropriate time. Be aware that the time elapsed between submitting a proposal and notification or actual receipt of a grant may be substantial. In planning your program, be sure to allow enough time to obtain the necessary funding. The review and processing of proposals that are seriously considered is rarely accomplished in less than three months and often takes substantially longer.

Beyond these basics, you will want to gather background information on the foundation's donor or sponsoring company as well as its current staff and trustees. You may find some unexpected connections between your organization and a potential funder that will help you to present a more convincing proposal.

Financial data is often mystifying to grantseekers, but these facts can provide important clues about the future funding patterns of a foundation. Has the foundation received any large contributions in recent years that might increase its grantmaking potential? Has there been an increase or decrease in the foundation's asset base in recent years? These factors can affect the amount of money available for grants, as well as the size and type of grants available. During the recent recession period, for example, many company-sponsored foundations received smaller contributions from their parent corporations and therefore had to confine their grantmaking activities temporarily to organizations where they had ongoing commitments.

The Final Prospect Worksheet in Figure 35 outlines the facts you need to gather about a foundation to determine whether your funding needs match its funding interests. Again, many grantseekers will want to develop their own forms for internal recordkeeping, but those forms should incorporate all of the essential facts we've outlined. It is also important to note the source and date of any information you gather to verify whether you have the most current and accurate facts.

FINDING INFORMATION ABOUT FOUNDATIONS

The amoung of information available on any particular foundation varies widely, depending largely on the foundation's size and staffing. The resources you will be using to investigate your foundation prospects will include directories of foundations, annual reports and other publications issued directly by the foundations themselves, the information returns (Form 990-PF) filed annually by each foundation with the Internal Revenue Service, and periodical and newspaper articles about foundations. Figure 36 diagrams what is generally the most effective process for reviewing all relevant materials for each foundation researched.

Foundation Annual Reports

Generally, an annual report issued directly by a foundation will provide the most complete and current information available about that foundation. These reports usually include detailed financial statements, a comprehensive list of grants awarded or committed for future payment, the names of officers and staff members, and a definition of program interests. Most annual reports also indicate the application procedures grantseekers should follow, including any application deadlines or particular proposal formats the foundation prefers. Some annual reports include information on the foundation's donor and essays on the operating philosophy that has or will guide their grantmaking decisions.

Foundations are not required by law to compile a separately printed annual report, and only about 600 foundations do so. These foundations are largely community foundations and larger foundations with assets of $1 million or more. Entries in each of the three major directories of foundations published by The Foundation Center—*The National Data Book, The Foundation Directory,* and *Source Book Profiles*—indicate whether the foundation has recently published an annual report. *The Foundation Grants Index Bimonthly* includes a listing of annual reports recently received by The Foundation Center with the addresses to which you can write to receive a copy of the report. Many Foundation Center libraries maintain collections of annual reports issued by foundations in their local communities and by national foundations located elsewhere. Because so few foundations publish annual reports, it is wise to check the resources in your local foundation library before you waste time and money requesting reports from foundations that don't publish them.

DIRECTORIES OF FOUNDATIONS

Although you have undoubtedly checked most directories of foundations to identify your initial prospects, you should now return to those sources to focus more specifically on your final prospects. After its own published report (or in the absence of such a report), the most comprehensive source of information about a foundation is *Source Book Profiles*. As you'll recall from Chapter 5, *Profiles* is The Foundation Center's quarterly information service which analyzes the nation's 1,000 largest foundations. *Profiles* operates on a two-year cycle with 500 profiles published each year. Changes in address, telephone, personnel, or program at a foundation profiled during the preceding year are noted in a special section, "Foundation Profile Updates," at the back of the current volume.

Your investigation should begin with the Index of Foundations at the back of the current *Profiles* volume to determine if and when a profile of the foundation was published and if there has been a subsequent update to the profile

FIGURE 35. Final Prospect Worksheet

The Final Prospect Worksheet is used to record the facts about a potential funding source you will need to determine whether your funding needs match its giving interests. Note the source and date of any information you gather to verify whether you have the most current and accurate facts.

FOUNDATION NAME: _____

ADDRESS: _____

APPLICATION ADDRESS: _____

CONTACT PERSON: _____ TELEPHONE: _____

OFFICERS, TRUSTEES AND KEY STAFF:

FINANCIAL DATA: Fiscal Year _____; Assets _____; Gifts Received _____; Total Giving _____; Grants Paid _____; Average Grant Range _____; Grant Range in Our Subject_____.

PURPOSE:

SUBJECT FOCUS:

   Restrictions:

GEOGRAPHIC FOCUS:

   Restrictions:

TYPES OF SUPPORT AWARDED:

   Restrictions:

TYPES OF ORGANIZATIONS FUNDED:

   Restrictions:

FIGURE 35. Final Prospect Worksheet

SAMPLE GRANTS:

APPLICATION PROCEDURES: Deadlines: _____

   Preferred First Contact: _____

   Information Requested:

   Board Meeting Dates:

   Funding Cycle/Time Required to Consider Requests:

OTHER NOTES/COMMENTS:

CONTACT RECORD:

Date	Type of Contact	Response

FIGURE 36. Learning All You Can About Your Foundation Prospects

Before you apply for a grant, you need to gather as much information as possible about your foundation prospects to determine whether your funding needs match their giving interests, whether they are likely to support organizations in your geographic area, whether they are likely to provide the type and amount of support you need, and how and when to submit your grant request. In using the materials below to complete a Final Prospect Worksheet for each foundation that seems likely to be interested in your proposals, be sure to note the date and source of the information gathered to be sure you have the most current and accurate information available.

STEP 1. FOUNDATION ANNUAL REPORTS are published by over 600 foundations. When available, these are generally the most complete source of information on the foundation's current and future interests, restrictions, and application procedures. Check entries in *Source Book Profiles, The Foundation Directory*, or *The National Data Book* or listings of "Grantmaker Publications" in the *Foundation Grants Index Bimonthly* to find out if a foundation publishes a report.

STEP 2. OTHER FOUNDATION PUBLICATIONS. Over 700 foundations that do not publish annual reports do publish information brochures, application guidelines, or other materials that describe their giving programs. Check entries in *Source Book Profiles, The Foundation Directory*, or listings of "Grantmaker Publications" in the *Foundation Grants Index Bimonthly* to determine if such materials are available.

STEP 3. SOURCE BOOK PROFILES analyzes the 1,000 largest foundations in depth. In the absence of material published by the foundation itself, this is the most complete source of information on the largest foundations.

STEP 4. THE FOUNDATION DIRECTORY provides basic descriptions of foundations with $1 million or more in assets or annual giving of at least $100,000. Also check **THE FOUNDATION DIRECTORY SUPPLEMENT** which updates entries for foundations that have had name, address, personnel, or program changes between editions of the major volume.

STEP 5. FOUNDATION GRANTS INDEX BIMONTHLY includes "Updates on Grantmakers" listing changes in name, address, personnel, or program reported by major foundations in preceding two months.

STEP 6. FOUNDATION INFORMATION RETURNS (IRS FORM 990-PF) are filed annually by all foundations and include complete lists of grants awarded during the tax year covered as well as other information on finances, giving interests and restrictions, and application procedures and deadlines. These are often the only source of information on smaller foundations. Available from the Internal Revenue Service or at Foundation Center libraries.

STEP 7. NEWSPAPER OR MAGAZINE ARTICLES often provide news or insights on personnel or program interests of foundations. Check with your local library for foundation files or indexes to relevant articles.

STEP 8. PEOPLE. Talk to your professional colleagues, board members, volunteers, past and current donors, and others interested in your work for advice on your project proposal and funding prospects.

(see Figure 37). Then read the profile carefully to complete your Final Prospect Worksheet.

If the foundation is not covered in *Source Book Profiles*, you should turn to *The Foundation Directory* which provides briefer descriptions of all grantmaking foundations that hold assets of $1 million or more or give at least $100,000 annually. There is also an Index of Foundations at the back of the *Directory* which provides the state locations and entry numbers for all foundations included. *Directory* entries will provide basic information on the foundation's giving interests and limitations; trustees and officers; current assets, gifts received, and grants; and application procedures. They also list the foundation's Employer Identification Number which you need to locate the foundation's current IRS Information Return for a full listing of the foundation's recent grants.

Changes in a *Directory* foundation's address, financial data, personnel, or program that occur after the publication of the biennial edition are incorporated in *The Foundation Directory Supplement* published the following September. Foundation changes are also published every two months in the "Updates on Grantmakers" section of *The Foundation Grants Index Bimonthly*. You will want to check both of these resources to ensure that you have the most current information on your foundation prospects.

If any of your foundation prospects are not large enough to be included in either *Source Book Profiles* or *The Foundation Directory*, you should check the entries in any local or state directories that include the state where the foundation is located. A bibliography of local foundation directories is provided in Appendix B. As we mentioned earlier, these directories vary greatly in the quantity and quality of information provided. Only by examining the directories themselves can you determine their usefulness for your funding research.

FOUNDATION INFORMATION RETURNS

As you'll recall from Chapter 5, a key source of information about private foundations is the information return (Form 990-PF) they are required to file annually with the Internal Revenue Service. The 990-PF provides basic financial data for the foundation, the names and addresses of foundation managers or trustees, the names and addresses of any individual who gave $5,000 or more to the foundation during the year, and a list of grants paid during the year with the name and location of the recipient, the amount of the grant, and the purpose of the grant. The current 990-PF form also requires foundations to indicate the name, address, and telephone number of the person to whom applications should be addressed, the form in which applications should be submitted, any submission deadlines, and any restrictions or limitations on awards. Unless there is a complete annual report available from the foundation, it is always

FIGURE 37. Index of Foundations and "Foundation Profile Updates" from SOURCE BOOK PROFILES

Abbott (The Clara) Foundation, IL, 86
Abbott Laboratories Fund, IL, 84
Abell (The A. S.) Company Foundation, Inc., MD, 84, 85U, 86U
Abell-Hanger Foundation, TX, 86
Abercrombie (The J. S.) Foundation, TX, 84
Abney Foundation, The, SC, 85
Abrons (Louis and Anne) Foundation, Inc., NY, 86
Achelis Foundation, The, NY, 86
Aetna Life & Casualty Foundation, Inc., CT, 85
Ahmanson Foundation, The, CA, 85
A.I.D. Foundation, CA, 84
Air Products Foundation, The, PA, 84
Alcoa Foundation, PA, 86
Alden (George I.) Trust, MA, 86
Allegheny Foundation, PA, 85

Allen-Bradley Foundation, Inc. (*see* Bradley (The Lynde and Harry) Foundation, Inc.)
Allied Corporation Foundation, NJ, 86
Allis-Chalmers Foundation, Inc., WI, 84
Alliss (Charles and Ellora) Educational Foundation, MN, 85
Allstate Foundation, The, IL, 84, 86U
Altman Foundation, NY, 85, 86U
Altschul Foundation, The, NY, 85
Amarillo Area Foundation, Inc., TX, 86
Amax Foundation, Inc., CT, 86
American Can Company Foundation, CT, 85
American Express Foundation, NY, 84, 85U
American Financial Corporation Foundation, The, OH, 85
American Foundation Corporation, The, OH, 85

Abell (The A. S.) Company Foundation, Inc., MD (84)
Governing body: C. Ruth Kratz, secretary-treasurer, is no longer with the foundation; Ronald E. Brown is now treasurer and Judith K. Keys is now secretary.

Allstate Foundation, The, IL (84)
Contact: Betty L. Wolfram, Exec. Dir.
Governing body: Betty L. Wolfram has succeeded John T. Murphy as executive director.

Altman Foundation, NY (85)
Address: 220 East 42nd St., Suite 411, New York, NY 10017
Contact: Paul B. Mott, Jr., Exec. Dir.
Telephone: (212) 682-0970
Purpose and activities: Support primarily for education, particularly programs benefitting underpriviliged youth; private voluntary hospitals and health centers to extend medical services to the underserved; artistic and cultural institutions for outreach projects; and social welfare programs providing long-term solutions for the needs of the disadvantaged.
Application information: Average grant range expected to increase in 1986 to $25,000-50,000. Application guidelines were published for the first time in March, 1986.
Other changes: The assets of the foundation increased by $86 million in 1985 as a result of the sale of seven B. Altman department stores. Annual giving is expected to rise to between $5 million and $6 million.

wise to examine the most current IRS returns for your final foundation prospects.

A full description and diagram of the components of the 990-PF form that are of interest to grantseekers is provided in Chapter 5, along with information about where to find copies of the 990-PF forms for your foundation prospects. Copies of 990-PF forms may be examined free of charge at most Foundation Center libraries or they can be purchased for a small fee from the Internal Revenue Service.

OTHER FOUNDATION PUBLICATIONS

A number of foundations issue brochures, pamphlets, news releases, or newsletters that provide information on application procedures, specific grant programs or recent grants, and occasionally foundation staff and trustees. Although such publications are most frequently issued by the larger, staffed foundations, there are some smaller foundations that publish descriptive brochures in lieu of a more extensive annual report. These documents are more than a source of facts about the foundation; they are also a good medium for determining its "personality."

Entries in *Source Book Profiles* and *The Foundation Directory* include information on publications issued by the foundation. *The Foundation Grants Index Bimonthly* includes a special section on "Grantmakers' Publications" which lists all foundation and corporate giving program annual reports, information brochures, and newsletters recently received by The Foundation Center's New York library.

The Foundation Center libraries in New York and Washington, D.C. collect as many foundation pamphlets and news releases as possible. Many of the Center's cooperating libraries also collect publications issued by grantmakers in their state or local area which you can examine free of charge. If you have identified grantmakers who are active in your subject or geographic area, you may also be able to have your name added to their mailing list by writing the foundation directly.

NEWSPAPER AND MAGAZINE ARTICLES

From time to time you may have seen articles about local foundations in newspapers. You have probably observed that a few foundations are mentioned frequently, while most are never covered. The Foundation Center subscribes to a newspaper clipping service that checks hundreds of newspapers and periodicals throughout the country and forwards to the Center any articles dealing with foundations and philanthropy. The Center also maintains files of general articles on foundation activity and editorials dealing with the field.

Occasionally, national magazines print articles on individual foundations or on foundations in general. You'll find it much easier to keep abreast of magazine articles than of those that appear in newspapers. You can look up such articles using the major periodical indexes like the *Reader's Guide to Periodical Literature, Business Periodicals Index,* or *Public Affairs Information Service* (PAIS), most of which are available in your local library.

The Foundation Center's libraries obtain copies of relevant articles, studies, and reports. You'll find that the files maintained by the Center libraries in

New York, Washington, D.C., Cleveland, and San Francisco provide the most comprehensive collection of information available on particular foundations, as well as on philanthropy and foundation activity generally. Most visitors to the Center's libraries are searching for funding and concentrate on using the materials described in this guide. However, because the Center serves an archival function for the field, its libraries are also used by foundation personnel, journalists, researchers, authors, and students interested in all aspects of philanthropic and nonprofit activity.

PEOPLE

Published directories and indexes of foundation grants and materials issued by the grantmakers themselves are an enormous help in identifying potential funders, sorting out funders who could not or are unlikely to provide grant support to your organization, and learning about appropriate application procedures. Thorough funding research also involves another important resource —*people*.

Talk to your professional colleagues about funding approaches they have tried and about their contacts with foundations active in your community or subject field. They may be able to provide useful insights into a foundation's decision-making process or funding interests. When you learn about an interesting grant to an agency from one of your foundation prospects, contact the agency's executive director and ask about their experiences with the grant and the foundation.

Know the affiliations of your board members, volunteers, and other individuals who have an active interest in your work. If they are familiar with or have worked with one of your foundation prospects, they might be able to advise you on preparing your proposal or direct you to the people within the foundation who should receive your application. Sources close to the foundation may be aware of impending changes in funding policies, staff, or application criteria that could affect your grant request.

Your past and current donors are also a useful source for learning more about potential funding sources or about the program interests of your foundation prospects. Share your idea and your proposal with your current supporters and let them know the basic facts you have already uncovered about the foundations you think will be interested in providing additional support. In addition to useful advice, supporters may be willing to write a letter or to contact foundation staff or managers about your programs and their experiences with your organization.

Finally, if your foundation prospect has staff, find out if they are able to meet with you or representatives from your organization to discuss your idea and the appropriate application procedures. Although most foundations do not have staff and are unable to meet individually with grantseekers, those foundations that do have program staff often prefer discussing proposed projects with applicants prior to the submission of a formal grant request. It is usually best to begin with a brief letter introducing your organization and describing your program, then follow up with a phone call to set up an appointment.

Personal contacts should not be viewed as a substitute for funding research, nor are they a requirement for obtaining foundation support. Still, your personal and professional contacts can be a valuable supplement to the published information on funding sources. A successful fundraising strategy involves hard effort that builds on *all* of your available resources.

10

Presenting Your Idea
to a Foundation

Bᵧ ɴᴏᴡ ʏᴏᴜ ʜᴀᴠᴇ ɪᴅᴇɴᴛɪꜰɪᴇᴅ a few foundations that seem likely to be interested in funding your project on the basis of your subject focus, the geographic area and population groups you serve, and the type and amount of support you need. Now you need to present your idea to those foundations and convince them to support it.

While many foundations are quite flexible about the form and timing of grant applications, others have developed specific procedures for applications to facilitate the decision-making process. You will want to review all of the notes you have made about the foundation prospect during the course of your research, and gather together the most recent copy of any annual report, application guidelines, or information brochures issued by the foundation. Knowing who to contact and how to submit your application can be essential in ensuring that your request gets a complete and careful hearing.

TIMING AND DEADLINES

Timing is often an essential element of the grant application process. Grant decisions are often tied to board meetings which can be held as infrequently as once or twice a year. Most foundations need to receive grant applications at least two to three months in advance of board meetings to allow time for review and investigation, and some may require a considerably longer lead time. If the foundation has not specified deadlines for submitting applications, try to determine when its board generally meets and submit your request as far in advance of the meetings as possible.

INITIAL INQUIRIES

Many foundations, both large and small, prefer grant applicants to send a brief letter of inquiry before or occasionally in lieu of a formal proposal. Some staffed foundations may offer advice or assistance in preparing the final proposal to applicants whose ideas seem particularly relevant to the foundation's funding program. The initial inquiry can also save you and the foundation a lot of valuable time if there are specific procedures you should follow in preparing your final proposal or if the foundation already knows it cannot provide funding because of prior commitments or a change in program focus. Still other foundations make their final funding decisions based solely on the letter of inquiry.

Your letter of inquiry should be brief, no more than three pages, and should state clearly the purpose of your organization and the program for which you are seeking funds. You should describe the particular problem you wish to address, the method you will use to address it, the total cost of the project, and the type and amount of support you are seeking from the foundation. Your opening paragraph should summarize the essential ingredients of your request, including the amount of money or the type of support you are seeking. All too often grant applicants bury these important facts in long descriptions of their organization or project, and the reader of the letter can't determine what they are asking of the foundation until the very last paragraph!

Most foundations will also want to see a copy of the Internal Revenue Service letter designating your organization's tax-exempt status. Depending on the information you have gathered about the foundation, offer to send a full proposal for their consideration or arrange a meeting to discuss your idea further with foundation staff or officials.

In the foreword to this book, James Richmond of the W. K. Kellogg Foundation urges grantseekers to be aggressive in their approach to foundations. Give the foundation time to respond to your inquiry, but don't be afraid to follow up with a phone call two or three weeks after you've sent your letter to make sure it was received and to find out if the foundation will need further information from you.

THE PROPOSAL

The full grant proposal is your opportunity to present your idea to a foundation and to convince that foundation that your program is worthy of its investment. Depending on what you've uncovered about the application procedures preferred by your foundation prospect, the proposal could be your first direct contact with the funder or it could follow an initial exchange of letters or discussions with foundation staff and trustees. In either case, the proposal should make a clear and concise case for funding your organization and its programs. Grantmakers have to review hundreds of proposals every year, and they need to be able to quickly see how you can put their money to work to benefit the community or to further the causes they are interested in.

At this point a number of nonprofits feel they should turn to experts and have a professional proposal developed for them. Although this might make you feel more confident, it is rarely necessary and may even be inadvisable. You and your colleagues understand best what you are trying to accomplish and therefore you can make the most persuasive case for funding your organization and its plans. Foundations aren't impressed by slick prose and fancy packages. They want the facts, presented clearly and concisely, and they want to get a feeling for the organization and its people.

There are a number of excellent books about how to write a grant proposal, and you may find it useful to review a number of them before you get started. Some of the better-known titles are listed in a bibliography in Appendix A. Many of these titles can be found in your local public library or Foundation Center cooperating collection.

While application criteria and proposal formats can vary, most funders expect to see the following elements in a grant proposal:

- **A cover letter** on the organization's letterhead signed by the chief executive officer. The cover letter highlights the features of your proposal most likely to be of interest to the foundation. It should point out how you selected the foundation and why you believe it will be interested in your proposal. It should also include the specific amount of money and type of support you are seeking.

- **A table of contents** will make it easy for the prospective funder to look up particular facts and figures in the proposal. Even though your proposal should be brief (most foundations recommend limiting proposals to ten pages), a table of contents helps to organize the presentation and outline the information it contains.

- **A summary of the project** that describes the purpose of the project, the total budget for the project and the specific amount requested from the funder, the plan of action, and the anticipated results. The summary may be incorporated into the cover letter or presented as the first section of the proposal. It can be as short as one or two paragraphs and should never exceed one page.

  Even though the summary appears first in the proposal, it should be the last thing you actually write. At that point you will have thought through and thoroughly documented the need, plan of action, and projected outcome of your proposed project and will be in the best position to pull out the most essential facts for the summary.

- **Introduction to your organization.** Even if your organization is large and relatively well-known, you cannot assume that the funders reading your proposal will be familiar with your programs and accomplishments. In fact, they may not even be aware of your existence! Therefore you need to provide them with enough background information to build confidence in your group and its ability to carry out the program you are proposing.

  State the mission of your organization and provide a brief history of your activities, stressing key accomplishments and describing your sources of support. A list of members of your board of directors should be included in the appendix, but you might wish to call attention here to individuals on your board or staff who have played a major role in the organization. Remember that your purpose is to convince the prospective funder that you are capable of producing the proposed program results and are worthy of his or her investment.

  You can do the groundwork for this section by keeping a "credibility file" that documents your progress and activities. Save letters of endorsement and support, newspaper articles, and studies that support your work. Soliciting letters of support from organizations that have or will benefit from your work is perfectly acceptable, and you may choose to include some of these letters in the appendix. Careful recordkeeping will help build a thorough and convincing chronicle of your work for submission with proposals.

- **Problem statement.** State as simply and clearly as possible the problem or need your project will address. Be sure to narrow the problem to limits that are solvable within the scope of your project. Identify the community or population groups to be served by the project and provide enough background information on them to put your project in context. Remember, however, that your focus should be the specific needs and problems you will address. A broad picture of all the problems that exist within your community will only detract from your presentation.

Document your perception of the problem with recent studies and current statistics, statements by public officials, other agencies, or professionals, and previous studies by private or public groups. What other efforts have been made (or are being made) to address the problem? You need to convince the funder that the problem or need is real and that the approach you wish to take builds upon the lessons others have learned. Show the funder that you have researched the problem carefully and that you have a new or unique contribution to offer towards its resolution.

In the 1984 Annual Report of the Mary Reynolds Babcock Foundation, Executive Director William Bondurant noted that "foundations have the opportunity to select programs and persons whose ability to contribute significantly to society's advancement is greater because it is grounded in an appreciation of what others have done before them. After reading many proposals over many years . . . I find myself increasingly conscious of the importance of an applicant's expressed awareness of historic antecedents for a proposed endeavor. This is not to ask for a history lesson in each application nor a disclaimer of an intention to 'reinvent the wheel.' But it is a plea for liberally educated *proposaliers!*"

- **Goals and objectives.** You have stated the problem, now you need to clarify exactly what you hope to accomplish. The goal is the ultimate accomplishment a project could achieve and, as such, is often unreachable. Objectives, on the other hand, are based on realistic expectations about the anticipated results of a project. Attainment of your stated objectives will be a measurable step in the process of working towards your goal.

The objectives you outline should promise a solution or reduction of the problem you have described. Clearly stated objectives provide the basis for evaluating the program, so be sure to make them measurable and time-limited. For example, if the *problem* is high unemployment among teenagers in your area, your *objective* might be to provide 100 new jobs for teenagers over the next two years. The *goal* of the project would be a significant reduction in or even the elimination of teenaged unemployment in your community.

Don't confuse the objective of a program with the means to be used in achieving that end. You might achieve your objective of providing new jobs for teenagers through a variety of methods, including working with local businesses to create jobs, running a job placement or job information center, or providing jobs within a program operated by your agency. But your measurable *objective* remains the same: to provide 100 new jobs for teenagers over the next two years.

- **Implementation methods and schedule.** Describe your specific plan of action for achieving your goals and objectives. Why have you chosen your particular approach? Who will actually implement the plan? If you are involving staff or volunteers already active in your program or consultants you have already identified, note their qualifications and include their résumés in the appendix to your proposal. If you will need to hire staff, include a job description and describe your plans for recruitment and training. You should also provide a timetable for the project and specify the most desirable starting and termination dates for the project activity.

- **Evaluation criteria and procedures.** Evaluation criteria provide a measure for judging how effective your project has been in reaching your objectives. If your objectives are specific and measurable, it will be easier to develop evaluation criteria. Although evaluating the outcome or product resulting from the project is a primary concern, don't overlook the need to evaluate the process or procedures employed. A good evaluation plan will enable you and others to learn from the successes and failures of your agency's efforts.

- **Budget.** Developing the budget you submit with your grant request requires honesty and common sense. It must be sufficiently detailed to demonstrate that you have considered the full range of needs and problems that may arise. For example, if your proposal involves hiring staff, don't forget that social security payments, workmen's compensation, and benefits all have to be included. It is unrealistic to expect additional funding to cover needs overlooked in your initial request.

  Foundation and corporate donors are experienced in evaluating costs. Don't pad your budget, but don't underestimate the amount you need. If other funding sources will be contributing to your program, say so. The fact that others have confidence in your organization is a plus. If you expect to receive donations of equipment, space, or volunteer time, be sure to mention these as well. A full list of your current and recent sponsors should be included in the appendix, but the dollar value of their contributions should be noted in the budget.

  When you are seeking funds for a special project, you should supply both the budget for the project and the overall operating budget of your agency. Some of the basic items you should consider as you prepare your budget include: personnel, including salaries and fringe benefits; consultant fees for legal, accounting, or other services; rent, utilities, equipment, and supplies; travel and meeting expenses; publicity costs;

insurance; postage; and publications and subscriptions. If you are relatively new to or uncertain about the budgeting process, there are a number of excellent handbooks listed in Appendix A that can lead you through the steps of preparing a budget.

- **Future funding plans.** Most foundations will want to know how you plan to support your project after their grant has been spent. Even with some requests for one-time support, such as the purchase of equipment, you should describe how you will handle related expenditures such as on-going maintenance. Vague references to alternative funding sources are not adequate. Foundations want evidence of specific plans. Do you expect the program to become self-supporting through client fees or sales of products or services? Do you have plans to solicit support from the public or other funding agencies? Is there a local institution or government agency that will support the program once it has demonstrated its value? Show the funder that you have thought through the problem of future funding and outline your specific alternatives.

- **Appendix.** The appendix should include all appropriate supporting documents for your request, including your agency's tax-exempt status letter from the IRS, a listing of your board of directors, your current operating budget and audited financial statement, a list of recent and current funding sources (both cash and in-kind), résumés of key project staff and consultants, letters of endorsement, and relevant news clippings or publications by or about your organization.

A WORD OF ADVICE

Make your proposal as readable as possible by using active language and by being clear and specific about what is to be accomplished. Despite the volume of information required, keep your proposal brief and to the point. Use the group approach to generate ideas, but let one writer develop a proposal draft. Committee writing usually doesn't work when you need a concise and organized final product.

You may wish to ask people who have been successful in securing foundation grants or other professionals in your field to review the proposal. It is also helpful to have someone unfamiliar with your project read the proposal to be sure it is clear and avoids specialized jargon.

Review the application requirements and other literature issued by the foundations from which you are seeking funds. Have you covered all of the concerns and requirements stated by the foundation? Do your proposal and cover letter point out the connections between your project and the foundation's interests? Grantseekers often ask if they should tailor proposals to individual foundations. It is generally not a good idea to develop a proposal or make major adjustments in your operation to conform to the interests of a particular funding source. Organizations can be all too easily sidetracked from their own basic program goals by developing proposals in direct response to the availability of funds. If, on the other hand, you begin with a solid program or idea and then identify funders who might be interested in funding that program, by all means let your proposal reflect that connection.

WHAT HAPPENS NEXT?

Submitting your proposal is not the end of your involvement in the grantmaking process. A few weeks after you have submitted your proposal, follow up with a phone call to make sure your materials were received and to find out if there are additional materials the foundation needs to process your application. You might wish to arrange a meeting with foundation officials to discuss your idea or invite them to visit your organization.

Grant review procedures vary widely from foundation to foundation, and the decision-making process can take from a few weeks to several months. During the review process, the foundation may request additional information from you or involve outside consultants or professional references to gather supplemental information on your organization or to review the proposal. You need to be patient, but persistent. Some foundations outline their review procedures and timetables in their annual reports or application guidelines. If you are unclear about the process or when to expect a decision, don't hesitate to ask.

Rejection Is Not the End

Most foundations receive far more worthy proposals than they can fund in a given year. In its 1983 Annual Report, the M. J. Murdock Charitable Trust described the situation as follows—

> It is seldom that the Trust is faced with having to decline a poor proposal. Rather, it is a matter of having to decide among a great many worthy proposals. A denial, therefore, is hardly ever a rejection on the merits of a proposal, but it is simply the result of a highly competitive system and the limitation of financial resources.

Simply because a foundation is unable to fund a particular proposal does not mean their door is closed forever. If you are unsure why your proposal was not funded, ask. Would the foundation consider the proposal at some other time?

Did they need additional information to support your case? Could they suggest other sources of support you should pursue? Such follow-up discussions can be particularly helpful if the foundation has demonstrated a commitment to funding in the geographic area or subject field your organization is involved in.

When You Get the Grant

Congratulations! You have received formal notification of your grant award and you're ready to get started with your program. Before you begin to hire staff or purchase supplies, take a few moments to acknowledge the foundation's support with a letter of thanks. You also need to find out if the foundation has specific forms, procedures, and deadlines for reporting progress and results on your grant activity. Clarifying your responsibilities as a grantee at the outset, particularly with respect to financial reporting, will prevent misunderstandings or more serious problems later on.

Some foundations request, and almost all appreciate, acknowledgment of their support in press releases, publications, and other products resulting from or concerning a grant activity. A few of the larger, staffed foundations offer assistance to grantees in developing press releases and other publicity materials. Again, if you are unsure about the foundation's expectations, ask.

Keep detailed records of all grant activities, including contacts with and payments from the funder. Prepare a schedule of deadlines for reports and follow-up calls. This is the beginning of what you hope will be a long and successful relationship—treat it with the care and attention it deserves.

Appendix A

Additional Readings

THE FOUNDATION CENTER's New York library has one of the most—if not the most—comprehensive collections of materials on philanthropy, fundraising, and nonprofit management in the country. In preparing this reading list, we decided not to attempt to include all of the hundreds of titles published in these areas and available in our library, but rather to concentrate on the most frequently used or recently published books and monographs that seemed most relevant to readers of this book. The listing is not intended to be comprehensive, and the inclusion—or omission—of any title does not imply an endorsement or rejection by The Foundation Center.

The list of additional readings is arranged in categories which roughly correspond to the chapters in this guide, i.e.:

- General Background on Foundations and Philanthropy
- Guides to Government and Religious Funding Sources
- Guides to Income-Generating Programs
- Getting Organized to Receive a Grant
- General Directories and Subject Guides to Funding Sources
- Presenting Your Idea to Funders
- General Periodicals

Directories of state and local funding sources, sources of information on grants for individuals, and guides to corporate funding sources are treated more extensively in Appendices B, C, and D, respectively. This bibliography does not include titles devoted to specific fundraising techniques, such as deferred giving, direct mail solicitation, or special events, or titles devoted to specific aspects of nonprofit management, such as board development, marketing and public relations, volunteer programs, etc. We have also decided not to include the hundreds of useful magazine and journal articles which provide information on funding sources, fundraising techniques, or trends in philanthropy. Instead, we have included a section listing the major journals which regularly treat issues of interest to grantmakers and grantseekers.

Copies of the titles listed here can be found in The Foundation Center's New York library, as well as in most of the Center's cooperating libraries. Anyone may examine and use these publications in our libraries free of charge, and we recommend that you take a look at any individual title to determine its relevance to your needs before making a purchase. When available, prices are noted with listings of particular titles, but please note that prices are subject to change and some publishers may add a surcharge for postage and handling. It is therefore advisable to check with publishers for current information before mailing your check.

GENERAL BACKGROUND ON FOUNDATIONS AND PHILANTHROPY

Andrews, F. Emerson. *Philanthropy in the United States: History and Structure.* New York: The Foundation Center, 1978. 35pp. $1.50
> This pamphlet presents a brief history of private foundations and philanthropy, emphasizing the structure and dimensions of the philanthropic world in the 1970s.

Bremner, Robert. *American Philanthropy.* Chicago: University of Chicago Press, 1960. 230pp. $11.00
> An historical review of the role and development of private philanthropy and voluntary activity from colonial times to the present.

Commission on Foundations and Private Philanthropy (The Peterson Commission). *Foundations, Private Giving, and Public Policy.* Chicago: University of Chicago Press, 1970. 287pp.
> The final report of the 15-member Commission, chaired by Peter G. Peterson, which was formed in 1969 to study American philanthropy and private foundations.

Commission on Private Philanthropy and Public Needs (The Filer Commission). *Giving in America: Toward a Stronger Voluntary Sector.* Washington, D.C.: U.S. Department of the Treasury, 1975. 240 pp.

The Filer Commission was formed in 1973 to study the role of private philanthropy in the U.S. Its final report summarizes the findings of the Commission's two-year study and presents its recommendations for broadening the base of philanthropy and improving the philanthropic process.

Council on Foundations. *The Grantmaking Process.* Washington, D.C.: Council on Foundations, 1983. $15.00
One of a series of "Resources for Grantmakers," this kit features articles, guidelines, and other materials on grantmaking procedures and practices.

Cuninggim, Merrimon. *Private Money and Public Service: The Role of Foundations in American Society.* New York: McGraw-Hill Co., 1972. 267pp.
Cuninggim, a former President of the Danforth Foundation, examines the criticisms and problems facing foundations after the 1969 Tax Reform Act and offers a rationale for private philanthropy in our society.

Freeman, David R. *Handbook on Private Foundations.* Washington, D.C.: Council on Foundations, 1981. 440pp. $20.00
Although designed primarily for foundation officials and those interested in forming a foundation, this handbook provides useful insights into the rules and regulations affecting foundations, grantmaking policies and practices, and other aspects of foundation operations.

Giving U.S.A. Annual Report 1985. New York: American Association of Fund-Raising Counsel, 1985. 112pp. $25.00
Annual study of contributions by individuals, foundations, and corporations to all types of nonprofit organizations. Includes analyses of trends and issues affecting private giving.

Heimann, Fritz F., ed. *The Future of the Foundation.* Englewood Cliffs, NJ: Prentice-Hall, 1973. 278pp.
These nine articles by foundation officials, tax specialists, and scholars examine the status and future roles for American foundations in light of the 1969 Tax Reform Act.

Hodgkinson, Virginia, and Weitzman, Murray. *Dimensions of the Independent Sector: A Statistical Profile.* Washington, D.C.: Independent Sector, 1984. 79pp. $35.00
This statistical compilation provides a wealth of data on the characteristics, growth, and financial status of all types of funders and nonprofit organizations. Section III details the changing sources of revenues for nonprofit organizations.

Internal Revenue Service, Department of the Treasury. *Instructions for Form 990-PF: Return of Private Foundation or Section 4947(a)(1) Trust Created as a Private Foundation.* Washington, D.C.: U.S. Government Printing Office, 1985. free.

Keele, Harold M., and Kiger, Joseph C., eds. *Foundations*. The Greenwood Encyclopedia of American Institutions, no. 8. Westport, CT: Greenwood Press, 1984. 516pp. $49.95
  Includes brief histories of the nation's 230 largest foundations (ca. 1981-82).

Maxwell, Joan. *Giving: A Comparison of the Philanthropic Resources of Seven Metropolitan Areas*. Washington, D.C.: Greater Washington Research Center, 1985. 62pp. $10.00
  Analyzes the philanthropic resources of Atlanta, Boston, Cleveland, Dallas/Ft. Worth, Minneapolis/St. Paul, San Francisco/Oakland, and Washington, D.C. and discusses the impact of these funding bases on local nonprofits.

McCarthy, Kathleen D. *Philanthropy and Culture: The International Foundation Perspective*. Philadelphia: University of Pennsylvania Press (for the Rockefeller Foundation), 1984. 189pp. $12.95
  Based on a Rockefeller Foundation conference, this collection of essays examines the history, impact, and changing roles of foundation and corporate funding abroad, focusing on support for humanities programs and concerns.

Mellon Bank Corporation. *Discover Total Resources: A Guide for Nonprofits*. Pittsburgh, PA: Mellon Bank Corporation, 1985. 43pp. free. (Order from Community Affairs Division, 1 Mellon Bank Center, Pittsburgh, PA 15258.)
  A basic guide to evaluating community-based organizations in order to build a more effective support base. Focus is using total community resources in addition to traditional funding sources.

Nason, John W. *Trustees and the Future of Foundations*. Washington, D.C.: Council on Foundations, 1977. 112pp. $10.00
  This analysis of the role of foundation trustees in today's society covers such topics as public accountability, professional staffs, and the 1969 Tax Reform Act.

Nielsen, Waldemar A. *The Big Foundations*. New York: Columbia University Press, 1972. 475 pp. $15.00
  A controversial examination of the 33 largest foundations, with a commentary of the patterns, processes, performance, and future outlook for large donor institutions.

Nielsen, Waldemar A. *The Golden Donors: A New Anatomy of the Great Foundations*. New York: E.P. Dutton, 1985. 468pp. $25.00
  A critical analysis of the nation's 36 largest foundations, focusing on their donors, development, governance, and funding activities. Nielsen also discusses the broad historical development of private foundations and the changing political context in which they operate.

O'Connell, Brian. *America's Voluntary Spirit.* New York: The Foundation Center, 1983. 450pp. $19.95; $14.95 pap.

The 45 selections in this anthology present a diverse picture of the history, philosophy, and impact of private philanthropy and voluntary action in America.

Odendahl, Teresa; Boris, Elizabeth; and Daniels, Arlene. *Working in Foundations: Career Patterns of Women and Men.* New York: The Foundation Center, 1985. 115pp. $12.95

Although the primary focus of this study is on gender differences in foundation career paths, it also provides a detailed picture of foundation management styles and grantmaking processes.

Pifer, Alan. *Philanthropy in an Age of Transition.* New York: The Foundation Center, 1984. 270pp. $12.50

These essays drawn from the annual reports of the Carnegie Corporation during Mr. Pifer's tenure as President examine some of the major issues confronting foundations and the nonprofit sector from 1966 to 1982.

Reeves, Thomas C., ed. *Foundations Under Fire.* Ithaca, NY: Cornell Unviersity Press, 1970. 235pp.

This anthology of 24 articles presents a wide variety of viewpoints on the role and the strengths and weaknesses of private foundations in America.

Riley, Margaret. "Private Foundations, 1982." *Statistics of Income S01 Bulletin* 5, no. 2 (Fall 1985): 1-27.

A detailed report on the financial status of private foundations in 1982, with an analysis of the impact of legislative changes on foundation operations.

Salamon, Lester M., and Abramson, Alan J. *The Federal Budget and the Nonprofit Sector.* Washington, D.C.: The Urban Institute Press, 1982. 116pp. $11.50

This monograph examines the scope and structure of the nonprofit sector, its relationships with government, and the impact of reduced Federal funding proposals on the sector.

Struckhoff, Eugene S. *The Handbook for Community Foundations: Their Formation, Development, and Operations.* 2 vols. Washington, D.C.: Council on Foundations, 1977. $50.00

The definitive guide to the history, governance, philosophy, and operations of community foundations.

Weaver, Warren. *U.S. Philanthropic Foundations: Their History, Structure, Management and Record.* New York: Harper and Row, 1967. 492pp.

Examines the historical origins, regulation, and operations of private foundations and the relationship of foundations to universities, government, and society. Part Two presents 19 essays by scholars and leaders in such fields as health and dance who discuss the impact of foundation funding in their area of activity.

Whitaker, Ben. *The Philanthropoids: Foundations and Society*. New York: William Morrow and Co., 1974. 256pp.

An often critical examination of the aims, politics, economics, and achievements of U.S. private foundations by a British scholar. Chapter 9 presents Whitaker's views on "How Not to Get a Grant."

A Window on the World of Philanthropy: A Compilation of Insights, 1973-1983. Arlington, VA: Council of Better Business Bureaus, 1984. 96pp. $25.00

A compilation of articles from the Philanthropic Advisory Service's monthly newsletter covering business giving, government funding, tax exemption, and standards and laws governing charitable solicitation.

Zurcher, Arnold J., and Dustan, Jane. *The Foundation Administrator*. New York: Russell Sage Foundation, 1972. 171pp.

The results of a 1970 study of the people who manage American foundations and determine their policies. Provides detailed information on employment patterns and policies and examines the pros and cons of increased professionalization of foundation service.

GUIDES TO GOVERNMENT AND RELIGIOUS FUNDING SOURCES

Church Funds for Social Justice: A Directory. Minneapolis, MN: Greater Minneapolis Council of Churches, n.d. 94pp. $8.00

Describes local, regional, and national church funding sources for social change organizations.

Congressional Staff Directory 1985. Mount Vernon, VA: Congressional Staff Directory Ltd., 1985. 1201pp. $45.00

Indexes members of Congress and their staff noting local and Washington, D.C. office addresses and phone numbers, committee assignments, and other useful information.

Federal Funding Guide. Arlington, VA: Government Information Service, 1985. $127.95

A detailed guide to federal programs which provide financial aid to state and local governments and to all types of nonprofit organizations. Issued annually with quarterly supplements that highlight statutory, regulatory, and budgetary changes.

Federal Grants Management Handbook. Washington, D.C.: Grants Management Advisory Service, 1978.
> Arranged in a loose-leaf format and updated monthly, this handbook provides practical advice on obtaining a federal grant, financial administration of federal grants, and compliance with federal regulations.

Fenton, Calvin W., and Edwards, Charles J., eds. *Guide to Federal Grants and Financial Aid for Individuals and Nonprofit Organizations*, 2nd ed. Dubuque, IA: Kendall/Hunt Publishing Co., 1983.
> Provides detailed descriptions of federal financial assistance programs, including project grants, loans, and other payments. Includes subject index and a "master index" by agency detailing type of support available and deadlines.

Greenly, Robert B. *How to Win Government Contracts.* New York: Van Nostrand Reinhold, 1983. 196pp. $24.95
> A practical guide to the government contracting system covering how to get on qualified bidders' lists, determine a budget, organize and write a proposal, etc.

Grisham, Roy, Jr., and McConaughy, Paul D., eds. *Encyclopedia of U.S. Government Benefits*, 2nd ed. Union City, NJ: Wm. H. Wise & Co., 1977. 1014pp. $17.95
> Provides background information on over 5,000 government services, including publications, funding programs, and contact person at each service agency.

Hillman, Howard. *The Art of Winning Government Grants.* New York: The Vanguard Press, 1977.
> Although much of the information on Federal agencies is now dated, Hillman's basic introduction to "the six grant-seeking phases" still contains relevant, practical advice for the government grantseeker.

Holtz, Herman. *Government Contracts: Proposalmanship and Winning Strategies.* New York: Plenum Press, 1979. 288pp. $19.50
> Reviews the workings of the government contract market and presents strategies for learning about and obtaining contracts.

Lesko, Matthew. *Getting Yours: The Complete Guide to Government Money.* New York: Viking Penguin, 1984. 292pp. $7.95
> Describes a number of Federal funding programs based on the *Catalog of Federal Domestic Assistance.* Includes descriptions of how specific individuals and organizations have used government funding.

The Philanthropy of Organized Religion. Washington, D.C.: Council on Foundations, 1985. 144pp. $10.00

The report on a survey of national and regional religious organizations on their philanthropic activities. Identifies grantmaking religious organizations and describes the nature of and trends in religious giving.

United States Government Manual. Washington, D.C.: U.S. Government Printing Office. $9.00
This official handbook of the Federal Government provides comprehensive information on agencies of the legislative, judicial, and executive branches. Entries generally describe the agency's purpose, history, and programs; list principal offices; and provide information on consumer activities, contracts and grants, employment, publications, etc. Updated annually in July to coincide with the Federal budget year.

U.S. Office of Management and Budget. *Catalog of Federal Domestic Assistance.* Washington, D.C.: U.S. Government Printing Office, 1984. 1063pp. $32.00
The essential guide to Federal funding assistance available to state and local governments, private profit and nonprofit agencies, and individuals.

Wright, Nancy D., and Allen, Gene P., comps. *The National Directory of State Agencies*, 6th Edition. Arlington, VA: Information Resources Press, 1984. 818pp. $82.50
Lists names, addresses, telephone, and contact of state agencies first by state, then by function, e.g., Aging, Housing, Mental health, etc.

GUIDES TO INCOME-GENERATING PROGRAMS

Center for Urban Economic Development. *Business Spinoffs: Planning the Organizational Structure of Business Activities.* Chicago: University of Illinois at Chicago Circle, 1982. 105pp. $12.00
This practical manual addresses legal questions, taxation issues, and managerial issues for nonprofit organizations that are deciding whether and how to set up profit-making ventures.

Duncan, William A. *Looking at Income-Generating Businesses for Small Nonprofit Organizations.* Berea, KY: Mountain Association for Community Economic Development, 1982. 25pp. $3.00
This useful pamphlet provides information to help small nonprofits decide whether or not to start a business and proposes an 11-step process for seeking business opportunities.

The Grantsmanship Center. *Profit Making by Nonprofits.* Los Angeles: The Grantsmanship Center, 1983. 23pp. $2.50

Reprints of a series of articles originally published in *The Grantsmanship Center News*, including case studies, guidelines for setting up a profit-making subsidiary, and tax implications of profit-making ventures.

Hunt, Susan, ed. *New Sources of Revenue: An Ideabook.* Washington, D.C.: Council for Advancement and Support of Education, 1984. 64pp. $16.50
Examines entrepreneurial and unrelated business enterprises for educational institutions, with case studies of several successful enterprises.

Internal Revenue Service, Department of the Treasury. *Tax on Unrelated Business Income of Exempt Organizations.* Washington, D.C.: U.S. Government Printing Office, 1984. 19pp. (Order from the IRS Forms Distribution Center for your state.)

Twin Cities Regenerative Funding Project. *In Search of Cash Cows: Exploring Money-Making Options for Nonprofit Agencies.* Minneapolis, MN: Peter C. Brown and Associates, 1983. 110pp. $15.00
Describes nonprofits' experiences with revenue-generating programs, types and potential sources of money-making programs, financing and developing business plans, and implementing the programs.

GETTING ORGANIZED TO RECEIVE A GRANT

Bauer, David G. *The How to Grants Manual.* New York: Macmillan Publishing Co., 1985. 229pp. $20.00
A manual for the novice grantseeker which explains how to develop a needs assessment, identify funding sources, and work with funders.

Belcher, Jane C., et al. *Ideas: A Process for Development of Ideas*, 3rd ed. Washington, D.C.: Association for Affiliated College and University Offices, 1984. 45 + pp. $15.00
This unusual handbook uses the proposal format to explain a process for developing new program ideas.

Breiteneicher, Joseph C. K. *Quest for Funds.* Washington, D.C.: Neighborhood Conservation Program, National Trust for Historic Preservation, 1983. 18pp. $1.50
A special issue of the bimonthly newsletter, *Conserve Neighborhoods*, this brief guide presents an overview of private fundraising with an emphasis on the planning process.

Connors, Tracy D., ed. *The Nonprofit Organization Handbook.* New York: McGraw-Hill, 1980. 740pp. $49.95

An anthology of articles by over 25 experts in all aspects of nonprofit management, including securing tax-exemption, program planning and fundraising, and financial management.

Flanagan, Joan. *The Grass Roots Fundraising Book*. Chicago: Contemporary Books, 1982. 334pp. $8.95

A basic guide on how to set up a fundraising program, choose the right strategy for your group, and raise money through a variety of approaches.

Flanagan, Joan. *The Successful Volunteer Organization*. Chicago: Contemporary Books, 1981. 376pp. $7.15

Subtitled: "Getting Started and Getting Results in Nonprofit, Charitable, Grass Roots, and Community Groups," this handbook provides practical advice on planning, fundraising, and managing nonprofits.

Godfrey, Howard. *Handbook on Tax-Exempt Organizations*. Englewood Cliffs, NJ: Prentice-Hall, 1983. 423pp. $39.95

Discusses exemption requirements for specific types of nonprofits and procedures for compliance, and offers practical advice on how to get and keep exempt status.

The Grantsmanship Center. *The Grantsmanship Book*. Los Angeles, CA: The Granstmanship Center, n.d. $59.95

This loose-leaf collection of reprints from *The Grantsmanship Center News* provides a wealth of practical advice and information on program planning and proposal writing, funding strategies, and other areas of interest to nonprofit managers.

Guzman, Carol. *Semillas de Prosperidad or How to Cultivate Resources from the Private Sector*. Albuquerque, NM: Neighborhood Housing Services of Albuquerque, 1982. 90pp. $3.95

A useful guide to organizing and conducting the funding search, with an emphasis on community-based organizations.

Hardy, James M. *Managing for Impact in Nonprofit Organizations*. Edwin, TN: Essex Press, 1984. 238pp. $29.95

Describes how corporate planning techniques can be applied in nonprofit organizations for both strategic and operational planning.

Hennessey, Paul, et. al. *Managing Nonprofit Agencies for Results*. San Francisco, CA: Institute for Fund Raising, 1978. $37.50

Subtitled "A Systems Approach to Long-Range Planning," this loose-leaf handbook describes a seven-step process for organizational planning with many forms, worksheets, and checklists.

Hopkins, Bruce R. *The Law of Tax-Exempt Organizations*, 4th ed. New York: John Wiley and Sons, 1983. 748pp. $60.00

A basic text on Federal laws governing income tax exemption and related rules for qualified organizations, including regulation of lobbying and other political activities, unrelated business income, etc. A detailed *Supplement* issued in 1985 is also available from the publisher for $35.

Internal Revenue Service, Department of the Treasury. *Tax Exempt Status for Your Organization*. Publication 557 (rev. Feb. 1984). Washington, D.C.: U.S. Government Printing Office, 1984. 44pp. free. (Order from the IRS Forms Distribution Center for your state.)

Mirkin, Howard R. *The Complete Fund Raising Guide.* Hartsdale, NY: Public Service Materials Center, 1981. 159pp. $13.50

Discusses the planning and financing of a fundraising campaign, with advice on specific funding sources and fundraising techniques.

O'Connell, Brian. *Effective Leadership in Voluntary Organizations.* New York: Walker and Co., 1981. 202pp. $5.95

A practical guide to nonprofit management, including constructive planning and fundraising.

Olenick, Arnold J., and Olenick, Philip R. *Making the Non-profit Organization Work: A Financial, Legal, and Tax Guide for Administrators.* Englewood Cliffs, NJ: Institute for Business Planning, 1983. 370pp. $79.50

Provides detailed explanations of how to obtain and keep tax-exempt status, set up budgets, and maintain financial records.

Public Management Institute. *Evaluation Handbook.* San Francisco, CA: Public Management Institute, 1980. 145pp. $47.50

This practical handbook in loose-leaf format discusses how to use evaluation as a tool for organizational planning, program management, and grants planning.

Setterberg, Fred, and Schulman, Kay. *Beyond Profit: The Complete Guide to Managing the Nonprofit Organization.* New York: Harper and Row, 1985. 271pp. $18.95

Contains practical advice on every aspect of nonprofit management, including budgeting, planning, and fundraising.

Smith, Craig, and Skjei, Eric W. *Getting Grants.* New York: Harper and Row, 1980. 286pp. $6.95

Designed as a guide to funding sources and grantsmanship, this manual also provides practical guidance on "mistakes to avoid in approaching the funder" and how to "become more believable."

Tenbrunsel, Thomas W. *The Fund Raising Resource Manual: Strategies for Non-profit Organizations.* Englewood Cliffs, NJ: Prentice-Hall, 1982. 182pp. $7.95
  Designed to serve as a self-learning tool, this guide includes numerous check-lists and worksheets for organizational planning and building a diversified funding strategy.

Treusch, Paul E., and Sugarman, Norman A. *Tax-Exempt Charitable Organizations*, 2nd Ed. Philadelphia, PA: American Law Institute-American Bar Association, 1983. 726pp. $95.00
  This basic text on tax law and charitable organizations discusses the pros and cons of operating as a tax-exempt organization, the categories under which exemption may be obtained, the tax consequences of unrelated business income, and other relevant legal information.

Vinter, Robert D. *Budgeting for Non-Profit Organizations.* New York: The Free Press, 1984. 390pp. $22.95
  A basic budget planning guide for program managers of small and mid-size nonprofit organizations.

Vogel, Frederic W., ed. *No Quick Fix (Planning).* New York: Foundation for the Extension and Development of the American Professional Theatre, 1985. 96pp. $9.95
  Although prepared primarily for theater groups, this handbook describes a process and tools for planning that can be used by all nonprofits.

Williams, M. Jane. *Foundation Primer*, 4th ed. Ambler, PA: Fund-Raising Institute, 1981. 152pp. $30.00
  A basic handbook on how to start and run a foundation solicitation program, including several examples of appeal letters and proposals.

GENERAL DIRECTORIES AND SUBJECT GUIDES TO FUNDING SOURCES

American Psychological Association's Guide to Research Support, 2nd ed. Washington, D.C.: American Psychological Association, 1984. 463pp. $25.00
  Describes public and private funding programs for the behavioral sciences.

Annual Register of Grant Support, 1985-1986 edition. Wilmette, IL: National Register Publishing Co, 1985. 923pp. $87.00
  Describes over 2900 grant programs for research in all disiplines and subject areas. Covers government, foundation, professional association, and other special interest group programs. Indexed by subject, sponsoring organization, geographic focus, and personnel.

Bauer, David G. *The Complete Grants Sourcebook for Higher Education*, 2nd ed. New York: American Council on Education, MacMillan, 1984.
    A directory of foundations, corporation and government programs that provide funding for higher education. Includes subject and geographic indexes to funding programs.

Boss, Richard W. *Grant Money and How to Get It: A Handbook for Librarians.* New York: R.R. Bowker, 1980. 138pp. $19.95
    A guide to funding sources for libraries with advice on proposal writing and approaching funders.

Butler, Frances J., and Farrell, Catherine E., eds. *Foundation Guide for Religious Grant Seekers*. Chico, CA: Scholars Press, 1984. 139pp. $11.95
    Provides brief descriptions of 384 foundations with a history of religious grantmaking and lists resources available to help religious grantseekers.

Chavers, Dean. *Funding Guide for Native Americans*. Broken Arrow, OK: Dean Chavers Associates, 1983. 339pp. $49.95
    Loose-leaf handbook and directory of foundation, corporate, and religious funders that support Native American programs and organizations.

Corry, Emmett. *Grants for Libraries: Guide to Public and Private Funding Programs and Proposal Writing Techniques.* Littleton, CO: Libraries Unlimited, 1982. 240pp. $22.50
    A guide to resources and fundraising strategies for library programs.

Dermer, Joseph, ed. *Where America's Large Foundations Make Their Grants*. 5th ed. Hartsdale, NY: Public Service Materials Center, 1983. 253pp. $44.50
    Brief listings of grants awarded by 651 foundations arranged by state and foundation name and noting grant amount and name and location of the organization receiving the grant. "Additional Insights" provide other information on 182 foundations.

Diehl, Richard, and Weger, Christine. *Mental Health Funding Service*. Honolulu, HI: Program Information Associates, 1985. 250pp. $45.00
    Describes federal government and foundation funding programs for alcoholism, drug abuse, and mental health programs.

Directory of Biomedical and Health Care Grants. Phoenix, AZ: Oryx Press, 1985. 275pp. $55.00
    Describes 1358 health-related funding programs sponsored by business and professional organizations, foundations, government agencies. Includes indexes by subject, sponsoring organization, and type of sponsor.

Directory of Research Grants 1986. Phoenix, AZ: Oryx Press, 1986. 748pp. $74.50
  Lists and describes over 4,000 funding programs sponsored by business and
  professional organizations, government agencies, and foundations. Entries
  describe the purpose, eligibility requirements, application procedures and
  deadlines, and contact for each program.

Eckstein, Burton J. *Handicapped Funding Directory, 1984-85 Edition.* Oceanside,
NY: Research Grant Guides, 1984. 189pp. $18.95
  Describes foundations, corporations, associations, and agencies that provide
  funding for programs and services for the emotionally, mentally, or physically handicapped.

Encyclopedia of Associations. Volume 1: National Organizations of the U.S. 20th
ed. Detroit, MI: Gale Research Co., 1985. 3 vols., 2290pp. $195.00
  Describes approximately 20,000 national and international nonprofit organizations, covering a variety of subject areas. Includes trade associations, professional societies, labor unions, fraternal and patriotic organizations, and
  other types of voluntary agencies. Useful for researching nonprofit organizations or agencies working in a particular field.

Foundation 500. 8th ed. New York: Douglas M. Lawson Associates, 1984. 76pp.
$29.50
  Guide to giving programs and geographical interests of 500 private foundations.

Hartman, Hedy A. *Fund Raising for Museums: The Essential Book for Staff and
Trustees.* Bellevue, WA: The Hartman Planning and Development Group, 1985.
530pp. $85.00
  A directory of foundations, corporations, and government agencies that have
  funded all types of museums, with a basic fundraising primer for museum
  fundraisers.

*International Funding Guide: Resources and Funds for International Activities at
Colleges and Universities.* Washington, D.C.: American Association of State Colleges and Universities, 1985. 167pp. $7.50
  Describes over 300 funding sources and service agencies that provide support
  to institutions and individuals for international studies and programs.

Jeffri, Joan. *Arts Money: Raising It, Saving It, and Earning It.* New York: Neal-
Schuman Publishers, 1983. 291pp. $17.95
  A general guide to fundraising techniques and strategies for arts organiza-
  tions.

Norback, Judith, ed. *Sourcebook of Aid for the Mentally and Physically Handicapped.* New York: Van Nostrand Reinhold Co., 1983. 506pp. $29.95

Describes a variety of services and funding programs offered by public and private agencies for the mentally and physically handicapped.

Pray, Francis C., ed. *Handbook for Educational Fund Raising.* San Francisco: Jossey-Bass Inc. Publishers, 1981. 442pp. $25.95
A collection of 71 articles that discuss philosophical and practical approaches to every aspect of fundraising for higher education institutions.

Public Management Institute, comp. *The Complete Grants Sourcebook for Higher Education.* Washington, D.C.: American Council on Education, 1980. 605pp. $69.50
A practical guide to setting up and implementing a fundraising program with a directory of foundations, corporate, and federal government funding programs.

Public Media Center's Index of Progressive Funders, 1985-86 edition. San Francisco, CA: Public Media Center, 1985. 466pp.
Lists over 130 funding sources that have provided support for social change and progressive causes. Each entry briefly describes funding interests and priorities and lists recent and typical grants. Indexed by subject.

Search for Security: A Guide to Grantmaking in International Security and the Prevention of Nuclear War. Washington, D.C.: The Forum Institute, 1985. 281pp. $45.00
Directory of 77 foundations that fund international security and anti-nuclear war programs with an analysis of funding trends.

Serving the Rural Adult: Private Funding Resources for Rural Adult Postsecondary Education. Manhattan, KS: Action Agenda Project, 1985. 67pp. $7.00
Directory of some 90 foundations that have funded rural postsecondary education programs. Includes advice for grantseekers.

Shellow, Jill, ed. *Grant Seekers Guide: Funding Sourcebook.* Mt. Kisco, NY: Moyer Bell Ltd., 1985. $19.95; $14.95 pap.
Describes over 160 grantmakers who provide funding for cultural, social, and economic justice projects.

Taft Foundation Reporter. Washington, D.C.: Taft Corporation, 1985. 804pp. $267.00
Directory of 500 major private foundations with indexes by state, types of grants, fields of interest, and officers and directors. The Taft Foundation Information System ($367) includes the *Reporter* and the monthly newsletter *Foundation Giving Watch.*

Tribal Economic Development Directory. Broken Arrow, OK: Dean Chavers and Associates, 1984. 468pp. $87.50

Describes strategies for economic development on American Indian Reservations, with a directory of public and private funding sources at the national and local level.

U.S. Department of Agriculture, Office of Rural Development Policy. *Rural Resources Guide: A Directory of Public and Private Assistance for Small Communities.* Washington, D.C.: Government Printing Office, 1984. 476pp. $12.00

Describes 400 public and private national organizations that provide financial and technical assistance to small communities.

White, Virginia. *Grants for the Arts.* New York: Plenum Press, 1980. 360pp. $22.50

A comprehensive guide to resources for fundraisers seeking grant support for all types of artistic activities. Includes descriptions of federal funding programs and advice on approaching funders.

PRESENTING YOUR IDEA TO FUNDERS

Coleman, William, et. al., eds. *A Casebook of Grant Proposals in the Humanities.* New York: Neal-Schuman Publishers, 1982. 248pp. $29.95

Presents examples of 14 proposals that resulted in individual or group research grants or program grants to institutions with annotated comments from the editors.

Conrad, Daniel Lynn. *The Quick Proposal Workbook.* San Francisco: Public Management Institute, 1980. 115pp. $19.00

A workbook on project planning, proposal writing, and evaluation techniques.

Dermer, Joseph. *The New How to Raise Funds from Foundations.* Hartsdale, NY: Public Service Materials Center, 1979. 96pp. $12.00

Practical advice on submitting funding requests to foundations.

Hall, Mary. *Developing Skills in Proposal Writing,* 2nd ed. Portland, OR: Continuing Education Publications, 1977. 339pp. $15.00

A thorough and practical guide to proposal development from the idea to submission of the funding proposal.

Kalish, Susan Ezell, et. al., eds. *The Proposal Writer's Swipe File.* Washington, D.C.: Taft Corporation, 1984. 162pp. $18.95

Includes 15 model fundraising proposals demonstrating different approaches, styles, and structures.

Lauffer, Armand, *Grantsmanship,* 2nd ed. Sage Human Services Guides, Vol. 1. Beverly Hills, CA: Sage Publications, 1983. 189pp. $9.95

A practical workbook for developing a fundraising/marketing strategy, identifying funding sources, and developing a budget and proposal.

Lee, Lawrence. *The Grants Game: How to Get Free Money.* San Francisco: Harbor Publishing, 1981. 177pp. $8.95
A basic introduction and handbook for identifying funding prospects, preparing a proposal, and following-up on funding requests.

Lefferts, Robert. *The Basic Handbook of Grants Management.* New York: Basic Books, 1983. 292pp. $21.95
A guide to managing grant-supported projects and funds to meet donors' accountability and reporting requirements.

Lefferts, Robert. *Getting a Grant in the 1980s: How to Write Successful Grant Proposals*, 2nd ed. Englewood Cliffs, NJ: Prentice-Hall, 1982. 168pp. $7.95
Provides guidelines for preparing, writing, and presenting proposals to foundations and government funding agencies.

McAdam, Robert E.; Maher, Michael; and McAteer, John F. *Research and Project Funding for the Uninitiated.* Springfield, IL: Charles C. Thomas, 1982. 72pp. $17.75
Designed for the novice, this brief handbook focuses on proposal writing and submission of grant requests to funders.

Meador, Roy. *Guidelines for Preparing Proposals.* Chelsea, MI: Lewis Publishers, 1985. 116pp. $19.95
A manual on preparing and writing proposals for foundation and government grants, venture capital, or research and development contracts.

Mitiguy, Nancy. *The Rich Get Richer and the Poor Write Proposals.* Amherst, MA: University of Massachusetts, Citizen Involvement Training Project, 1978.
A workbook on program planning, identifying funding sources, and writing and submitting proposals with tips on approaching government, corporate, and foundation funders.

White, Virginia P. *Grants: How to Find Out About Them and What to Do Next.* New York: Plenum Press, 1979. 354pp. $19.50
Designed for the novice, this guide explains government, foundation, and corporate funding sources; how to find the right funder; and how to submit a proposal.

GENERAL PERIODICALS

Association Management. American Society of Association Executives, 1575 Eye St., NW, Washington, D.C. 20005. Monthly. $24.00

Articles and news reports on management, legal issues, member meetings and services, and other concerns of primary interest to membership organizations.

Board Letter. Duca Associates, P.O. Box 6496, Denver, CO 80206. Quarterly. $30.00
Articles on effective use of board members, annual giving campaigns, and case studies of nonprofit organizations and their boards.

CASE Currents. Council for Advancement and Support of Education, Publishers Service, Inc., 80 S. Early St., Arlington, VA 22304. 10/yr. $45.00
Articles on fundraising and management for educational institutions. Book reviews and conference listings included.

Channels. Dudley House, P.O. Box 600, Exeter, NH 03833-0600. Monthly. $40.
New ideas about communications in the nonprofit area; articles on coping with economic hardship, tax issues, approaching corporations, and public relations.

Chronicle of Nonprofit Enterprise. 138 Wyatt Way NE, Bainbridge Island, WA 98110. 6/yr. $23.00
Brief articles and book reviews focusing on a variety of nonprofit concerns.

Chronicle of Higher Education. 1255 23rd St., NW, Washington, DC 20037. Weekly. $48.00
Includes general articles on philanthropy and fundraising as well as funding announcements and lists of grants for higher education programs.

Conserve Neighborhoods. Preservation Press, National Trust for Historic Preservation, 1785 Massachusetts Ave., NW, Washington, D.C. 20036. 10/yr. $15.00
Contains practical information to aid community improvement efforts. Articles on fundraising, nonprofit management, public relations and current trends analysis are included.

Council on Foundations Newsletter. 1828 L Street, NW, Washington, DC 20036. Biweekly. $60.00
Features updates on legislative/regulatory activities of Congress, and key events and activities of the Council and its members as well as brief articles on corporate grantmaking, community foundations and affinity groups, research and professional development, and regional associations.

Foundation News. Foundation News Fulfillment Service, P.O. Box 501, Martinsville, NJ 08836. Bimonthly. $24.00
Features articles about grantmakers, grantmaking activities and trends; book reviews, people news, and classifieds.

FRI Monthly Portfolio. Fund-Raising Institute, Box 365, Ambler, PA 19002. Subscription information on request.

>   Provides practical advice to fundraisers, with focus on direct mail and capital campaigns.

Foundation Giving Watch. Taft Corporation, 5125 MacArthur Blvd., NW, Washington, D.C. 20016. Monthly. $127.00

>   Brief reports on new foundation programs, giving trends, and lists of recent grants. Updates the annual *Taft Foundation Reporter.*

Fundraising Management. Hoke Communications, 224 Seventh St., Garden City, Long Island, NY 11530. Monthly. $36.00

>   How-to articles on all aspects of fundraising; reports on successful campaigns and methods; advertisements on services and products useful to fundraisers is stressed; book reviews and calendar events.

FRM Weekly. Hoke Communications, 224 Seventh St., Garden City, Long Island, NY 11530. Weekly. $72.00

>   Short notes on all aspects of philanthropy; practical information and statistical analyses included.

Grants Magazine. Plenum Press, 233 Spring St., New York, NY 11013. Quarterly. $80.00

>   Articles for grantmakers and grantseekers covering issues in both public and private philanthropy; how-to articles, legislative information, and book reviews included.

Grantsmanship Center News. The Grantsmanship Center, 1031 S. Grand Ave., Los Angeles, CA 90015. 6/yr. $28.00

>   Information on public and private sources of funding and how to get it; articles review current issues in philanthropy; grants lists with deadlines and book reviews included.

Grassroots Fundraising Journal. P.O. Box 14754, San Francisco, CA 94114-0754. Bimonthly. $20.00

>   Articles on alternative sources of funding; book reviews and bibliographies.

KRC Letter. KRC Development Council, Box 53, Hastings-on-Hudson, NY 10706. 10/yr. $35.00

>   Articles serving as an exchange of information and ideas for fundraisers.

LRC-W Newsbriefs. Lutheran Resources Commission, Dupont Circle Bldg., Suite 923, 1346 Connecticut Ave., NW, Washington, D.C. 20036. Monthly. $60.00

>   Short notes on subjects such as aging, including information on funding, legislation, publications, conferences, and a variety of programs.

Nonprofit Executive. Taft Corporation. 5130 MacArthur Blvd., NW, Washington, D.C. 20016. Monthly. $97.00

Articles helpful in nonprofit management area; job listings included.

Nonprofit World. The Society for Nonprofit Organizations, 6314 Odana Rd., Suite 1, Madison, WI 53719. Bi-monthly. $59.00

Articles, book reviews, and advisory columns on legal, fundraising programs, and management issues.

NSFRE Journal. National Society for Fund Raising Executives, Inc., Suite 1000, 1511 K St., Washington, D.C. 20005. 2/yr. $15.00

How-to articles and reports on successful campaigns; advertisements of professional fundraisers.

Philanthropic Digest. Brakeley, John Price Jones, Inc., 1100 17th St., NW, Washington, D.C. 20036. Monthly. $35.00

Listings of recent foundation and corporate grants and large gifts and bequests from individuals, with brief reports on other fundraising issues.

Philanthropy Monthly. Non-Profit Report, Inc., P.O. Box 989, New Milford, CT 06776. 11/yr. $72.00

Articles concentrating on general issues in philanthropy and tax and legal aspects of fundraising for grantmakers and grantseekers.

The Philanthropy Resource Letter. Cerise Communications Co., 1821 San Ramon Ave., Berkeley, CA. 94707. Monthly. $54.00

Brief articles on fundraising sources and techniques.

Research Reports. Program on Nonprofit Organizations, Institution for Social and Policy Studies, Yale University, P.O. Box 154, Yale Station, 88 Trumbull St., New Haven, CT 06520. Occasional. Free.

Articles reporting on the progress or results of research related to the nonprofit sector conducted under the Program's auspices.

Tax Exempt News. Capitol Publications, Inc. 1300 North 17th St., Arlington, VA 22209. Monthly. $117.00

Short articles of interest to all nonprofits; analysis of trends, corporate information, legislative information, and special features on news from IRS, Treasury and Congress.

Taxwise Giving. 13 Arcadia Road, Old Greenwich, CT 06870. Monthly. $115.00

Brief reports on tax issues affecting charitable giving.

Voluntary Action Leadership. Volunteer: The National Center for Citizen Involvement, 1111 N. 19th St., Room 500, Arlington, VA 22209. Quarterly. $14.00

How-to articles for volunteers; calendar section lists programs and courses of interest; book reviews included.

Appendix B

Directories of State and Local Grantmakers

Compiled by Lydia Motyka

Alabama (184 foundations). *Alabama Foundation Directory.* Compiled by the Reference Department, Birmingham Public Library. 56 p. Based primarily on 1982 and 1983 990-PF returns filed with the IRS. Main section arranged alphabetically by foundation; entries include areas of interest and officers; no sample grants. Indexes of geographic areas and major areas of interest. Available from Reference Department, Birmingham Public Library, 2100 Park Place, Birmingham, Alabama 35203. $5.00 prepaid. New edition available Fall of 1986.

Alabama (212 foundations). *Foundation Profiles of the Southeast: Alabama, Arkansas, Louisiana, Mississippi.* Compiled by James H. Taylor and John L. Wilson. 1983. vi, 119 p. Based on 1978 and 1979 990-PF and 990-AR returns filed with the IRS. Main section arranged by state and alphabetically by foundation name; entries include principal officer, assets, total grants and sample grants. No indexes. Available from James H. Taylor Associates, Inc., 804 Main Street, Williamsburg, Kentucky 40769. $39.95 prepaid.

Arizona. The first directory of private, corporate and community foundations in Arizona will be published in 1986. For further information, contact Junior League of Phoenix, 1949 East Camelback Road, P. O. Box 10377, Phoenix, Arizona 85064.

Arkansas (148 foundations). See **Alabama.**

Arkansas (120 grantmakers). *Guide to Arkansas Funding Sources.* Compiled by Jerry Cronin and Earl Anthes, 1985. Based on 1982–1984 990-PF returns filed with the IRS. Main section arranged alphabetically under three categories: Arkansas foundations, foundations from neighboring states that make grants in Arkansas, religious funding sources and private scholarship and educational sources. Entries include assets, revenues and expenses, list of officers and trustees and sample grants. Appendix of smaller Arkansas foundations. Available from Independent Community Consultants, P.O. Box 1673, West Memphis, Arkansas 72301. $13.50 plus $1.50 postage and handling.

California (approximately 749 foundations). *Guide to California Foundations.* 6th edition. Researched by Morgan Gould, Ph.D. 1985. 585 p. Based primarily on 1983 990-PF returns filed with the IRS or records in the California Attorney General's Office; some additional data supplied by foundations completing questionnaires. Main section arranged alphabetically by foundation; entries include statement of purpose, sample grants and officers. Also section on applying for grants. Indexes of all foundations by name and by county location; index of primary interests only for those foundations completing questionnaire. Available from Northern California Grantmakers, 334 Kearny Street, San Francisco, California 94108. $17.00 plus $2.00 tax and postage, prepaid.

California (620 corporations). *National Directory of Corporate Charity: California Edition.* Compiled by Sam Sternberg. x, 450+ p. Based on annual reports, questionnaires, reference directories, grants lists, corporate donors lists of non-profit organizations, and news releases. Main section arranged alphabetically by corporation; entries include categories of giving, giving policies, geographic preference, and contact person; no sample grants. Also sections describing corporate giving patterns, nonprofit strategy and corporate giving, how to conduct a corporate solicitation campaign, and a bibliography. Indexes of operating locations of corporations, support categories, and companies and their California subsidiaries. Available from Regional Young Adult Project, 330 Ellis Street, Room 506, San Francisco, California 94102. $14.95 plus $2.00 shipping and $.97 sales tax for California residents.

California (67 foundations and 56 corporations) *San Diego County Foundation Directory.* Produced by the Junior League of San Diego, Inc. and the San Diego Community Foundation. 1985. 125 p. Based on 990-PF returns filed with the IRS. Main sections arranged alphabetically. Entries include contact person, type of support, range of grants, total amount and number of grants, application procedures and directors; no date of financial information indicated. Available from San Diego Community Foundation, 625 Broadway, Suite 1015, San Diego, California 92101. $20.00 includes postage.

California (97 + foundations). *The Directory of the Major California Foundations.* First Edition. Prepared by Logos Associates. 1986. 94p. Based on 1983 and 1984 990-PF returns and annual reports. Main section arranged alphabetically by foundation; entries include contact person, activities, categories of giving, board meeting dates, officers and directors and grants. No indexes. Available from Logos Associates, 7 Park St., Rm. 212, Attleboro, Massachusetts 02703. $19.95 plus $.63 shipping.

California (45 Bay Area foundations). *Small Change from Big Bucks: A Report and Recommendations on Bay Area Foundations and Social Change.* Edited by Herb Allen and Sam Sternberg. 1979. 226 p. Based primarily on 1976 990-AR returns filed with the IRS, CT-2 forms filed with California, annual reports, and interviews with foundations. Main section arranged alphabetically by foundation; entries include statement of purpose and contact person; no sample grants. Also sections on the Bay Area Committee for Responsive Philanthropy, foundations and social change, the study methodology, the committee's findings, and the committee's recommendations. No indexes. Appendixes of Bay Area resources for technical assistance, bibliography, nonprofit organizations in law and fact, and glossary. Available from Regional Young Adult Project, 330 Ellis Street, Room 506, San Francisco, California 94102. Make check payable to: Regional Young Adult Project. $3.00 plus $1.50 postage.

California (525 foundations). *Where the Money's At, How to Reach Over 500 California Grant-Making Foundations.* Edited by Patricia Blair Tobey with Irving R. Warner as contributing editor. 1978. 536 p. Based on 1975 through 1977 (mainly 1976) California CT-2 forms in the California Registry of Charitable Trusts Office. Main section arranged alphabetically by foundation; entries include statement of purpose, sample grants, and officers. Indexes of foundation names, foundation names within either Northern or Southern California, counties, and foundation personnel. Available from Irving R. Warner, 3235 Berry Drive, Studio City, California 91604. $17.00

Colorado (approximately 250 foundations). *Colorado Foundation Directory 1986–1987.* 5th edition. Co-sponsored by the Junior League of Denver, Inc., the Denver Foundation, and the Attorney General of Colorado. 1984. Based on 1983 and 1984 (mostly 1984) 990-PF returns filed with the IRS and information supplied by foundations; entries include statement of purpose, sample grants and officers. Also sections on proposal writing, sample proposal, and sample budget form. Available from Colorado Foundation Directory, Junior League of Denver, Inc., 6300 East Yale Avenue, Denver, Colorado 80222. Make check payable to: Colorado Foundation Directory. $10.00 prepaid.

Connecticut (61 foundations). *Directory of the Major Connecticut Foundations.* Compiled by Logos, Inc. 1982. 49 p. Based on 1979–80 990-PF and 990-AR IRS returns, foundation publications and information from the Office of the Attorney General in Hartford. Arranged alphabetically by foundation; entries include grant range, sample grants, geographic limitations, officers and directors. Index of subjects. Available from Logos, Inc., 7 Park Street, Room 212, Attleboro, Massachusetts 02703. $19.95 prepaid.

Connecticut (approximately 865 foundations). *1985–1986 Connecticut Foundation Directory.* Edited by Michael E. Burns. 1985. 148 p. Based primarily on 1984 and 1985 990-PF returns filed with the Connecticut Attorney General and survey of foundations. Main section arranged alphabetically by foundation; entries include selected grants list and principal officer, statements of purpose. Index of foundations by city and alphabetical index. Available from DATA, 880 Asylum Avenue, Hartford, Connecticut 06103. $25 prepaid.

Connecticut (approximately 890 corporations). *1986–1987 Guide to Corporate Giving in Connecticut.* Edited by Michael E. Burns. 1986. 350 p. Based on information supplied by corporations. Main section arranged alphabetically by corporation; entries for most corporations include areas of interest, giving policies, geographic preference, high, low, average grants, total grants, non-cash giving, products, related foundation and contact person; no sample grants. Indexes of corporations by town. Available from DATA, 880 Asylum Avenue, Hartford, Connecticut 06105. $26.50 plus $2.00 prepaid.

Delaware (154 foundations). *Delaware Foundations.* Compiled by United Way of Delaware, Inc., 1983. x, 120 p. Based on 1979 through 1981 990-PF and 990-AR returns filed with the IRS, annual reports, and information supplied by foundations. Main section arranged alphabetically by foundation; entries include statement of purpose and officers, grant analysis, type of recipient; no sample grants. Detailed information on 111 private foundations, a list of 27 operating foundations and a sampling of out-of-state foundations with a pattern of giving in Delaware. Two indexes; alphabetical listing of all foundations, all trustees and officers. Available from United Way of Delaware, Inc., 701 Shipley Street, Wilmington, Delaware, 19801. $14.50 prepaid.

District of Columbia (approximately 500 foundations). *The Directory of Foundations of the Greater Washington Area.* Edited by Elizabeth Frazier. 1984. 125 p. Based on primarily 1982 990-PF returns filed with the IRS. Sections on large foundations, small foundations and publicly supported institutions arranged alphabetically; entries include areas of interest, officers and directors, high and low grant and five highest grants. Glossary of terms. Indexes of trustees and managers, foundations by asset size and alphabetical index of foundations. Available from the Community Foundation of Greater Washington, 3221 M Street, NW, Washington, DC 20007 or College University Research Institute, Inc., 1701 K Street, NW, Washington, DC 20006. $10.00 plus $1.50 postage.

Florida (954 foundations). *The Complete Guide to Florida Foundations 1985/1986.* Compiled by Mary Ann M. Harris. 1985. 239 + p. Based primarily on 1983 and 1984 990-PF returns. Main section arranged alphabetically by foundation name; entries include officers, contact person, assets, total grants amount, high, low and average grants, funding priorities and geographic preferences; no indexes. Appendix of foundations and their subject and geographic preferences. Available from Adams and Co., Inc., Publications Department, P. O. Box 561565, Miami, Florida 33156. $55.00.

Florida (780 foundations). *Foundation Profiles of the Southeast: Florida.* Compiled by James H. Taylor and John L. Wilson. 1983. vi, 130 + p. Based on 1978 and 1979 990-PF and 990-AR returns filed with the IRS. Main section arranged alphabetically by foundation name; entries include principal officer, assets, total grants and sample grants. No indexes. Available from James H. Taylor Associates, Inc., 804 Main Street, Williamsburg, Kentucky 40769. $39.95 prepaid.

Georgia (457 foundations). *Foundation Profiles of the Southeast: Georgia.* Compiled by James H. Taylor and John L. Wilson. 1983. vi, 85 p. Based on 1978 and 1979 990-PF and 990-AR returns filed with the IRS. Main section arranged alphabetically by foundation name; entries include principal officer, assets, total grants and sample grants. No indexes. Available from James H. Taylor Associates, Inc., 804 Main Street, Williamsburg, Kentucky 40769. $39.95 prepaid.

Georgia (530 foundations). *Guide to Foundations in Georgia.* Compiled by the Georgia Department of Human Resources. 1978. xv, 145 p. Based on 1975 through 1977 990-PF and 990-AR returns filed with the IRS. Main section arranged alphabetically by foundation; entries include statement of purpose, sample grants, and principal officer. Indexes of foundation names, cities, and program interests. Available from Atlanta–Fulton Public Library, #1 Margaret Mitchell Square, Atlanta, Georgia 30303. Free.

Hawaii (143 foundations, 25 local service organizations, 13 church funding sources). *A Guide to Charitable Trusts and Foundations in the State of Hawaii.* 1986. Based on 1982 and 1983 990-PF returns filed with the IRS, annual reports and contact with foundations. Main section arranged alphabetically by foundation; entries include date established, purpose and activities, type of foundations, assets, total giving, officers and directors and number of grants, if available. Sections on program planning and proposal writing, forming a tax-exempt organization, mainland foundations, national church funding sources and local service organizations. Alphabetical index. Available from Alu Like, Inc., 401 Kamakee Street, 3rd floor, Honolulu, Hawaii 96814. $35.00 ($30.00 for nonprofits).

Idaho (89 foundations). *Directory of Idaho Foundations, 1984.* Prepared by the Caldwell Public Library. 1984. 23 p. Based on 1982 or 1983 990-PF returns filed with the IRS and questionnaires. Main section arranged alphabetically by foundation; entries include areas of interest, sample grants, directors and trustees, and application deadlines. Indexed by subject and foundation name. Appendixes of inactive foundations, foundations with designated recipients and national foundations with a history of Idaho giving. Available from Caldwell Public Library, 1010 Dearborn, Caldwell, Idaho 83605. $3.00 prepaid.

Illinois (approximately 200 corporations). *The Chicago Corporate Connection: A Directory of Chicago Area Corporate Contributors, Including Downstate Illinois and Northern Indiana.* 2nd edition. Edited by Susan M. Levy. 1983. xiii, 213 p. Based on information supplied by corporations. Main section arranged alphabetically by corporation; entries include principal business activity, local subsidiaries, giving policies, geographic preference, availability of printed materials, matching gift information, and contact person; no sample grants. Also section on guidelines for seeking corporate funding and a bibliography. Indexes of geographic locations, fields of business and matching gifts. Available from Donors Forum of Chicago, 208 South LaSalle Street, Chicago, Illinois 60604. $18.50 plus $1.50 postage and handling, prepaid.

Illinois (approximately 103 grantmakers). *Donors Forum Members Grants List 1984.* Edited by Susan M. Levy. 1985. xii, 253 p. A collection of grants of $500 or more awarded by Donors Forum members to organizations within the Chicago Metropolitan Area. Grantmakers arranged alphabetically under ten subject categories; entries include name of donee, amount of grant and whether the grant is new or a renewal of a previous grant; no address, financial data or officers. Appendix of miscellaneous grants. Available from Donors Forum of Chicago, 208 South LaSalle Street, Chicago, Illinois 60604. $35 plus $2.00 postage and handling. New edition published annually in September.

Illinois (approximately 1900 foundations). *Illinois Foundation Directory*. Edited by Beatrice J. Capriotti and Frank J. Capriotti III. 1985. ix, 327 + p. Based on 1983 990-PF and 990-AR returns filed with the IRS plus questionnaires completed by foundations. Main section arranged alphabetically by foundation; entries include financial data: statement and purpose; listing of all grants; officers; and principal contributors; Table of Contents alphabetical by foundation name; Index section: Summary Report of Foundations with special purpose or assets under $200,000; Banks/Trusts as Corporate Trustees; Donors, Trusteees & Administrators; Survey of Foundation Interests; Foundation Guidelines & Deadlines. Available from the Foundation Data Center, Kenmar Center, 401 Kenmar Circle, Minnetonka, Minnesota 55343. (612) 542-8582. $275 (includes annual seminar). Update service by annual subscription, $210.

Indiana (288 foundations). *Indiana Foundations: A Directory*. 3rd edition. Edited by Paula Reading Spear. 1985. iv, 164 p. Based on 1983 and 1984 990-PF returns filed with the IRS and information supplied by foundations. Main section arranged alphabetically by foundation; entries include officers, areas of interest, sample grants, high and low grants. Indexes of financial criteria, subjects, counties, and officers. Appendixes of restricted foundations, foundations for student assistance only, and foundations without funding. Available from Central Research Systems, 320 North Meridian, Suite 515, Indianapolis, Indiana 46204. $24.75 prepaid.

Iowa (247 foundations). *Iowa Directory of Foundations*. Compiled by Daniel H. Holm. 1984. iv, 108 p. Based primarily on returns filed with the IRS and information supplied by foundations; date of information is 1982 in most cases, no date is given in other entries. Main section arranged alphabetically by foundation; most entries include address, telephone number, Employer Identification Number, total assets, total grants, purpose and activities, officers and trustees, and contact person. Appendix of cancelled foundations. Index by city. Available from Trumpet Associates, Inc., P.O. Box 172, Dubuque, Iowa 52001. $19.75 plus $2 postage and handling.

Kansas (approximately 255 foundations). *Directory of Kansas Foundations*. Edited by Connie Townsley. 1979. 128 p. Based on 990-PF and 990-AR returns filed with the IRS. Fiscal date of information not provided. Main section arranged alphabetically by foundation; entries include areas of interest, sample arts grants and officers. Index of cities. Available from Association of Community Arts Agencies of Kansas, P.O. Box 62, Oberlin, Kansas 67749. $5.80 prepaid.

Kentucky (117 foundations). *Foundation Profiles of the Southeast: Kentucky, Tennessee, Virginia.* Edited by James H. Taylor and John L. Wilson. 1981. vi, 153 p. Based on 1978 and 1979 990-PF and 990-AR IRS returns. Main section arranged alphabetically by foundation; entries include assets, total number and amount of grants, sample grants and officers. No indexes. Available from James H. Taylor Associates, Inc., 804 Main Street, Williamsburg, Kentucky 40769. $39.95 prepaid.

Kentucky (101 foundations). *A Guide to Kentucky Grantmakers.* Edited by Nancy C. Dougherty. 1982. 19 p. Based on questionnaires to foundations, 1981 990-PF and 990-AR IRS returns. Arranged alphabetically by foundation; entries include assets, total grants paid, number of grants, smallest/largest grant, primary area of interest and contact person. No indexes. Available from Louisville Community Foundation, Inc., Three Riverfront Plaza, Louisville, Kentucky 40202. $6 prepaid.

Louisiana (229 foundations). See **Alabama.**

Maine (74 foundations). *A Directory of Foundations in the State of Maine.* 6th edition. Compiled by the Center for Research and Advanced Study. 1985. 39 p. Based on 1981 and 1982 990-PF returns filed with the IRS. Main section arranged alphabetically by city location of foundation; entries include areas of interest, sample grants, and principal officer. Also sections on basic elements in a letter of inquiry, a description of IRS information returns, a sample report to funding source, and a list of recent grants. Index of subjects. Available from Center for Research and Advanced Study, University of Southern Maine, 246 Deering Avenue, Portland, Maine 04102. $3.50 prepaid.

Maine (approximately 75 corporations). *Maine Corporate Funding Directory.* 1984. 100 p. Based on information supplied by corporations. Main section arranged alphabetically by corporation; entries include contact person and, for a few corporations, the areas of interest. Available from the Center for Research and Advanced Study, University of Southern Maine, 246 Deering Avenue, Portland, Maine 04102. $5.50 prepaid.

Maine (218 corporations). *Guide to Corporate Giving in Maine.* Michael E. Burns, editor. 1984. 72 + p. Based on questionnaires and telephone interviews. Main section arranged alphabetically; entries include product, plant locations, contributions and giving interests, if available. Index of foundations by city. Available from OUA/DATA, 81 Saltonstall Avenue, New Haven, Connecticut 06513. $15.00.

Maryland (approximately 380 foundations). *1984 Annual Index Foundation Reports.* Compiled by the Office of the Attorney General. 1985. Based on 1984 990-PF returns received by the Maryland State Attorney General's Office. Main section arranged alphabetically by foundation; entries include statement of purpose and complete list of grants, and officers. Available from the Office of the Attorney General, 7 North Calvert Street, Baltimore, Maryland 21202. Attention: Sharon Sullivan. $35.00 prepaid.

Massachusetts (385 foundations and corporations). *Massachusetts Grantmakers.* Edited by Gracelaw Simmons and Linda C. Coe. 1986. Based on 1985 returns filed with the IRS and questionnaire responses. Main section arranged alphabetically by foundation name; entries include emphasis and program areas, total grants, range, assets, trustees and contact person; no sample grants. Indexes by program areas, population groups, city; index of corporate grantmakers, regional associations of grantmakers and recently terminated foundations. Available from Associated Grantmakers of Massachusetts, Inc., 294 Washington St., Suite 501, Boston, Massachusetts 02108. $25.00 plus $3.00 handling.

Massachusetts (56 Boston area foundations). *Directory of the Major Greater Boston Foundations.* 1981. 48 p. Based on 1975 through 1980 990-PF and 990-AR returns filed with the IRS. Main section arranged alphabetically by foundation; entries include statement of purpose, sample grants, and officers. Index of fields of interest. Available from Logos Associates, 12 Gustin, Attleboro, Massachusetts 02703. $19.95 prepaid.

Massachusetts (737 corporations). *Guide to Corporate Giving in Massachusetts.* Michael E. Burns, editor. 1983. 97 p. Based on questionnaires and telephone interviews. Main section arranged alphabetically by city and zip code; entries include product, amount given annually, frequency, area of interest and non-cash contributions. Index of corporations by city. Available from OUA/DATA, 81 Saltonstall Avenue, New Haven, Connecticut 06513. $30.00 plus $1.50 postage and handling.

Massachusetts (approximately 150 foundations). *Private Sector Giving: Greater Worcester Area.* Prepared by The Social Service Planning Corporation. 1983. 184 p. Based on 1978 through 1981 information from 990-PF and 990-AR forms filed with the IRS and surveys. Main section arranged alphabetically by foundation; entries include financial data, trustees and grants. Indexes of foundations and areas of subject interest. Available from The Social Service Planning Corporation, 340 Main Street, Suite 329, Worcester, Massachusetts 01608. $12.50 plus $2.25 postage and handling for photocopy (printed edition depleted).

Michigan (859 foundations). *The Michigan Foundation Directory.* 5th edition. Prepared by the Council of Michigan Foundations and Michigan League for Human Services. 1986. vi, 213 p. Based on information compiled from foundations, The Foundation Center, and primarily 1984–1985 990-PF returns filed with the IRS. Main section arranged in four parts: Section 1 is mainly an alphabetical listing of 412 Michigan foundations having assets of $200,000 or making annual grants of at least $25,000 with entries including statement of purpose and officers, geographic priority, limitations, application procedures, and grant analysis; Section I also provides brief information on 398 foundations making grants of less than $25,000 annually, geographical listing of foundations and corporate giving programs by city, terminated foundations and special purpose foundations; Section II is a listing of 64 corporate giving programs and corporate foundations; Section III is a survey of Michigan foundation philanthropy; and Section IV provides information on seeking grants. Indexes of subjects/areas of interest; donors, trustees, officers; and foundation names. Available from Michigan League for Human Services, 300 North Washington Square, Suite 401, Lansing, Michigan 48933. $15.00 for members, $18.00 for nonmembers.

Minnesota (approximately 700 foundations) *Minnesota Foundation Directory.* Edited by Beatrice J. Capriotti and Frank J. Capriotti III. 1985. ix, 327+ p. Based on 1983 990-PF and 990-AR returns filed with the IRS plus questionnaires completed by foundations. Main section arranged alphabetically by foundation; entries include financial data; statement and purpose; listing of all grants; officers; and principal contributors; Table of Contents alphabetical by foundation name; Index section: Summary Report of Foundations with special purpose or assets under $200,000; Banks/Trusts as Corporate Trustees; Donors, Trustees & Administrators; Survey of Foundation Interests; Foundation Guidelines & Deadlines. Available from the Foundation Data Center, Kenmar Center, 401 Kenmar Circle, Minnetonka, Minnesota 55343. (612) 542-8582. $275 (includes annual seminar). Update service by annual subscription, $210.

Minnesota (420+ grantmakers). *Guide to Minnesota Foundations and Corporate Giving Programs.* Prepared by the Minnesota Council on Foundations. 1983. xxiv, 149 p. Based primarily on 1981 and 1982 IRS 990-PF returns and a survey of grantmakers. Main section arranged alphabetically by foundation name; entries include program interests, officers and directors, assets, total grants, number of grants, range, and sample grants. Some entries include geographic orientation, types of organizations funded and types of support. Indexes of foundations, types of organizations funded by specific grantmakers, and grantmakers by size. Appendixes of inactive foundations, foundations with designated recipients, foundations making grants only outside of Minnesota and foundations not accepting applications. Also section on funding research in Minnnesota. Available from University of Minnesota Press, 2037 University Avenue S.E., Minneapolis, Minnesota 55414. $14.95 plus 6% sales tax or tax exempt number for Minnesota residents.

Mississippi (54 foundations). See **Alabama**.

Missouri (788 foundations). *The Directory of Missouri Foundations.* Compiled and edited by Wilda H. Swift, M.A. 1985. 126p. Based on 1983 and 1984 990-PF returns and questionnaires. Sections on foundations making grants to organizations, foundations giving assistance to individuals, foundations with designated recipients, foundations which contribute scholarship funds to educational institutions, inactive, operating and terminated foundations. Entries include contact person, assets, total grants amount, low and high grant amounts and funding priorities; alphabetical index of foundations and listing of foundations by city. Available from Swift Associates, P. O. Box 28033, St. Louis, Missouri 63119. $15.00 plus $2.10 shipping.

Montana (65 + Montana and 20 + Wyoming foundations) *The Montana and Wyoming Foundations Directory.* 4th Edition. Compiled by Kendall McRae and Kim Pederson. 1986. Based on 990-PF, returns filed with the IRS, the National Data Book, and information supplied by foundations. Main section arranged alphabetically by foundation; entries include areas of interest, geographic preference, application process and contact person; no sample grants. Indexes of foundation names and areas of interest. Available from Grant Assistance, Eastern Montana College Library, 1500 North 30th Street, Billings, Montana 59101. $6.00 prepaid.

Nebraska (approximately 200 foundations). *Nebraska Foundation Directory.* Compiled by the Junior League of Omaha. 1985. 30 p. Based on mostly 1982 and 1983 990-PF returns filed with the IRS. Main section arranged alphabetically by foundation; entries include statement of purpose and officers. No sample grants or indexes. Available from Junior League of Omaha, 808 South 74th Plaza, Omaha, Nebraska 68114. $6.00.

Nevada (41 foundations). *Nevada Foundation Directory.* Prepared by Vlasta Honsa and Annetta Yousef. 1985. 64 p. Based on 1982 and 1983 990-PF forms filed with the IRS and interviews with foundations. Main section arranged alphabetically by foundation; entries include contact person, financial data, funding interests and sample grants. Section on inactive and defunct Nevada foundations. Section on 30 national foundations that fund Nevada projects. Index of fields of interest and index by foundation location. Available from: Community Relations Department, Las Vegas–Clark County Library District, 1401 East Flamingo Road, Las Vegas, Nevada 89109. $10.00 plus $2.00 postage.

New Hampshire (239 corporations). *1984–1985 Guide to Corporate Giving in New Hampshire.* Edited by Michael E. Burns. 1984. 89p. Based on questionnaires answered by corporations. Main section arranged alphabetically by corporation; entries include contact person, product, plants and giving interests. List of corporations by city. Available from OUA/DATA, 81 Saltonstall Avenue, New Haven, Connecticut 06513. $15.00.

New Hampshire (approximately 400 foundations). *Directory of Charitable Funds in New Hampshire.* 3rd edition. June 1976. 107 p. Based on 1974 and 1975 records in the New Hampshire Attorney General's Office. Updated with cumulative, annual supplement published in June. Main section arranged alphabetically by foundation; entries include statement of purpose and officers; no sample grants. Indexes of geographical areas when restricted, and of purposes when not geographically restricted. Available from the Division of Charitable Trusts, 400 State House Annex, Concord, New Hampshire 03301-6397. $2.00. Annual supplement, which includes changes, deletions, and additions, available from the same address for $2.00 prepaid. Make check payable to "State of N.H."

New Jersey (approximately 116 foundations and approximately 500 corporations). *The New Jersey Mitchell Guide: Foundations, Corporations, and Their Managers.* Edited by Janet A. Mitchell. 1985. 150+p. Based primarily on 1984 990-PF returns filed with the IRS and information supplied by foundations. Main section arranged alphabetically by foundation; entries include sample grants and officers, restrictions and program priorities. Section on corporations includes address, telephone, and contact person; no indexes. Available from The Mitchell Guide, P.O. Box 413, Princeton, New Jersey 08542. $65.00 prepaid.

New Jersey (approximately 66 foundations). *The Directory of the Major New Jersey Foundations.* First edition. Prepared by Logos Associates. 1983. 56 p. Based on 1980 through 1982 financial information. Arranged alphabetically by foundation; entries include contact person, activities, officers and directors, geographic limitations, financial data, and sample grants. No indexes. Available from Logos Associates, Room 212, 7 Park Street, Attleboro, Massachusetts 02703. $19.95.

New Mexico (approximately 41 foundations). *New Mexico Private Foundations Directory.* Edited by William G. Murrell and William M. Miller. 1982. 77 p. Main section arranged alphabetically by foundation; entries include contact person, program purpose, areas of interest, financial data, application procedure, meeting times and publications. Also sections on proposal writing, private and corporate grantsmanship and bibliography. No indexes. Available from New Moon Consultants, P.O. Box 532, Tijeras, New Mexico 87059. $10.00 plus $1.00 postage. New edition available mid-1984.

New York (approximately 125 organizations). *Guide to Grantmakers: Rochester Area.* 2nd Edition. Compiled by the Monroe County Library System. 1983. vii, 220 p. Based on contact with organizations and 1980 through 1982 (mostly 1981) 990-PF and 990-AR returns filed with the IRS. Main section arranged alphabetically by organization, including foundations, corporations, associations, nonprofit organizations offering funds, services, or products; entries include statement of purpose and officers; no sample grants. Also a section on liquidated and relocated foundations. Index of fields of interest. Appendixes of glossary of terms and bibliography. Published by Reynolds Information Center, Monroe County Library System. May be used in libraries of Monroe County Library System.

New York (62 foundations and 125 corporations). *The Mitchell Guide to Foundations, Corporations and Their Managers: Central New York State* (includes Binghamton, Corning, Elmira, Geneva, Ithaca, Oswego, Syracuse and Utica). Edited by Rowland L. Mitchell. 1984. Based on 990-PF returns filed with the IRS. Main sections arranged alphabetically by foundation and by corporation; entries include managers, financial data and sample grants. Alphabetical indexes of foundations and corporations and index to managers. Available from The Mitchell Guide, P. O. Box 413, Princeton, New Jersey 08542. $25.00 prepaid.

New York (149 foundations and 125 corporations). *The Mitchell Guide to Foundations, Corporations and Their Managers: Long Island* (includes Nassau and Suffolk Counties). Edited by Rowland L. Mitchell. 1984. Based on 990-PF returns filed with the IRS. Main sections arranged alphabetically by foundation and by corporation; entries include managers, financial data and sample grants. Alphabetical indexes of foundations and corporations and index to managers. Available from The Mitchell Guide, P. O. Box 413, Princeton, New Jersey 08542. $30.00 prepaid.

New York (61 foundations and 125 corporations). *The Mitchell Guide to Foundations, Corporations and Their Managers: Upper Hudson Valley* (includes the Capital Area, Glenns Falls, Newburgh, Plattsburgh, Poughkeepsie and Schenectady). Edited by Rowland L. Mitchell. 1984. Based on 990-PF returns filed with the IRS. Main sections arranged alphabetically by foundation and by corporation; entries include managers, financial data and sample grants. Alphabetical indexes of foundations and corporations and index to managers. Available from The Mitchell Guide, P. O. Box 413, Princeton, New Jersey 08542. $25.00 prepaid.

New York (148 foundations and 58 corporations). *The Mitchell Guide to Foundations, Corporations and Their Managers: Westchester* (includes Putnam, Rockland and parts of Orange Counties). Edited by Rowland L. Mitchell. 1984. Based on 990-PF returns filed with the IRS. Main sections arranged alphabetically by foundation and by corporation; entries include managers, financial data and sample grants. Alphabetical indexes of foundations and corporations and index to managers. Available from The Mitchell Guide, P. O. Box 413, Princeton, New Jersey 08542. $30.00 prepaid.

New York (125 foundations and 132 corporations). *The Mitchell Guide to Foundations, Corporations and Their Managers: Western New York State* (includes Buffalo, Jamestown, Niagara Falls and Rochester). Edited by Rowland L. Mitchell. 1984. Based on 990-PF returns filed with the IRS. Main sections arranged alphabetically by foundations and by corporation; entries include managers, financial data and sample grants. Alphabetical index of foundations and corporations and index to managers. Available from The Mitchell Guide, P. O. Box 413, Princeton, New Jersey 08542. $30.00 prepaid.

New York (1,832 foundations and 750 corporations). *The New York City Mitchell Guide: Foundations, Corporations and Their Managers.* Edited by Rowland L. Mitchell. 1983. xi, 413 p. Based on 1980 through 1982 990-PF and 990-AR returns filed with the IRS. Main sections arranged alphabetically by foundation and by corporation; foundation entries include managers, financial data and sample grants; no statement of purpose. Alphabetical indexes of foundations and corporations. Available from The Mitchell Guide, P.O. Box 413, Princeton, New Jersey 08542. $75.00 prepaid.

North Carolina (492 foundations). *Foundation Profiles of the Southeast: North Carolina, South Carolina.* Compiled by James H. Taylor and John L. Wilson. 1983. vi, 100+ p. Based on 1978 and 1979 990-PF and 990-AR returns. Main sections arranged alphabetically by foundation name; entries include principal officer, assets, total grants and sample grants. No indexes. Available from James H. Taylor Associates, Inc., 804 Main Street, Williamsburg, Kentucky 70769. $39.95 prepaid.

North Carolina (589 Foundations and 362 Corporations). *Grantseeking in North Carolina: A Guide to Foundation and Corporate Giving*. Compiled by Anita Gunn Shirley. 1985. vi, 637 p. Based on 1981–1983 990-PF returns filed with the IRS and questionnaires. Main sections arranged by type of foundation; entries include financial data, trustees, sample grants, limitations and application procedures. Alphabetical index of foundations and corporations; indexes by county, funding interest and index of officers, directors and trustees. Appendixes on proposal writing and corporate fundraising. Available from North Carolina Center for Public Policy Research, P. O. Box 430, Raleigh, North Carolina 27602. $35.00 plus $2.50 postage and handling.

Ohio (1800 foundations). *Charitable Foundations Directory of Ohio*. 6th edition. 1984. 105 p. Based on 1977 through 1983 records in the Ohio Attorney General's Office and returns filed with the IRS. Main section arranged alphabetically by foundation; entries include statement of purpose and contact person; no sample grants. Indexes of foundation by county location and purpose. Available from Charitable Foundations Directory, Attention: Faye Sebert, Attorney General Celebrezze's Office, 30 East Broad Street, 15th floor, Columbus, Ohio 43215. $6.00 prepaid.

Ohio (38 foundations). *Guide to Charitable Foundations in the Greater Akron Area*. 2nd edition. Prepared by Grants Department. 1981. 48 p. Based on United Way files, the Charitable Foundations Directory of Ohio, 990-PF and 990-AR returns filed with the IRS, and information supplied by foundations. Main section arranged alphabetically by foundation; entries include statement of purpose, sample grants, and officers. Also section on proposal writing. Appendixes include indexes of assets, grants, and officers and trustees. Available from Grants Department, United Way of Summit County, P.O. Box 1260, 90 North Prospect Street, Akron, Ohio 44304. $7.50.

Ohio (22 foundations). *Directory of Dayton Area Grantmakers*. 1983 Edition. Prepared by Carol Richardson and Judy Tye. 1983. xii, 29 p. Based on 1980 through 1982 data. Main section arranged alphabetically by foundation; most entries include contact person, fields of interest and limitations, and total assets, total and number of grants. Section on "Applying for a Grant" and glossary of grantmaker terms. Alphabetical index and index of interests. Available from: Belinda Hogue, 449 Patterson Road, Apt. A, Dayton, Ohio 45419. Free plus $1.25 postage and handling.

Ohio (259 Foundations). *The Source: A Directory of Cincinnati Foundations*. Prepared by Cynthia Hastings Roy and the Junior League of Cincinnati. 1985. 120 p. Based primarily on 1982 and 1983 990-PF returns filed with the IRS and questionnaires. Main section arranged alphabetically by foundation; entries may include financial data, sample grants, area of interest, officers and trustees and application information. Index of areas of interest. Available from the Junior League of Cincinnati, Grantsmanship Committee, Regency Square, 2334 Dana Avenue, Cincinnati, Ohio 45208. $9.85 ($10.32 Ohio residents).

Oklahoma (approximately 150 foundations). *Directory of Oklahoma Foundations.* 2nd edition. Edited by Thomas E. Broce. 1982. 284 p. Based on data from cooperating foundations or from 1974 through 1981 990-PF and 990-AR returns filed with the IRS. Main section arranged alphabetically by foundation; entries include statement of purpose and officers for some foundations; no sample grants. Index of foundation grant activities. Available from University of Oklahoma Press, 1005 Asp Avenue, Norman, Oklahoma 73019. $22.50 plus $.86 postage.

Oregon (approximately 300 foundations). *The Guide to Oregon Foundations.* 3rd edition. Produced by the United Way of the Columbia-Willamette. 1984. xv, 208 p. Based on 990-PF and CT-12 forms filed with the Oregon Register of Charitable Trusts and information supplied by foundations. Main section arranged alphabetically by foundation within six subdivisions: general purpose foundations, special purpose foundations, student aid or scholarship funds, service clubs, dedicated purpose and national foundations with an active interest in Oregon; entries include statement of purpose, officers, assets, total grants, sample grants and application information. Appendixes include Oregon foundations having assets of $500,000 or more, terminated foundations, inactive foundations, new foundations, regional breakdown of foundations and national foundation grants to Oregon. Index of foundation names. Available from Bonnie Smith, the United Way of the Columbia-Willamette, 718 West Burnside, Portland, Oregon 97209. $15.00 prepaid.

Pennsylvania (2300 + foundations). *Directory of Pennsylvania Foundations.* 3rd edition. Compiled by S. Damon Kletzien, Executive Editor. Published by Triadvocates Associated in cooperation with The Free Library of Philadelphia. 1986. 300 p. Based primarily on 1984 990-PF returns filed with IRS and information supplied by foundations. Organized in five geographical regions. Full profile-entries for about 975 foundations—those with assets exceeding $75,000 or awarding grants totaling $5,000 or more on a discretionary basis—include a statement on geographical emphasis of giving, a descending listing of all grants down to $250, listing of major interest codes, application guidelines and/or statement on giving policy when available, and a list of directors, trustees, and donors. Other foundations not meeting above criteria listed by name, address and status code only. Appendix article on broadening the foundation search. Indexes of officers, directors, trustees and donors; major giving interests; and foundation names. Make check payable to "Directory of Pa. Foundations"; mail to P.O. Box 336, Springfield, Pennsylvania 19064. $37.50 postpaid (plus Pa. sales tax of $2.25, unless exempt).

Rhode Island (91 foundations). *Directory of Grant-Making Foundations in Rhode Island.* Compiled by the Council for Community Services. 1983. 47 p. Based on 1980 and 1981 990-PF and 990-AR returns filed with the IRS, information from the Rhode Island Attorney General's Office and information from foundations. Main section arranged alphabetically by foundation; entries include officers and trustees, assets, total dollar amount of grants and total number of grants, statement of purpose, geographic restrictions, application information and sample grants. Includes "Introduction to Foundations"; indexes of foundations by total dollar amount of grants made, foundations by location and by area of interest. Available from the Council for Community Services, 229 Waterman Street, Providence, Rhode Island 02906. $8.00 prepaid.

Rhode Island (188 corporations). *Guide to Corporate Giving in Rhode Island.* Michael E. Burns, editor. 1984. 58 p. Based on questionnaires and telephone interviews. Main section arranged alphabetically; entries include product, plant location, giving interests and non-cash giving, where available. Index of corporations by city. Available from OUA/DATA, 81 Saltonstall Avenue, New Haven, Connecticut 06513. $15.00.

South Carolina (174 foundations). *South Carolina Foundation Directory.* 2nd edition. Edited by Anne K. Middleton. 1983. 51 p. Based on 1981 and 1982 990-PF returns filed with the IRS. Main section arranged alphabetically by foundation; entries include areas of interest, principal officer, assets, total grants, number of grants, range and geographic limitations. Indexes of foundations by city and field of interest. Out of print. Available on inter-library loan from South Carolina State Library, Columbia, South Carolina.

South Carolina (49 foundations). See **North Carolina.**

Tennessee (58 foundations; 21 corporations and corporate foundations). *Tennessee Directory of Foundations and Corporate Philanthropy.* 3rd edition. Published by City of Memphis, Bureau of Intergovernmental Management. 1985. Based primarily on 990-PF returns filed with the IRS and questionnaires. Two main sections arranged alphabetically by foundation and alphabetically by corporation; entries include contact person, contact procedure, fields of interest, geographic limitations, financial data, officers and trustees and sample grants. Indexes of foundations and corporations by name, fields of interest and geographic area of giving. Appendixes of foundations giving less than $10,000 a year, and major corporations in Tennessee which employ more than 300 persons. Available from Executive and Management Services, Room 508, City Hall, 125 North Mid-America Mall, Memphis, Tennessee 38103. $30.00 plus $2.50 postage and handling. Diskette available ($30.00).

Tennessee (202 foundations). See **Kentucky.**

Texas (approximately 1232 foundations). *The Hooper Directory of Texas Foundations.* 8th edition. Compiled and edited by John Cavnar-Johnson and Faith Edwards. 1984. 288p. Based on 1983 990-PF returns and information provided by foundations. Main section on larger foundations arranged alphabetically; entries include funding emphasis and restrictions, total assets and grants, application information, trustees and contact person. Available from Funding Information Center of Texas, 507 Brooklyn, San Antonio, Texas 78215. $30.00. Companion Supplement listing 267 foundations also available. $20.00 ($45.00 for both publications).

Texas (268 foundations). *Directory of Dallas County Foundations.* Compiled by Sharon Herfurth, Karen Fogg, and Lynn Bussey. 1984. 310p. Based on 1982 and 1983 990-PF returns and information provided by the Funding Information Library and The Foundation Center. Main section arranged alphabetically by foundation; entries include contact person, interests, total assets, total amount and number of grants, and officers. Appendix of Dallas foundations ranked by assets; index of foundations by giving interests and index of trustees and officers. Available from Urban Information Center, Dallas Public Library, 1515 Young St., Dallas, Texas 75201. $14.75 plus $2.35 postage and handling.

Texas (approximately 115 foundations). *Directory of Tarrant County Foundations.* 3rd edition. Prepared by Catherine Rhodes and the Junior League of Fort Worth. 1984. 150 + p. Based on 1982 and 1983 990-PF forms filed with the IRS and foundation questionnaires. Main section arranged alphabetically by foundation; entries include financial data, background and program interest, officers and trustees, types of support and geographic focus. Indexes of foundations, trustees and officers, types of support and fields of interest. Appendixes of foundations by asset amount and foundations by total grants. Available from Funding Information Center, Texas Christian University Library, P.O. Box 32904, Fort Worth, Texas 76129. $6.00 plus $1.00 postage and handling.

Utah (163 foundations) *A Directory of Foundations in Utah.* Compiled by Lynn Madera Jacobsen. 1985. xi, 265 p. Based on 1980–1982 990-PF returns filed with the IRS and questionnaires. Main section arranged alphabetically by foundation name; entries include officers and directors, financial data, area of interest, types of support, grant analysis and sample grants. Alphabetical index of foundations as well as index by area of interest and index of officers, directors, and advisors. Available from University of Utah Press, 101 University Services Building, Salt Lake City, Utah 84112. $50.00.

Utah (200 Foundations). *The Directory of Utah Foundations.* Compiled by Mary Gaber. 1984. 200 p. Based primarily on 1982 990-PF returns filed with the IRS. Main section arranged alphabetically; some entries include contact person, total contributions, highest and lowest grant, type of grant and type of recipient. Tables of Foundations ranked by assets, type of grant, highest grant and type of recipient. Available from MG Enterprises, 839 East South Temple #107, Salt Lake City, Utah 84102. $35.00 plus $2.50 postage and handling.

Vermont (132 corporation and 56 foundations). *OUA/DATA's 1984–1985 Guide to Corporate and Foundation Giving in Vermont.* Edited by Michael E. Burns. 1984. 28p. Based on 1982 and 1983 990-PF returns and information provided by foundations. Main sections arranged alphabetically by foundation and corporation. Foundation entries include contact person, assets, total grants, purpose, and grantmaking policies; no sample grants. Corporation entries include contact person, product, plants, giving policies and interests, and non-cash giving. Listings of corporations and foundations by city. Available from OUA/DATA, 81 Saltonstall Avenue, New Haven, Connecticut 06513. $15.00.

Virginia (approximately 500 foundations). *Virginia Foundations 1985.* Published by the Grants Resource Library of Hampton, Virginia. 1984. 200+ p. Based on 1980 through 1984 990-PF and 990-AR returns filed with the IRS. Main section arranged alphabetically by foundation; entries include officers and directors, assets, total grants and sample grants. Index by foundation name. Available from Sharen Sinclair, Grants Resources Library, Hampton City Hall, 9th Floor, 22 Lincoln Street, Hampton, Virginia 23669. $16.00 prepaid.

Virginia (326 foundations). See **Kentucky.**

Washington (approximately 968 organizations). *Charitable Trust Directory.* Compiled by the Office of the Attorney General. 1985. 202 p. Based on 1984 records in the Washington Attorney General's Office. Includes information on all charitable organizations and trusts reporting to Attorney General under the Washington Charitable Trust Act. Main section arranged alphabetically by organization; entries may include statement of purpose, officers, sample grants, and financial data. Available from the Office of the Attorney General, Temple of Justice, Olympia, Washington 98504. $4.00 prepaid.

Wisconsin (626 foundations). *Foundations in Wisconsin: A Directory 1984.* 6th edition. Compiled by Susan H. Hopwood. 1984. 282 p. Based on 1982 and 1983 990-PF returns filed with the IRS. Main section arranged alphabetically by foundation; entries include areas of interest and officers; no sample grants. Also sections listing inactive foundations, terminated foundations, and operating foundations. Indexes of areas of interest, counties, and foundation managers. Available from The Foundation Collection, Marquette University Memorial Library, 1415 West Wisconsin Avenue, Milwaukee, Wisconsin 53233. $16.00 prepaid plus $2.00 shipping. New edition available Fall 1986.

Wyoming (45 foundations). *Wyoming Foundations Directory.* Prepared by Joy Riske. 1982. 2nd edition. 54 p. Based on 1980 through 1982 990-PF and 990-AR returns filed with the IRS and a survey of the foundations. Main section arranged alphabetically by foundation; entries include statement of purpose and contact person when available. Also sections on foundations based out-of-state that award grants to Wyoming and a list of foundations awarding educational loans and scholarships. Index of foundations. Available from Laramie County Community College Library, 1400 East College Drive, Cheyenne, Wyoming 82007. Free. $1.00 postage for out-of-state orders.

Wyoming (20 foundations). See **Montana.**

Appendix C

Where to Find Information on Grants to Individuals

by Zeke Kilbride

How can you get a grant to help pay for your education, write a book, make a film, conduct research, pay medical expenses, or to fund any charitable activity?

There are a broad range of funding programs offered by government agencies, universities, foundations, and other nonprofit organizations, and there are a number of resources available to help you learn about them. As with all grant-seeking, however, the keys to obtaining grant support are planning, research, and persistence.

Every two years, The Foundation Center compiles a directory of foundation funding programs that are open to individuals. Now in its fifth edition, *Foundation Grants to Individuals* describes the purposes, the type and amount of support available, and the application requirements and procedures for the approximately 950 foundation programs that award grants directly to individuals. These programs include scholarships, fellowships, internships, residences, and travel programs for individuals in a variety of fields, as well as medical and emergency assistance for the needy. Because many of these programs have very specific application requirements, the book is as much a guide to those programs to which you should not apply as it is a guide to funding programs for which you may qualify.

Foundation Grants to Individuals includes several indexes to help you identify foundations that provide grants in your subject field or geographic area, that provide the type of support you are seeking (e.g., scholarships, fellowships, travel funds, etc.), that support students at or graduates of specific educational institutions, or that offer support to employees (and their relatives) of specific corporations. If you find a foundation program that provides the amount and type of support you need, you should carefully read the foundation's application requirements and program description. By demonstrating your knowledge of the foundation's programs and your qualifications for them, you have a better chance of having your request considered favorably. Foundations have only a limited amount of money available and a large number of applications from which to choose. The people who review your application will be looking for the candidate who best meets the standards and purposes of their programs.

This directory is limited to foundation funding programs, but there are many other sources of funding that should be fully investigated in your search for grant support.

FINANCIAL AID FOR EDUCATION

If you are a student and need financial support to further your education, your first stop should be the financial aid office of your current school as well as of the school you plan to attend. Financial aid officers usually have information about special scholarships or awards given by government agencies, local corporations, trade associations, or foundations, as well as programs offered by the school itself. Their advice can get you started in the right direction.

You might also research the general financial aid directories, as well as directories of funding sources in your academic area. A representative list of resources appears at the end of this article. Many public and school libraries maintain collections of funding directories relevant to students in their areas. In addition, many of the resources described here are available for free use at The Foundation Center Cooperating Libraries listed in Appendix G.

The best approach is to consider your own attributes and the connections you have to associations, corporations or other organizations. Many scholarships are not based solely on academic merit or financial need. For example, there are scholarships for dependents of Armed Forces veterans, scholarships for residents of a particular county, scholarships for art history majors, scholarships for the physically handicapped, scholarships for women, etc. Consider your background, the type of support you need and apply to those programs for which you qualify. Some of the more useful directories include: *The College Blue Book* (New York: MacMillan Information, published annually), *The Scholarship Book: The Complete Guide to Private Sector Scholarships, Grants and Loans for Undergraduates* (Englewood Cliffs, NJ: Prentice-Hall, Inc., 1984), *Financial Aids* for *Higher Education Catalog* (Dubuque, IA: William C. Brown Company, published biennially), and *The Chronicle Student Aid Annual* (Moravia, NY: Chronicle Guidance Publications, published annually). These books are well-indexed and may suggest additional funding possibilities to you.

GENERAL RESOURCES FOR GRANTSEEKERS

In addition to the directories of financial aid for education, there are directories covering noneducational funding possibilities. For example, *The Annual Register of Grant Support* (Wilmette, IL: National Register Publishing Co., published annually) covers grants for academic and scientific research, project development, travel and exchange programs, publication support, equipment and construction, in-service training, and competitive awards and prizes in a variety of fields. *The Grants Register* (New York: St. Martin's Press, published biennially) is tailored for grantseekers at or above the graduate level and others who require further professional or advanced vocational training. It is international in scope and is especially useful to students from other countries seeking exchange opportunities or international scholarships. Volume 1 of *Awards, Honors and Prizes* (Detroit: Gale Research, published irregularly) contains details about more than 6,000 prizes and awards for all types of service and special achievement in the United States and Canada. Volume 2 covers awards in more than 58 foreign countries. *The Directory of Research Grants* (Phoenix: Oryx Press, annual) is a useful source for scholars, grant administrators, faculty members and others seeking support for research projects. Over 2,000 programs are listed, including programs supported by private foundations, corporations, professional organizations, and a few state and foreign governments. Also of interest to the researcher is the *Research Centers Directory*, 10th Edition (Detroit: Gale Research Company, 1986) which lists approximately 8,300 university-related and other nonprofit research organizations in the U.S. and Canada.

SPECIALIZED RESOURCES

In addition to the general directories, there are specialized resources written for specific groups of people (women, minorities, etc.) or for specific disciplines and professional fields (grants in the arts, medicine, sciences, etc.). Some of the titles include: the *Directory of Financial Aids for Women* (Los Angeles: Reference Service Press, 1985), the *Directory of Financial Aids for Minorities* (Los Angeles: Reference Service Press, 1986), *Grants in the Humanities*, 2nd Edition (New York: Neal-Schuman, 1984), *Money Business: Grants and Awards for Creative*

Artists (Boston: The Artists Foundation, 1982), *Grants and Awards Available to American Writers* (New York: PEN American Center, biennial), *Fellowships and Grants of Interest to Historians* (Washington, DC: American Historical Association, annual) and *The ARIS Funding Messengers* (San Francisco: Academic Research Information System, subscription service). There are three separate *ARIS Messengers:* "Creative Arts and Humanities," "Medical Sciences Report," and "Social and Natural Sciences Report," issued 8 times a year.

For information on federal funding, the main source is the *Catalog of Federal Domestic Assistance* (Washington, DC: U.S. Superintendent of Documents, Government Printing Office, annual). Use this catalog as a starting point because much of the information is dated by the time it's published. Follow up by calling the local or regional office listed under "Information Contacts."

Typically, these publications provide addresses of funders, program descriptions, financial data, and deadline dates. Keep in mind that researching takes time and effort. You will need to carefully read each book's introduction, scan indexes, and study program descriptions to identify grant programs for which you qualify. Always request guidelines or applications before submitting a proposal.

AFFILIATING WITH A TAX-EXEMPT ORGANIZATION

If you are seeking support other than for your education, you should know that few private foundations and corporations make grants directly to individuals. Most only make grants to nonprofit tax-exempt organizations (universities, hospitals, museums, and other organizations with educational, scientific, religious or other charitable purposes) to whom contributions are deductible. Some individual grantseekers such as artists or writers become affiliated with non-profit organizations which have the federal tax-exempt status that funders require. This type of affiliation may also lead to greater credibility and exposure for their work. For a complete list of organizations to whom contributions are deductible, see the *Cumulative List of Organizations* published annually by the U.S. Internal Revenue Service, Publication 78. Order from the U.S. Government Printing Office, Washington, D.C. For a good discussion of affiliation and of grantseeking generally, see Judith Margolin's *The Individual's Guide to Grants* (New York: Plenum Press, 1983) and Ron Gross' *Independent Scholars Handbook* (Reading, MA: Addison-Wesley, 1982). Margolin suggests a number of affiliation possibilities including: forming a consortium with other individuals interested in the same subject, finding a temporary "in name only" tax-exempt sponsor or umbrella group to serve as a fiscal agent for your project, making use of your current affiliations to professional societies, trade associations, clubs, alumni groups, etc., or becoming an employee of a nonprofit institution. Gross offers suggestions like teaching in a college or university continuing education program on a part-time basis, developing a "scholar-in-residence" role, etc.

If you don't have organizational affiliations, there are a number of directories of nonprofit organizations that might help you find them. One, for example, is *The Encyclopedia of Associations*, Volume 5: Research Activities and Funding Programs (Detroit: Gale Research, 1983). Let's say, for example, that you are writing a book on the contributions of Hispanic Americans to American society. Looking in the index of *The Encyclopedia of Associations*, you'll find under "Hispanic" an organization called "The Institute for the Study of the Hispanic American in U.S. Life and History." It says "research is conducted both in-house and through the awarding of research contracts, project grants, scholarships, fellowships, and institutional grants." Perhaps the Institute or a similar organization would be worth affiliating with. Some organizations might fund your project directly or serve as "conduits" for your funding. A "conduit" is an organization which will accept funds on your behalf. It makes formal application for the grant and retains fiscal responsibility over the project. If you choose to work with a conduit organization, be sure that it has federal tax-exempt status, and be aware that there may be strings attached. For example, the organization might impose administrative controls on your work; it might want a percentage of your grant; it might want rights as a joint author, etc. No two conduit relationships are exactly alike. Proceed with caution.

FORMING YOUR OWN NONPROFIT ORGANIZATION

Still a third option is to consider forming your own nonprofit, tax-exempt organization. This will require careful thought and a good deal of administrative work on your part. It also entails legal and financial responsibilities requiring a lawyer. Don't try it alone. If you'd like to learn more about what's involved in incorporating or in forming an unincorporated association, there are a number of useful sources, including: *Starting and Running a Nonprofit Organization* (Minneapolis, MN: University of Minnesota Press, 1980), *To Be or Not To Be: An Artist's Guide to Not-for-Profit Incorporation* (New York: Volunteer Lawyers for the Arts, 1982), *The Nonprofit Organization Handbook* (New York: McGraw-Hill, 1980), and *Arts Money: Raising It, Saving It, and Earning It*, by Joan Jeffri (New York: Neal-Schuman, 1983). Books covering incorporation for your particular state can be more useful; for example, *The California Non-Profit Corporation Handbook*, 4th Edition (Berkeley, CA: Nolo Press, 1984), or *The New York Not-for-Profit Organization Manual* (New York: Council of New York Law Associates, Volunteer Lawyers for the Arts, 1985).

Keep in mind that forming a nonprofit organization is not the same as getting tax-exempt, tax-deductible status. Nonprofit incorporation is a procedure handled on the state level; tax-exempt status is a federal procedure. For information on getting federal tax-exempt status, see IRS publication 557, *Tax Exempt Status for Your Organization*. You can obtain copies from the U.S. Government Printing Office, Washington, D.C. or by calling the Tax Information number in the phone book listed under "United State Government, Internal Revenue Service." Forming a nonprofit organization is not for everyone. In fact, many nonprofit organizations fail in their first few years because the people who formed them did not understand what they were getting into. By reviewing the resources mentioned and discussing your options with a lawyer, you should be better able to decide if this approach is right for you.

This article has discussed a number of ideas and resources for individual grantseekers to consider. It's meant as a starting point for further research. The following is a list of representative resources that can be valuable to you as you research further. The categories are not mutually exclusive. When grantseeking, a good approach is to scan the general resources first. Then, check to see if there are specific resources related to your interests.

Publisher's addresses, book prices, and editions are constantly changing. Before ordering a particular title, check with the publisher to verify that you have the most current information. Copies of many of the works are available for free reference use in The Foundation Center's New York, Washington, D.C., Cleveland, and San Francisco libraries and in many of its cooperating libraries. Many publications are also available in local libraries and college financial aid offices.

GENERAL SOURCES OF INFORMATION ON GRANTS TO INDIVIDUALS

Annual Register of Grant Support, 1985-86. 19th ed. Wilmette, IL: National Register Publishing Co., 1985. 923p. (3004 Glenview Rd., 60091) $87.00

Includes information on nearly 3,000 programs sponsored by funding sources, including government agencies, public and private foundations, educational and professional associations, special interest organizations and corporations. Covers a broad range of interests including academic and scientific research, publication support, equipment and construction support, in-service training, competitions and prizes, and travel and exchange programs. Organized by broad subject areas with four indexes: subject, organization and program, geographic, and personnel.

Awards, Honors, and Prizes. 6th ed. Volume I: United States and Canada. Paul Wasserman, ed. Detroit: Gale Research Co., 1985. approx. 950p. (Book Tower, 48226) $145.00

Directory of awards in advertising, public relations, art, business, government, finance, science, education, engineering, literature, technology, sports, religion, public affairs, radio and television, politics, librarianship, fashion, medicine, law, publishing, international affairs, transportation, architecture, journalism, motion pictures, music, photography, and theater and performing arts.

Directory of Research Grants, 1986. Betty L. Wilson and William K. Wilson, eds. Phoenix: The Oryx Press, 1986. xii,748p. (2214 North Central at Encanto, 85004) $74.50

Information about almost 3,000 grants, contracts, and fellowships available from federal and state governments, private foundations, professional organizations, and corporations for research projects. Lists grants programs by specific funding areas; indexed by sponsoring organization and grant name.

Foundation Grants to Individuals. 5th ed. New York: Foundation Center, 1986. (79 Fifth Ave., 10003) $18.00

Profiles the programs of about 1100 foundations that make grants to individuals. The foundations described have made grants to students, artists, scholars, foreign individuals, minorities, musicians, scientists and writers. The book includes information on foundation sources of funds for scholarships, fellowships, internships, medical and emergency assistance, residences and travel programs.

The Grants Register, 1985-1987. Norman Frankel, ed. New York: St. Martin's Press, 1984. 870 p. (175 Fifth Ave., 10010) $39.95

Lists scholarships and fellowships at all levels of graduate study, from regional, national and international sources. Also includes research grants, exchange opportunities, vacation study awards, travel grants, all types of grants-in-aid, project grants, competitions, prizes and honoraria—including awards in recognition of support of creative work, professional and vocational awards, and special awards—for refugees, war veterans, minority groups, and students in unexpected financial difficulties, etc.

The Independent Scholar's Handbook. Ronald Gross. Reading, MA: Addison-Wesley Publishing Co., Inc., 1982. 256p. (01867) $8.95 pap.

Designed to give direction and advice to anyone who wishes to become an independent scholar or a more effective researcher. There is also information on how to obtain grants and funding, rather than listings of specific sources of funding.

The Individual's Guide to Grants. Judith B. Margolin. New York: Plenum Press, 1983. 295p. (233 Spring St., 10013) $15.95

Aimed at a wide audience of individual grantseekers, it discusses getting a sponsor, finding the right funder, refining your idea, facts about funders and preparing the proposal, and follow up information. It is an excellent source to start with.

U.S. Office of Management and Budget. *Catalog of Federal Domestic Assistance.* Washington, DC: Government Printing Office, Annual. Looseleaf, various pages (Superintendent of Documents, 20402) approx. $36.00

   Official compendium of federal programs, projects, services, and activities which provide assistance or benefits to American organizations, institutions, and individuals. Includes programs open to individual applicants or for individual beneficiaries in the areas of agriculture, commerce, community development, consumer protection, cultural affairs, disaster prevention and relief, education, employment, energy, environmental quality, nutrition, health, housing, social services, information sciences, law, natural resources, regional development, science and technology, and transportation.

SOURCES OF SCHOLARSHIPS, FELLOWSHIPS, AND LOANS

ARIS Funding Messenger: Creative Arts & Humanities Report. approx. $49 per year/8 issues per year.
ARIS Funding Messenger: Bio Medical Sciences Report. $79 per year/8 issues per year + 8 supplements.
ARIS Funding Messenger: Social and Natural Sciences Report. $79 per year/8 issues per year + 8 supplements. Academic Research Information System. San Francisco, 1976–. (2940 16th St., Suite 314, 94103).
   Reports which provide up-to-date information about grant opportunities, current agency activities, new programs, and funding policies. Includes addresses, telephone numbers of relevant program personnel, concise guidelines, and deadline dates.

After Scholarships, What? Creative Ways to Lower Your College Costs—and the Colleges That Offer Them. Princeton, NJ: Peterson's Guides, 1981. x,385p. (P.O. Box 2123, 08540) $8.00.

Aids to Individual Scholars: Competitions to be Held 1985-1986. New York: American Council of Learned Societies, Annual. 19p. (228 E. 45th St., 10017) free.
   Annual guide to ACLS fellowships and grant programs; awards mainly to support postdoctoral humanistic research.

The Career Education and Financial Aid Guide. Robert L. Bailey, Ph.D. New York: Arco Publishing, Inc., 1982. xi,209p. (215 Park Ave. South, 10003) $7.95
   This publication devotes a chapter to financial support. Emphasis is on gov-

ernment aid (BEOG, SEOG, etc.), and a few other sources of financial support are listed.

Chronicle Student Aid Annual. Moravia, NY: Chronicle Guidance Publications, Inc., 1985. v,410p. (13118) $16.50
Contains information on financial aid programs offered nationally or regionally, primarily by non-collegiate organizations. Awards are for undergraduate, graduate and postdoctoral students.

The College Blue Book: Vol. 5: Scholarships, fellowships, grants, and loans. 20th ed. New York: Macmillan Information, 1985. xv,718p. (866 Third Ave., 10022) $44.00
Lists financial aid programs offered by agencies and institutions, excluding colleges and universities. Individual programs listed by grant-making organization and arranged under broad and specific subject areas.

The College Cost Book, 1985-86. College Scholarship Service. New York: College Board, 1985. vii,244p. (888 Seventh Ave., 10106) $10.95
Explains how college financial planning can be done in advance and how to estimate your need and eligibility for financial aid.

The College Financial Aid Emergency Kit. Joyce Lain Kennedy and Dr. Herm Davis. Cardiff, CA: Sun Features, Inc., 1986. 48p. (Box 368-F, 92007). $3.50

College Grants from Uncle Sam: Am I eligible—and for how much? 1986-87. Alexandria, VA: Octameron Associates, l985. (P.O. Box 3437, 22302) $2.00

College Loans from Uncle Sam: The borrower's guide that explains it all—from locating lenders to loan forgiveness. 1986-87. Alexandria, VA: Octameron Associates, 1985. (P.O. Box 3437, 22302) $2.00

College Money Handbook: The Complete Guide to Expenses, Scholarships, Loans, Jobs and Special Aid Programs at Four-Year Colleges. Princeton, NJ: Peterson's Guides. 1985. 550p. (P.O. Box 2123, 08540) $8.95

Complete Grants Sourcebook for Higher Education, 2nd ed. American Council on Education. New York: Macmillan Publishing Co. 1985. 608p. (866 Third Ave., 10022) $85.00.
A guide to grantsmanship and a directory to more than 500 funding sources for higher education.

Don't Miss Out: The Ambitious Student's Guide to Financial Aid, 1986-87. 10th ed. Robert Leider. Alexandria, VA: Octameron Associates, 1985. 86p. (P.O. Box 3437, 22302) $4.00
Planning guide suggesting procedures and strategies for students seeking financial aid. Updated annually in September.

The Dow Jones-Irwin Guide to College Financial Planning. Paul M. Lane. Homewood, IL: Dow Jones-Irwin, 1981. xii,260p. (60430) $18.95

Earn and Learn: Cooperative education opportunities offered by the federal government. 7th ed. 1986-87. Alexandria, VA: Octameron Associates, Inc. 1985. approx. 20p. (P.O. Box 3437, 22302) $2.50
   Includes sponsors, occupational fields, and participating colleges.

Financial Aid for College-Bound Athletes. Marlene Lazar and Dr. Stephen H. Lazar. New York: Arco Publishing, Inc., 1982. x,323p. (215 Park Ave. South, 10003) $8.95 pap.
   Covers 850 colleges and universities. Entries include name of school, address, athletic director's name, teams (both men's and women's), conferences participated in, deadlines, and other scholarship information. Also an index by sport—under name of sport are the schools with awards in that sport.

Financial Aids for Higher Education Catalog: A Catalog for Undergraduates. 12th ed. Oreon Keesler. Dubuque, IA: William C. Brown Company Publishers, 1984. approx. 750p. (2460 Kerper Blvd., 52001) $32.95
   Lists over 3,200 programs intended for both college freshmen and advanced students. Index includes donor agencies and foundations, common program names, subject areas, types of awards, and special eligibility characteristics. Updated every two years.

Financing College Education. 3rd ed. Kenneth A. Kohl and Irene C. Kohl. New York: Harper & Row, 1983. x,304p. (10 East 53rd St., 10022) $5.95
   A practical guide to scholarships, loans, grants, and work-study programs for both parents and students.

Five Federal Financial Aid Programs, 1985-1986 A Student Consumer's Guide. Washington, DC: U.S. Department of Education, 1984. 17p. (Box 84, 20044) free.
   Briefly describes eligibility and application process for Pell Grants, Supplemental Educational Opportunity Grants, College Work-Study, National Direct Student Loans and Guaranteed Student Loans available from the federal government.

Need a Lift? To Educational Opportunities, Careers, Loans, Scholarships, Employment. Indianapolis, IN: American Legion Education and Scholarship Program, Fall, 1986. 144p. (The American Legion, Need a Lift? P.O. Box 1055, 46206) $1.00 prepaid
   Emphasis on scholarship opportunities for veterans, dependents of veterans, and children of deceased or disabled veterans. Includes information on federal, state, and private sources of funding, financial benefits of the American Legion and American Legion Auxiliary Programs, and annotated bibliography.

Paying for Your Education: A Guide for Adult Learners. 2nd ed. New York: College Board Publications, 1983. 160p. (Box 886, 10101) $7.95

The Scholarship Book: The Complete Guide to Private Sector Scholarships, Grants and Loans for Undergraduates. Englewood Cliffs, NJ: Prentice-Hall, Inc., 1985. 391p. (West Nyack, NY 10995) $14.95 + $3.50 postage & handling.

Directory of over 1100 potential sources of aid for undergraduates. Describes scholarships awarded by foundations, associations, armed forces, state and local governments, and individual colleges. Entries include scholarship name, address, phone number, amount of award, deadline, subject area, and an abridged description. Provides a list of over 300 career organizations and a bibliography. Includes indexes by major fields of study and by scholarship name.

Scholarships, Fellowships, and Loans. Vol. 6. S. Norman Feingold and Marie Feingold. Arlington, MA: Bellman Publishing Co., 1977. v,514p. (02174-0164) $45.00.

Lists a wide range of scholarships, fellowships, loans, grants, and awards not controlled by a college or university. Includes index which lists awards according to specific educational or occupational goals. Material is dated. Check with funder before applying.

Scholarships, Fellowships, and Loans. Vol. 7. S. Norman Feingold and Marie Feingold. Arlington, MA: Bellman Publishing Co., 1982. v,804p. (02174-0164) $75.00

Similar to Volume 6 in format but includes different awards.

Scholarships Guide for Commonwealth Postgraduate Students, 1983-85. The Association of Commonwealth Universities. London, England: John Foster House, 1982. 328p. (36 Gordon Square, WCH OPF) $25.00

A guide to scholarships, grants, loans, assistantships, and other aid open to graduates of Commonwealth universities who want to undertake postgraduate study or research at a Commonwealth university outside their own country.

Your Own Financial Aid Factory: The Guide to Locating College Money. 4th ed. Alexandria, VA: Octameron Assocciates, Inc., 1983. 212p. (P.O. Box 3437, 22302) $6.20

GRANTS FOR MINORITIES AND WOMEN

Better Late Than Never: Financial Aid for Older Women Seeking Education and Training. Washington, DC: Women's Equity Action League, 1985. 43p. (1250 I St., NW, Suite 305, 20005) $8.00

Focuses on programs that provide financial aid for women who need to train or retrain for a career. Apprenticeships are also included.

Directory of Financial Aids for Minorities, 1986-1987. Gail A. Schlachter, ed. Santa Barbara, CA: ABC-Clio Information Service, 1986. 345p. (P.O. Box 4397, 93103) $35.00

The Directory is divided into four separate sections: financial aids designed primarily or exclusively for minorities, a list of state sources for educational benefits, an annotated bibliography of directories and five sets of indexes by program title, sponsoring organization, geography, subject and calendar filing dates. Over 1,500 references and cross references to scholarships, fellowships, loans, grants, awards, internships, state sources of educational benefits and general financial aid directories are included.

Directory of Financial Aids for Women. 1985-1986. Gail Schlachter, ed. Santa Barbara, CA: ABC-Clio Information Services, 1985. 370p. (P.O. Box 4397, 93103) $35.00

Lists scholarships, fellowships, loans, grants, internships, awards, and prizes designed for women. Also includes women's credit unions and sources of state educational benefits, international programs, more than 1,100 references to scholarships, and an annotated bibliography. Indexed by sponsoring organization, geographic location, and subject.

Directory of Special Opportunities for Women. Martha Merrill Doss, ed. Garrett Park, MD: Garrett Park Press, 1981. 290p. (20896) $18.00

Lists over 1,000 funding sources for women seeking educational and career opportunities.

Directory of Special Programs for Minority Group Members: Career Information Services, Employment Skills Banks, Financial Aid Sources. Willis L. Johnson, ed. 3rd ed. Garrett Park, MD: Garrett Park Press, 1980 612p. (20896) $16.00

Educational Financial Aids: A Guide to Selecting Fellowships, Scholarships and Internships in Higher Education. Washington, DC: American Association of University Women, 1984. (Sales Office, 2401 Virginia Ave., NW, 20037) $5.00 + $1.00 postage & handling.

Lists financial assistance available to undergraduate, graduate and postgraduate women.

Financial Aid for Minorities in Allied Health. Lois S. Cofield and Ruth N. Swann, eds. Garrett Park, MD: Garrett Park Press, 1980. iii,58p. (20896) $2.00

Financial Aid for Minorities in Business. Howard F. Wehrle, III and Ruth N. Swann, eds. Garrett Park, MD: Garrett Park Press, 1980. iii,48p. (20896) $3.00

Financial Aid for Minorities in Education. Mary T. Christian and Ruth N. Swann, eds. Garrett Park, MD: Garrett Park Press, 1980. iv,58p. (20896) $3.00

Financial Aid for Minorities in Engineering. Clayton G. Holloway and Ruth N. Swann, eds. Garrett Park, MD: Garrett Park Press, 1981. 53p. (20896) $3.00

Financial Aid for Minorities in Law. Novelle J. Dickenson and Ruth N. Swann, eds. Garrett Park, MD: Garrett Park Press, 1980. iv,34p. (20896) $3.00
This booklet, one of a series on financial aid to minorities, includes grants available to all persons interested in law, along with 32 awards available to minority students. Another section is devoted to the minority financial aid program at specific law schools.

Financial Aid for Minorities in Mass Communications. Leslie L. Lawton and Ruth N. Swann, eds. Garrett Park, MD: Garrett Park Press, 1981. iv,63p. (20896) $3.00

Financial Aid for Minorities in Medicine. Sterling H. Hudson III and Ruth N. Swann, eds. Garrett Park, MD: Garrett Park Press, 1981. iv,66p. (20896) $3.00

Financial Aid for Minorities in Science. Ruth N. Swann and Sharon F. White, eds. Garrett Park, MD: Garrett Park Press, 1980. ii,49p. (20896) $2.00

Financial Aid: A Partial List of Resources for Women. Washington, DC: Project on the Status and Education of Women, Association of American Colleges, Jan., 1982. 12p. (1818 R St., NW, 20009) $2.50
Includes programs geared toward older women, returning students, minority women, and those in professional and technical programs, as well as programs open to students of both sexes. Selected bibliography.

Higher Education Opportunities for Minorities and Women: An Annotated Selection. Washington, DC: U.S. Education Department, 1982 ed. 128p. (20402) $5.00
Includes specific loan, scholarship, and fellowship opportunities, as well as information on how to seek guidance about educational and career goals.

How to Get Money for Research. Mary Rubin and the Business and Professional Women's Foundation. Westbury, NY: The Feminist Press, 1983. xiii,78p. (P.O. Box 334, 11568) $6.95
A guide to research funding opportunities for and about women at the pre- and post-doctoral levels. This book was compiled for women scholars, researchers, and others pursuing research questions about women.

Minority Student Opportunities in United States Medical Schools 1985-86. 9th ed. Mary T. Cureton, ed. Washington, DC: Association of American Medical Colleges, 1985. approx. 295p. (One Dupont Circle, NW, 20036) $7.50

"1984 Scholarship Guide." Women's Sports. San Francisco, CA: Women's Sports Foundation, 1984. 12p. (195 Moulton St., 94123) $1.00
   Lists over 800 institutions offering financial aid to women athletes.

GRANTS IN PARTICULAR SUBJECT FIELDS

Arts

American Art Directory 1984. New York: Jaques Cattell Press, R.R. Bowker Co., 1984. x,740p. (205 East 42nd St., 10017) $85.00
   Includes a section listing art scholarships and fellowships available through various organizations including museums and colleges.

Artist Colonies. Laura Greer. New York: Center for Arts Information, 1986. 5p. (625 Broadway, 10012) $1.50.
   25 artist colonies are briefly covered including the name of the colony, address, and phone number. Also includes information on the residency season, application deadline and financial assistance available.

Cultural Directory II: Federal Funds and Services for the Arts and Humanities. Barbara Coe, ed. Washington, DC: Smithsonian Institution Press, 1980. approx. 250p. (1111 N. Capitol St., 20560) $8.95
   Describes many federal funding programs for the arts and the humanities which are included in the *Catalog of Federal Domestic Assistance*.

Dance Magazine's Performing Arts Directory. New York: Danad Publishing Co., Inc., 1986. 450p. (33 W. 60th St., 10023) $30.00
   Emphasis on all aspects of dance, but of particular interest are sections on funding agencies and programs, sponsors and spaces for dance, organizations and councils for dance and the arts, sources and resources (information and merchandise for the dance world), and dance education directory.

Dramatists Sourcebook 1985-86. New York: Theatre Communications Group, Inc., 1985. 206p. (355 Lexington Ave., 10017) $10.95
   A guide to fellowships and grants, contests and awards, emergency funds, artist colonies for translators, lyricists, librettists, composers, as well as playwrights. Also includes information on conferences, festivals, workshops, residencies and artist colonies.

Film Service Profiles; A directory of organizations offering services to independent filmakers and film users in New York State. Kay Salz. New York: Center for Arts Information, 1980. xiv,50p. (625 Broadway, 10012) $2.50

Guide to Women's Art Organizations & Directory for the Arts. Cynthia Navaretta. New York: Midmarch Associates, 1982. vi,174p. (Box 3304, Grand Central Station, 10163) $8.50

>Information on visual and performing arts, crafts, writing, film. The financial help and work opportunities section has information on emergency funds, artists' colonies and residences, studying abroad, and grants, awards, and fellowship resources.

Introduction to the Arts Endowment. Washington, DC: National Endowment for the Arts, Annual. 25p. (2401 E St., NW, 20506) free.

>Overview of funding programs offered by the NEA.

Money Business: Grants and Awards for Creative Artists. Rev. ed. Boston, MA: The Artists Foundation, Inc., 1982. 130p. (110 Broad St., 02110) $9.50

>Directory of organizations that offer financial assistance to poets, fiction writers, playwrights, filmmakers, video artists, composers, choreographers, painters, printmakers, sculptors, craftsmen and photographers. Aid is for both independent artists and students for special projects.

Money for Artists: A guide to grants, awards, fellowships and artists-in-residence programs. New York: Center for Arts Information, 1983. 6p. (625 Broadway, 10012) $3.00

National Directory of Grants and Aid to Individuals in the Arts, International. 5th ed. Daniel Millsaps. Washington, DC: Washington International Arts Letter, 1983. 231p. (Box 15240, 20003) $15.95

>Brief listings of grants, prizes, and awards for professional work in the U.S. and abroad; includes information about universities and schools with special aid to students.

Crafts

The Crafts Business Encyclopedia: Marketing, Management, and Money. Michael Scott. New York: Harcourt Brace Jovanovich, 1979. xviii,286p. (1250 Sixth Ave., San Diego, CA 92101) $4.95 + .75¢ postage & handling.

>Focuses primarily on managing a crafts business covering such areas as management, insurance, labor and employees, legal affairs, accounting, banking, pricing, taxes, selling and marketing. A section on organizations of interest to craftspeople and a chapter on grants is included.

How to Enter and Win Fabric and Fiber Crafts Contests. Alan Gadney. New York: Facts on File Publications, 1983. xviii,202p. (460 Park Ave. South, 10016) $14.95

How to Enter and Win Jewelry and Metal Crafts Contests. Alan Gadney. New York: Facts on File Publications, 1983. xviii,204p. (460 Park Ave. South, 10016) $14.95

Engineering (*See also* Internships/Employment)

Official Register. 1986. New York, NY: American Society of Civil Engineers, 1986. 332p. (345 East 47th St., 10017) free.
   Includes a section on the Society's awards.

History

Fellowships and Grants of Interest to Historians, 1986-87. Washington, DC: American Historical Association, 1986. approx. 90p. (400 A St., SE, 20003) $5.00
   Lists 190 sources of funding for graduate students, postdoctoral researchers and scholars in history. Published annually in June.

Humanities

Grants in the Humanities: A scholar's guide to funding sources, 2nd ed. William E. Coleman. New York: Neal Schuman Publishers, Inc., 1984. xiv,152p. (23 Cornelia Place, 10014) $24.95
   This publication focuses on grantsmanship for the individual grantseeker and covers preparation of the essential parts of a proposal, along with a sample proposal and budget. Covers about 150 funders in the humanities. The audience for which this book was compiled is the humanities scholar interested in sources of funding for postdoctoral research.

Overview of Endowment Programs. Washington, DC: National Endowment for the Humanities, Annual. (1100 Pennsylvania Ave., NW, 20506) free.
   Annual overview of funding programs offered by the NEH.

Internships/Employment

1986 Internships: 35,000 on-the-job training opportunities for all types of careers. Lisa Hulse, ed. Cincinnati, OH: Writer's Digest Books, 1985. approx. 423p. (9933 Alliance Road, 45242) $14.95

Peterson's Guide to Engineering, Science, and Computer Jobs, 1984. Sandra Grundfest, ed. Princeton, NJ: Peterson's Guides, 1983. 795p. (P.O. Box 2123, 08540) $13.95
   This guide is more career-oriented and includes information on job-related graduate study, postdoctoral appointments, summer employment, co-op education programs, and advice on getting a job.

1984 Summer Employment Directory of the United States. Barbara Norton Kuroff, ed. Cincinnati, OH: Writer's Digest Books, 1983. 245p. (9933 Alliance Road, 45242) $8.95

Lists over 50,000 paying jobs including summer, seasonal, part-time and some full-time. An International section lists jobs abroad for U.S. students.

Library Sciences

Financial Assistance for Library Education, Academic Year 1986-87. Chicago, IL: American Library Association, Annual. approx. 42p. (Standing Committee on Library Education, 50 East Huron St., 60611) $1.00

Annually revised list of awards from state library agencies, national and state library associations, local libraries, academic institutions, national associations, foundations, and other agencies giving financial assistance for library education.

Mathematics and Sciences

"Assistantships and Fellowships in the Mathematical Sciences." *NOTICES of the American Mathematical Society*, December issue annually. (American Mathematical Society, P.O. Box 1571, Annex Station, Providence, RI 02901) $7.00 prepaid.

Free Money for Science Students. Laurie Blum. New York: Harper & Row, 1985. 204p. (10 East 53rd St., 10022) $5.95

State-by-state listings of scholarships and grants from over 1,000 foundations. Some are "science" oriented but many are general.

Graduate Assistantships Directory in the Computer Sciences. New York: Association for Computing Machinery. Biennial. (Association for Computing Machinery, P.O. Box 64145, Baltimore, MD 21264) $10.00/nonmembers.

Lists U.S. universities that offer fellowships and scholarships for the study of computer sciences.

National Science Foundation Guide to Programs. Washington, DC: National Science Foundation. Annual. (Publications Office, 1800 G St., NW, 20550) free.

Lists foundation programs in various areas of scientific research. Describes NSF criteria for selection of research projects.

Media and Communications

Film/Video Festivals and Awards #3. Washington, DC: The American Film Institute, National Information Services/Education Services, 1980. 88p. (ES Publications, 2021 N. Western, P.O. Box 27999, Los Angeles, CA 90027) $4.00/members; $5.00/nonmembers.

Foundation Radio Funding Guide I. San Francisco, CA: Audio Independents, Inc., 1982. 63p. (1232 Market St., 94102) $15.00
  Lists and describes those foundations which have given grants to radio-related projects, and includes contact data, brief guidelines, criteria and a sample listing of grants.

Gadney's Guide to 1800 International Contests, Festivals & Grants in Film and Video, Photography, TV-Radio Broadcasting, Writing, Poetry, Playwriting, and Journalism. Alan Gadney. Glendale, CA: Festival Publications, 1980. xv, 578p. (P.O. Box 10180, 91209) $15.95 plus $1.75 postage.
  Includes national and international contests, festivals, competitions, exhibitions, markets, and award/sales events, as well as grants, loans, scholarships, fellowships, residencies, apprenticeships, internships, and training programs. Indexed by event, sponsor, award, and subject area. Awarded Outstanding Reference Book of the year by the American Library Association.

Get the Money and Shoot: The DRI guide to funding documentary films. Bruce Jackson. Buffalo, NY: Documentary Research, Inc., 1981. v,167p. (96 Rumsey Road, 14209) $15.00
  This volume, aimed at filmmakers, covers how to find out about money, getting a sponsor, and preparing your budget and proposal.

Guidelines for Film Fund Grants Program 1984. New York: The Film Fund, 1984. 4p. + application. (80 East 11th St., 10003) free.

How to Enter and Win Film Contests. Alan Gadney. New York: Facts on File Publications, 1981. xx,193p. (460 Park Ave. South, 10016) $5.95

How to Enter and Win Video/Audio Contests. Alan Gadney. New York: Facts on File Publications, 1981. xviii,193p. (460 Park Ave. South, 10016) $6.95
  Covers all events for those interested in contests, festivals, competitions, markets, trade fairs and other award events. Also describes grants, loans, scholarships and internships.

How to Get Grants to Make Films and Video: A guide to media grants, film, video, audio visual projects and media scholarships. Steve Penny. Santa Barbara, CA: Film Grants Research, 1978. 128p. (P.O. Box 1138, 93102) $15.95
  Practical advice for the filmmaker.

1986 Journalism Career and Scholarship Guide: What to study in college; Where to study journalism & communications; Where the jobs are & how to find them. Princeton, NJ: The Newspaper Fund, 1986. approx. 139p. (P.O. Box 300, 08540) Single copies free; two or more at $.50 copy.
  Annual guide to aid offered through schools and departments of journalism in U.S. and Canadian colleges and universities, by newspapers, professional so-

cieties, and miscellaneous sources. Section on grants specifically designed for minority students.

Making Films Your Business. Mollie Gregory. New York: Schocken Books, 1979. xiv,256p. (200 Madison Ave., 10016) $7.95

Briefly covers writing proposals to foundations, foundations as sources of support, and the appendix mentions foundations which have an interest in funding films.

Medicine/Health

Arthritis Fellowships and Research Grants for Non-Physician Health Professionals: Information for applicants. Atlanta, GA: Arthritis Foundation, brochure. (3400 Peachtree Road, NE, 30326).

Barron's Guide to Financial Aid for Medical Students. Dr. Stephen H. Lazar. Woodbury, NY: Barron's Educational Series, Inc., 1979. 264p. (113 Crossways Park Drive, 11797) $6.95

Medical School Admission Requirements 1986-87, United States and Canada. Washington, DC: Association of American Medical Colleges, Annual. Approx. 360p. (One Dupont Circle, NW, 20036) $8.50

Includes information on undergraduate financial planning, sources of financial aid at the medical school and post-M.D. levels, and financial resources for minority and disadvantaged students.

Research Fellowships Related to the Rheumatic Diseases: Information for applicants. Atlanta, GA: Arthritis Foundation, brochure. (3400 Peachtree Road, NE, 30326).

Scholarships for Nursing Education. New York: National League for Nursing, 1985. approx. 30p. (10 Columbus Circle, 10019) $6.95

Music

Career Guide for the Young American Singer. Central Opera Service Bulletin. New York: Central Opera Service, 1985. approx. 70p. (Metropolitan Opera, Lincoln Center, 10023) $9.50 (includes update).

Provides information on grants for American singers, grants for study abroad, American vocal competitions, foreign vocal competitions, apprenticeships. A section on American and Canadian opera companies is also provided. Updates published biennially.

Music Industry Directory. 7th ed., 1983. Chicago, IL: Marquis Academic Media, 1983. 678p. (Marquis Who's Who, Inc., 200 East Ohio St., 60611) $67.50

Has sections on foundations, music competitions and festivals and information on scholarships and awards.

Songwriter's Market, 1986: Where to sell your songs. Rand Ruggeberg, ed. Cincinnati, OH: Writer's Digest Books, 1985. 432p. (9933 Alliance Road, 45242) $15.95
Focuses on music publishers, record companies and record producers, managers and booking agencies, but does include a section on awards and contests.

Pharmacology

Clinical Pharmacology: A Guide to Training Programs. 6th ed. Barbara C. Ready, ed. Princeton, NJ: Peterson's Guides, 1985. 150p. (Box 2123, 08540)

Philosophy

Grants and Fellowship Opportunities of Interest to Philosophers: 1986-87. Newark, DE: American Philosophical Association, 1986. approx. 50p. (University of Delaware, 19716) approx. $3.50
Annual publication lists fellowships and grant opportunities available from sixty different sources.

Photography

Photographer's Market 1986: Where to sell your photography. Robin Weinstein, ed. Cincinnati, OH: Writer's Digest Books, 1985. 576p. (9933 Alliance Road, 45242) $16.95

Political Science

Guide to Graduate Study in Political Science, 1986. rev. 12th ed. Patricia Spellman, comp. Washington, DC: American Political Science Association, 1986. 430p. (1527 New Hampshire Ave., NW, 20036) $20.00 for non-APSA members.
Describes approximately 300 masters and doctoral programs in political science; includes financial aid information and faculty listings for each program.

Research Support for Political Scientists: A Guide to Sources of Funds for Research Fellowships, Grants, and Contracts. Stephen F. Szabo, comp. Washington, DC: American Political Science Association, 1981. viii,126p. (Departmental Services Program, 1527 New Hampshire Ave., NW, 20036) $6.00
Includes information on research fellowships, doctoral dissertation grants and fellowships, foundation research grants and U.S. government grants and contracts.

Psychology

APA Guide to Research Support, 2nd ed. Ralph E. Dusek, et. al., eds. Washington, DC: American Psychological Association, 1984. 376p. (1200 17th St., NW, 20036) $25.00
  Covers over 150 federally-funded programs for behavioral science research.

Sciences (*See* Mathematics and Sciences)

Social Sciences

Fellowships and Grants for Research to be Offered in 1986-87. New York: Social Science Research Council, 1985. 43p. (605 Third Ave., 10158) free.
  Describes the fellowship and grant programs the Council sponsors jointly with American Council of Learned Societies. Research Training Fellowships offer support for training in the social sciences. Foreign-area programs offer dissertation fellowships and postdoctoral research grants in both the social sciences and the humanities.

Grants and Awards Available to American Writers. 13th ed. New York: P.E.N. American Center, 1984. approx. 90p. (47 Fifth Ave., 10003) $8.50
  A comprehensive list of awards available to American and Canadian writers for use in the U.S. or abroad. Appendix of American State Arts Councils.

Dramatists Sourcebook 1985-86 Edition. New York: Theatre Communications Group, Inc., 1985. 216p. (355 Lexington Ave., 10017) $10.95

Literary and Library Prizes. New York: R. R. Bowker Co., 1980. viii,651p. (1180 Ave. of the Americas, 10036) $26.95

Literary Market Place with Names and Numbers, 1986: Directory of American Book Publishing. New York: R. R. Bowker Co., 1985. 967p. (205 East 42nd St., 10017) $59.95
  Includes literary awards, contests, fellowships, and grants.

Writer's Market: 1986. Paula Deimling, ed. Cincinnati, OH: Writer's Digest Books, 1985. 1056p. (9933 Alliance Road, 45242) $19.95

Grants for International Study, Travel, and Study Abroad

Basic Facts on Foreign Study. New York: Institute of International Education, 1985. approx. 6p. (809 United Nations Plaza, 10017) single copies free.
  A guide for U.S. students planning study abroad.

Directory of Financial Aids for International Activities. 4th ed. Minneapolis, MN: Office of International Programs, University of Minnesota, 1985. approx. 440p. (201 Nolte West, 315 Pillsbury Drive, SE, 55455) $20.00
> Covers grants to individuals interested in international activities or in studying abroad.

Fellowship Guide to Western Europe. 6th ed. New York: Council for European Studies, 1985. approx. 100p. (1509 International Affairs, Columbia University, 10027) $5.00

Fellowships, Scholarships, and Related Opportunities in International Education. Knoxville, TN: University of Tennessee, 1985. unpaged. (Division of International Education, 205 Alumni Hall, 37916) $5.00 + $1.45 postage & handling.

Fulbright and Other Grants for Graduate Study Abroad. New York: Institute of International Education, Annual. (809 United Nations Plaza, 10017) free.
> Lists IIE-administered financial assistance programs available to U.S. graduate students for study abroad.

Financial Resources for International Study: A selected bibliography. New York: Institute of International Education, 1985. 23p. (809 United Nations Plaza, 10017) free.
> Annotated list of reference sources on awards for international studies.

Study Abroad, 1983-84, 1984-85, 1985-86. Paris: UNESCO, 1983. approx. 1000p. (UNIPUB, Box 433, Murray Hill Station, New York 10157) $20.50
> Listing in three languages of scholarships and courses offered by foreign universities and international and national organizations and institutions. The term scholarship is used to include all forms of financial or material aid for study abroad.

The Learning Traveler: Volume I: U.S. College Sponsored Programs Abroad. Gail A. Cohen, ed. New York: Institute of International Education, Annual. (809 United Nations Plaza, 10017) $9.95
> Lists by country over 800 semester and academic year study programs abroad (for undergraduates) that are sponsored by accredited U.S. colleges and universities.

The Learning Traveler: Volume II: Vacation Study Abroad. Gale A. Cohen and Diane D'Angelo, eds. New York: Institute of International Education, Annual. (809 United Nations Plaza, 10017) $9.95
> Lists by country about 900 spring, summer, and early fall study programs offered in countries around the world by U.S. and foreign institutions and private organizations.

Sources for Affiliating with or Forming a Nonprofit Organization

Arts Money: Raising It, Saving It, and Earning It. Joan Jeffri. New York: Neal-Schuman Publishers, 1983. 291p. (23 Cornelia St., 10014) $19.95
  As the title suggests, plus useful advice on considering and choosing an organizational format.

The California Non-Profit Corporation Handbook. Anthony Mancuso. Berkeley, CA: Nolo Press, 1984. 288p. (950 Parker St., 94710) $21.95
  A guide to preparing articles and bylaws, obtaining exempt status, keeping legal records, choosing a lawyer, etc.

Cumulative List of Organizations—Publication 78. Department of the Treasury. Internal Revenue Service. Washington, DC: U.S. Government Printing Office, Annual. various pages. (Superintendent of Documents, 20402) approx. $35.00
  Lists organizations to whom contributions are deductible. The list is not all-inclusive. If an organization is not listed but has a ruling or an IRS determination letter holding contributions to be deductible, generally the letter will serve as evidence to contributors of the deductibility of their contributions.

Encyclopedia of Associations. Volume 1: National Organizations of the United States-1986, 20th ed. Detroit, MI: Gale Research, 1985. 2290p. (Book Tower, 48226) $210
  Updated every two years in three volumes, the 20th edition includes about 20,000 organizations within 17 broad subject categories, e.g., scientific, cultural, social welfare, fraternal, etc. Many associations can offer or suggest funding possibilities and other types of support for your work.

How to Set Up and Operate a Non-Profit Organization. Carole C. Upshur. Englewood Cliffs, NJ: Prentice-Hall, Inc., 1982. 252p. (07632) $18.95
  Guidelines for incorporating, raising funds and writing grant proposals.

National VLA Directory, 1986. Volunteer Lawyers for the Arts. New York: Volunteer Lawyers for the Arts, 1986. 52p. (1560 Broadway, Suite 711, 10036) free.
  Describes Volunteer Lawyers for the Arts programs throughout the U.S.—and one in Canada. VLAs are groups of lawyers that will provide legal services for free or at a reduced rate to artists and nonprofit groups.

New York Not-for-Profit Organization Manual. ed. New York: Council of New York Law Associates, 1985. 190p. (99 Hudson St., 10013) $25.00
  An attorney's guide to incorporating in New York State and gaining tax-exempt status.

The Nonprofit Organization Handbook. Tracy D. Connors, ed. New York: McGraw-Hill, 1980. 740p. (1221 Ave. of the Americas, 10020) $36.75
  A desk reference on organizing and operating nonprofit organizations.

Research Centers Directory, 10th ed., 1986. Detroit, MI: Gale Research, 1985. 1561p. (Book Tower, 48226) $340
  A guide to approximately 8,300 university-related and other nonprofit research organizations in 17 broad subject areas. An excellent guide to finding out what's being done where.

Starting and Running a Nonprofit Organization. Joan Hummel. Minneapolis: University of Minnesota Press, 1980. 343p. (2037 University Ave. Southeast, 55414) $20.00
  Basic guide for putting together a small, nonprofit organization.

Tax Exempt Status for Your Organization. Publication 557. Department of the Treasury. Internal Revenue Service. Washington, DC: U.S. Government Printing Office. (Superintendent of Documents, 20402) free.
  IRS instructions for organizations seeking exempt status.

To Be or Not To Be: An Artist's Guide to Not-for-Profit Incorporation. New York: Volunteer Lawyers for the Arts, 1982. 12p. (1560 Broadway, Suite 711, 10036).
  Covers the critical questions you should ask yourself and your attorney about nonprofit incorporation.

Appendix D

Where to Find Information on Corporate Funding

According to estimates by The Conference Board and the Council on Financial Aid to Education, American corporations contributed over $4 billion to nonprofit institutions and causes in 1985—an amount roughly equal to charitable contributions awarded by independent and community foundations. In addition to these substantial cash awards, a growing number of corporations are making non-cash contributions in the form of loaned personnel, product or property donations, use of corporate facilities or services, low-cost loans, and cooperative service programs. Corporations, like foundations, do not represent a limitless pool of funding and resources, but they are clearly an important source of support for many nonprofits.

There are some significant differences between corporate and foundation philanthropy. Corporations may choose to make charitable contributions directly from corporate funds or they may establish a separate corporate foundation to administer their philanthropic giving. Corporate foundations are private foundations under the tax law and are controlled by the same rules and regulations as independent private foundations. Corporate foundations must make charitable contributions equal to five percent of the market value of their assets each year and they must file an annual information return (Form 990-PF) with the Internal Revenue Service. They are legally separate from the corporation, but in practice, company-sponsored foundations generally maintain close ties with the profit-making companies from which they derive their funding.

Generally, company-sponsored foundations maintain relatively small endowments and rely on contributions from their parent companies to support their giving programs, but they do provide a vehicle for corporations to set aside funds in years of heavy profits that can be used to sustain giving in years when corporate earnings are lower. Direct giving programs, on the other hand, are administered within the corporations and are based solely on the corporation's annual operating budget. The amount of funds contributed through direct giving programs is therefore more susceptible to the rise and fall of corporate profit cycles.

Many corporations choose to make charitable contributions through both direct giving and foundation programs. Although these two programs are often coordinated under the same general policy and may even be administered by the same staff, they are legally separate and are subject to different regulations and reporting requirements. Corporations are not required to disclose information about direct giving programs to the public, nor are they required to sustain prescribed levels of funding. Corporations are allowed by tax laws to deduct charitable contributions at a rate up to ten percent of their pre-tax income for federal tax purposes, but they may also choose to make "contributions" such as advertisements, loaned personnel, etc., that are treated as operating expenditures.

Although there are many exceptions, corporate giving tends to be in fields related to corporate activities or in communities where the company operates, regardless of whether the contributions are administered within the corporation or through a foundation. Recent studies and reports indicate that education, primarily higher education institutions, is still the highest priority for corporations, accounting for 39 percent of corporate contributions in the Conference Board's 1983 survey. Changes in federal funding of nonprofit activities since 1980 have effected some changes in corporations' giving policies, and a growing percentage of corporate contributions is being allocated to civic and community organizations. While these general trends are important to note, fundseekers in all fields will generally find it more helpful to focus on the particular business activities and community interests of corporations to identify prospective donors.

IDENTIFYING CORPORATE PROSPECTS

As in any fundraising effort, the search for corporate funding begins with a careful evaluation of your organization's needs and an evaluation of the community in which it operates. Corporate fundraising strategy also demands careful attention to the expectations of the business community and the special nature of corporate philanthropy. Your search for corporate sponsors may focus on local businesses as well as major corporations, and it should take into account the wide variety of resources those businesses may be able to provide.

Due to the different reporting requirements, there is generally more information available about corporate foundations than there is about direct giving programs. Nonetheless, there are a growing number of reference directories that focus on both types of corporate giving programs, as well as specific business directories that can help you to identify companies by principal business activity or geographic location. The bibliography below lists most of the current directories of corporate contributions programs, as well as some of the major business directories fundraisers have found useful. These general business directories can be helpful in learning more about corporations that have active giving programs, as well as in identifying other funding prospects.

In addition to the resources listed in the bibliography, nonprofits should consult their local public library to find out if there are any regional or local business indexes for your area. Consult with your local Chamber of Commerce or Better Business Bureau, organizations that often publish guides to businesses operating in your city or town. One readily available, but often overlooked, resource is the yellow pages of your local telephone directory which can be used to identify manufacturers or distributors of particular products or services your organization needs, as well as to identify local subsidiaries of larger corporations that have community giving programs.

DEVELOPING A RESEARCH STRATEGY

Although the resources and the amount of information available to research corporate donors are somewhat different from those used to identify foundation prospects, the research strategies you will follow incorporate the same considerations. **The Subject Approach** would lead you to corporations that have a stated interest in funding programs in your subject field as well as those whose principal area of business is related to the programs and services your organization offers. Some relationships between nonprofit activities and corporate interests may seem relatively obvious: a sporting goods manufacturer or distributor might be interested in funding a recreational program for young people; a manufacturer or distributor of musical instruments might provide support for a music education program; funding for a drug education program for the elderly might be provided by a pharmaceutical firm; and so forth. As you think about how your program relates to specific business activities and interests, allow yourself to look beyond the more obvious connections. In the introduction to *The National Directory of Corporate Charity*, Sam Sternberg points out some reasons for corporate giving that might help to broaden your search, including:

1. Developing a pool of trained individuals who are potential employees;

2. Supporting research of interest to the company;

3. Improving the market for a company's products; and

4. Responding to social issues related to their products and services.

The Geographic Approach, as applied to corporate giving, focuses on major corporations that have subsidiaries or operating plants in your community as well as local manufacturers, retailers, and service companies. Companies that operate in your community might be convinced to support your organization because you provide services that benefit their employees and families, because a contribution would bring public recognition or prestige to the company or its senior management, because it would improve customer relations or build a future customer base, or simply because they have an interest and investment in your community's future.

In following a **Types of Support Approach** to identify potential corporate donors, you will generally want to think beyond cash contributions and focus on the types of products and services your organization needs. Corporations are often able to provide space, equipment, personnel, products, and a wide range of services. Many of the guides, reports, and studies listed in the bibliography below focus specifically on non-cash contributions and provide extensive suggestions on the types of products and services nonprofits might appropriately request, as well as advice on how to approach companies with those requests.

This Appendix is offered only as a very general starting point for your investigation of corporate donors. In addition to the books, reports, and periodicals below, many of the resources listed in Appendix A as general fundraising guides provide useful information on corporate philanthropy as well. The major fundraising periodicals, such as *Foundation News, Grantsmanship Center News, Philanthropy Monthly*, and others, frequently include articles and news items related to corporate giving.

Foundation Center publications described in this guide currently include information on corporate foundations, and *The Foundation Grants Index Bimonthly* includes publications issued by corporate direct giving programs in its section on "Grantmaker Publications." The Center is currently gathering other types of information on corporate giving programs for inclusion in its publications and libraries. Consult with your local Foundation Center cooperating library (listed in Appendix G) for further information and materials to help you in your funding search.

DIRECTORIES

Burns, Michael E. *1983 Guide to Corporate Giving in Connecticut.* New Haven, CT: OUA/DATA, 1983. 393pp. $20.00 plus $1.50 postage and handling.
  Describes the cash and non-cash giving of 769 corporations with headquarters or operating units in Connecticut.

Burns, Michael E. *OUA/DATA's 1983–84 Guide to Corporate Giving in Massachusetts.* New Haven, CT: OUA/DATA, 1983. 97pp. $30.00 plus $1.50 postage and handling.
  Provides brief descriptions of cash and non-cash giving programs of 737 corporations headquartered or operating in Massachusetts.

Charitable Contributions by Arkansas Business. Hampton, AR: Independent Community Consultants, 1982. $10.50
  Brief report of a study examining the size and scope of contributions to charities by Arkansas corporations.

Chicago Corporate Connection: A Directory of Chicago Area Corporate Contributors, 2nd ed. Chicago, IL: Donors Forum, 1983. 212pp. $13.50
  Describes 200 corporations making charitable contributions in the Chicago metropolitan area, downstate Illinois, and northern Indiana. Indexed by geographic area, field of business, and matching gift programs.

Corporate 500: The Directory of Corporate Philanthropy, 4th ed. San Francisco: Public Management Institute, 1985. 942pp. $265.00
  Describes giving interests, eligibility requirements, and application procedures for corporate foundations and direct giving programs. Indexed by funding interest, types of support, contact persons, corporate headquarters, subsidiaries, principal business activity, and foundation names.

Corporate Foundation Profiles, 4th ed. New York: The Foundation Center, 1985. 622pp. $55.00
  Provides detailed analyses of over 250 major corporate foundations and brief descriptive listings of nearly 470 smaller corporate foundations. Indexed by subject interest, type of support offered, and geographic location.

The Corporate Fund Raising Directory, 1985–86 Edition. Hartsdale, NY: Public Service Materials Center, 1984. 400pp. $65.00
  Describes the giving programs of over 600 corporations with indexes by headquarters state, geographic preference, contact persons, and corporations that issue guidelines.

Corporate Giving Yellow Pages. Washington, DC: The Taft Group, 1985. 101pp. $47.50

Lists the name and address of the contact persons for over 1300 corporate giving programs and corporate foundations in the U.S.

The Corporate 1000: A Directory of Who Runs the Top 1000 U.S. Corporations. Washington, DC: The Washington Monitor, Inc., 1985. 604pp. $79.95

Lists board members and chief officers and management staff of 1000 corporations and their subsidiaries. Indexed by industry and personal names.

Directory of Corporate Affiliations 1986: Who Owns Whom. Wilmette, IL: National Register Publishing Co., 1986. 1152pp.

An annual guide to major U.S. corporations and their subsidiaries, divisions, and affiliates. Section 1 is an alphabetical list cross-referencing affiliates, divisions, and subsidiaries with their parent companies. Section 2 lists over 4000 parent companies with assets, approximate sales, number of employees, type of business, and top corporate officers. Indexed by state and city and by type of business.

Guide to Corporate Giving, 3rd ed. New York: American Council for the Arts, 1983. 567pp. $39.95

Describes the giving programs of 711 U.S. corporations with indexes by location, kinds of arts organizations/activity supported, and types of support offered. Although the emphasis is on arts support, giving for other programs is also covered.

Maine Corporate Foundation Directory. Portland, ME: University of Maine, Center for Research and Advanced Study, 1984. 77pp. $10.00

Provides brief descriptions of the giving programs of 75 corporations with headquarters or companies in Maine.

National Directory of Corporate Public Affairs 1986. Washington, DC: Columbia Books, Inc., 1986. 575pp. $55.00

Part I lists 1500 companies with information on their political action committees, foundation or corporate giving programs, corporate publications, and public affairs staff. Part II is an alphabetical list of corporate public affairs staff with their institutional affiliations. Indexed by principal business activity and headquarters location.

Standard & Poor's Register of Corporations, Directors and Executives. 3 vols. New York: Standard & Poor's Corporation, 1986.

Volume 1 is an alphabetical list of 45,000 corporations with address and telephone number; officers, directors and key staff; principal business and products and services; divisions and subsidiaries; annual sales and number of employees. Volume 2 is an alphabetical list of corporate officials. Volume 3 includes indexes by standard industrial classification, state and city location, and "corporate family," with division and subsidiary cross-references.

Sternberg, Sam. *National Directory of Corporate Charity*. San Francisco, CA: Regional Young Adult Project, 1984. 613pp. $80.00 (New Publisher: The Foundation Center, 79 Fifth Avenue, New York, NY 10003)

Describes 1600 corporate giving programs with information on application policy and procedures, contact, etc. Indexed by headquarters state and giving interests. Introduction provides advice and guidelines for conducting a corporate solicitation campaign.

Taft Corporate Giving Directory, 7th ed. Washington, DC: The Taft Group, 1985. 733pp. $267.00

Directory of 540 major corporate giving programs and company foundations, with indexes by grant type, areas of interest, headquarters state and operating locations, and individual directors and administrators.

GUIDES, REPORTS, AND STUDIES

Bertsch, Kenneth A. *Corporate Philanthropy*. Washington, DC: Investor Responsibility Research Center, 1982. 84pp. $25.00

A report on current issues and trends in corporate philanthropy, including a discussion of the motivations that guide corporate contributions officers.

Brownrigg, W. Grant. *Effective Corporate Fundraising*. New York: American Council for the Arts, 1982. 161pp. $14.95

Outlines a strategy for securing corporate funding for nonprofit activities, including sample calendar and budget for the campaign, introductory and appeal letters, etc.

Coro Foundation. *An Examination of Bay Area Corporate Non-Cash Contributions: Programs and Policies for the 80's*. San Francisco: Coro Foundation, 1982. 82pp. $10.00

Describes strategies and approaches for non-cash giving and provides brief profiles of 38 corporations active in non-cash giving in the Bay Area.

Corporate Contributions Programs: A Sampler of Policies and Statements. Alexandria, VA: United Way of America, 1983. 69pp. $5.00

Reprints of 12 brochures that describe giving policies and application procedures of corporate giving programs.

Corporate Philanthropy. Washington, DC: Council on Foundations, 1982. 160pp. $12.00

Contains 42 articles dealing with the major issues surrounding corporate giving, including management requirements, tax considerations, non-cash giving, etc.

Dermer, Joseph, and Wertheimer, Stephen, eds. *The Complete Guide to Corporate Fund Raising.* Hartsdale, NY: Public Service Materials Center, 1982. 112pp. $16.75

Eleven articles offering advice and strategies on conducting corporate fundraising efforts.

Dunkle, Margaret. *Cracking the Corporations: Finding Corporate Funding for Family Violence Programs.* Washington, DC: Center for Women Policy Studies, 1981. 26pp. $5.00

Offers tips for developing a corporate fundraising campaign, applicable to all types of nonprofits.

Guidelines: How to Develop an Effective Program of Corporate Support for Higher Education. New York: Council for Financial Aid to Education, 1982. 20pp. $5.00

Discusses the rationale for corporate support of higher education and the types of aid companies can provide to colleges and universities.

Hillman, Howard. *The Art of Winning Corporate Grants.* New York: Vanguard Press, 1980. 180pp. $10.00

A general guide to raising funds from corporations, including a section on questions most proposal evaluators ask and a sample proposal.

How to Get Corporate Grants. San Francisco, CA: Public Management Institute, 1981. $47.50

A "how-to" workbook with numerous forms, worksheets, and checklists for use in corporate grantseeking.

Klepper, Anne. *Corporate Social Programs: Nontraditional Assistance.* New York: The Conference Board, 1983. 11pp. $15.00

The report of the Conference Board's first survey of non-cash giving programs of corporations.

Knauft, E.B. *Profiles of Effective Corporate Giving Programs.* Washington, DC: Independent Sector, 1985. 14pp. $4.00

Report based on a research study of decision-making practices in 48 corporate giving programs.

Koch, Frank. *The New Corporate Philanthropy: How Society and Business Can Profit.* New York: Plenum Press, 1979. 305pp. $18.50

Directed primarily towards corporate executives, this book focuses on how philanthropy works within the corporation but also provides useful insights for the nonprofit seeking corporate support.

Murphy, Dennis J. *Asking Corporations for Money*. Port Chester, NY: Gothic Press, 1982. 33pp. $9.95
   Analyzes the criteria and characteristics of the decision-making process in corporate contributions programs.

Other Than Grants . . . A Sampling of Southern California's Corporate Gift-Matching, Volunteer, and In-kind Giving Programs. Los Angeles: California Community Foundation, 1984. 48pp. $3.00 plus $1.50 postage and handling.
   General advice on non-cash corporate philanthropy with brief profiles of 31 California corporations' giving programs.

Partners: A Practical Guide to Corporate Support of the Arts. New York: Cultural Assistance Center, 1982. 112pp. $10.95
   Designed as a guide for corporate officials, this report also suggests ways non-profits, particularly arts groups, can improve and build corporate support.

Platzer, Linda Cardillo. *Annual Survey of Corporate Contributions*, 1985 ed. New York: The Conference Board, 1985. 37pp. $125.00
   Annual report giving trends and statistics on corporate giving, including non-cash giving, with breakdowns by pretax income, type of industry, etc.

Plinio, Alex, and Scanlon, Joanne. *Resource Raising: The Role of Non-Cash Assistance in Corporate Philanthropy*. Washington, DC: Independent Sector, 1986. $10.00
   A report on the ways that corporations can offer non-cash assistance to non-profits, covering legal and tax considerations, new roles for corporate giving officers, brokerage services, and numerous examples of non-cash gifts.

Sinclair, James P. *How to Write Successful Corporate Appeals—with Full Examples*. Hartsdale, NY: Public Service Materials Center, 1982. 110pp. $19.75
   Provides samples of initial requests, renewal letters, and other fundraising letters with commentary.

Smith, Craig. *How to Increase Corporate Giving to Your Organization*. San Francisco, CA: Public Management Institute, 1984. 25pp.
   Provides advice on how to identify prospective corporate donors and when and how to ask for cash and non-cash gifts.

Smith, Hayden W. *A Profile of Corporate Contributions*. New York: Council for Financial Aid to Education, 1983. 46pp. $10.00
   A detailed research report on the development of corporate contributions from 1936 to 1981.

Troy, Kathryn. *Managing Corporate Contributions*. New York: The Conference Board, 1980. 95pp. $10.00

> Written for the corporate executive, this report details how to establish and operate a contributions program.

Troy, Kathryn. *Meeting Human Needs: Corporate Programs and Partnerships*. New York: The Conference Board, 1986. 55pp.

> Report of a study of corporate contributions and human-resource executives that examines trends in the funding of human service programs for employees and the broader community.

Volunteerism Corporate Style, 2nd ed. Minneapolis, MN: Corporate Volunteerism Council of Minnesota, 1984. 77pp. $25.00

> Uses case studies from the Minneapolis/St. Paul area to explain how to initiate, operate, and evaluate corporate volunteer programs.

Yankelovich, Skelly and White. *Corporate Giving: The Views of Chief Executive Officers of Major American Corporations*. Washington, DC: Council of Foundations, 1982. 101 + pp. $30.00

> Report of a study of corporate CEO's that examined current giving practices and projections of future giving.

PERIODICALS

Corporate Giving Watch. The Taft Group, 5130 MacArthur Blvd., NW, Washington, DC 20016. Monthly. $127.00

> Articles analyzing corporate philanthropy, corporate sources of support and fundraising ideas.

Corporate Philanthropy Report. Public Management Institute, 358 Brannan St., San Francisco, CA 94107. Monthly. $127.00

> Brief articles on issues and trends in corporate philanthropy, advice on corporate fundraising, and news items.

Fund Raising Management. Hoke Communications, 224 Seventh St., Garden City, Long Island, NY 11530. Monthly. $36.00

> Includes regular column on corporate philanthropy by Alex Plinio of the Prudential Insurance Company as well as occasional articles on corporate solicitation.

Response. Center for Corporate Public Involvement, 1850 K St., NW, Washington, DC 20006-2284. Quarterly. Subscription information on request.
Published primarily for the life and health insurance business, includes articles on corporate philanthropy, special programs, and public/private partnerships.

Appendix E

National Organizations Serving Grantmakers and Grantseekers

IN ADDITION TO the numerous print resources listed in this guide and its appendices, there are a number of service organizations that provide training and consultation to both grantmakers and grantseekers in the areas of nonprofit management, fundraising, and voluntary action. The following listing provides addresses, contact information, and brief descriptions of 48 national organizations that provide broad services to the philanthropic and nonprofit sector. Entries were compiled on the basis of questionnaire responses and materials housed in The Foundation Center's New York library.

Although we have attempted to cover the major nonprofit publishers and service providers in the philanthropic field, this listing does not include the many important professional and trade associations serving specific nonprofit fields which may publish materials or provide training and consultation on fundraising to their members as part of their broader service mission. We urge nonprofit groups to consult *The Encyclopedia of Associations* published by Gale Research Company in Detroit, Michigan, for information about organizations serving their specific service areas. We also welcome comments and suggestions from our readers of other organizations which should be listed in future editions of *Foundation Fundamentals*.

The Advertising Council
825 Third Avenue
New York, NY 10022
(212) 758-0400

The Council is a nonprofit organization which conducts public service advertising campaigns that promote voluntary citizen actions to help solve national problems. It is supported by annual grants and volunteer assistance from business firms and advertising and media groups. The Council reviews requests for assistance from nonprofit groups on an annual basis to select those that best suit its guidelines and mission.

The Alliance for Justice
600 New Jersey Avenue, N.W.
Washington, DC 20001
(202) 624-8390
Nan Aron, Exec. Dir.
Contact: Nan Aron or Monica Hauck, Assistant to the Director

The Alliance is an association of public interest legal organizations which serves as a clearinghouse for information on public interest law. Its purpose is to pool the resources and talents of the public interest community to address issues affecting the financial well-being of nonprofits and to ensure access to the courts and governmental agencies for persons who have historically been unrepresented in the legal and administrative process. It publishes a directory of public interest law centers, reports and articles on funding of public interest law projects, and a newsletter, the *Pipeline*.

American Association of Fund-Raising Council
500 Fifth Avenue
New York, NY 10036
(212) 354-5799
John J. Schwartz, Pres.

AAFRC is a national membership organization composed of professional fundraising counseling firms that assist all types of nonprofit agencies in managing and planning fundraising programs. The Association welcomes requests for information on any aspect of philanthropic fundraising or the services of its members. It is committed to the study of economic and social trends in American philanthropy and to sharing this information with the general public through the publication of surveys; an annual review of philanthropy, *Giving USA*; and a newsletter, *The Fund Raising Review*.

American Council for the Arts
570 Seventh Avenue
New York, NY 10018
(212) 354-6655

ACA is a national arts service organization which works to promote and strengthen cultural activities in the U.S. It publishes the monthly magazine, *American Arts*, and a wide variety of materials on arts management, fundraising, corporate giving, and related topics. ACA sponsors a number of seminars and provides limited telephone and personal consulting services for arts groups.

American Management Association (AMA)
135 W. 50th Street
New York, NY 10020
(212) 586-8100
Dr. Thomas R. Horton, Pres.

AMA is a membership organization of managers in industry, commerce, government, and charitable and non-commercial organizations, and university faculty and administrators. It provides educational programs including conferences, seminars, courses, briefings, and workshops on various management topics. AMA operates a library, bookstore, and Management Information Service, and publishes a number of periodicals and monographs on organizational management, financial administration, personnel issues, and communications.

American Society of Association Executives (ASAE)
1575 Eye Street, N.W.
Washington, DC 20005
(202) 626-2723
R. William Taylor, CAE, Pres.

ASAE is a professional society of paid executives of national, state and local professional, technical and business associations. It works to promote the proper functioning of associations and professional standards of association executives, and conducts referral, resume, guidance, and consultation services. Additionally, ASAE maintains a central reference library. Its monthly journal, *Association Management*, features articles on membership recruitment, conference planning, fundraising, earned income opportunities, etc.

Association of Black Foundation Executives (ABFE)
1828 L Street, N.W.
Washington, DC 20036

(202) 466-6512
Hugh Burroughs, Chair.

ABFE is a membership organization of men and women on the staffs or boards of corporate and foundation grantmaking organizations. Its purpose is to encourage grantmaking that addresses the issues and problems facing blacks and to promote the status and number of blacks as grantmaking professionals.

Association of Governing Boards of Universities and Colleges (AGB)

One Dupont Circle, N.W., Suite 400
Washington, DC 20036
(202) 296-8400
Robert L. Gale, Pres.

AGB is a membership organization of governing boards of colleges and universities, regents, trustees, presidents, supervisors, visitors, and other board members of colleges and universities. AGB focuses on the problems and responsibilities in the relationships between trustees, regents/presidents, and faculty/students. It operates a Trustee Information Center and offers training for members of governing boards. Its monthly newsletter, *AGB Notes*, and bimonthly journal, *AGB Reports*, include articles on fundraising and funding trends in higher education, as well as other issues of concern to trustees.

Association of Hispanic Arts (AHA)

200 E. 87th Street
New York, NY 10028
(212) 369-7054
Jane Delgado, Exec. Dir.

AHA works to advance the general concept of Hispanic arts as an integral part of the arts community in the U.S. It provides services to all nonprofit arts organizations, community organizations, and individual artists. AHA maintains a funding resource library of information related to government and private funding and publishes *AHA!-Hispanic Arts Newsletter*.

Association of Voluntary Action Scholars

S-126 Human Development Bldg.
Pennsylvania State Univ.
University Park, PA 16802
(814) 863-2944
Drew Hyman, Pres.

AVAS is a membership organization of scholars and professionals engaged in research, scholarship, or programs related to citizen participation and voluntary action. The association coordinates research projects and makes their results accessible to the field, as well as sponsoring collaborative research proposals. It publishes two quarterly journals, *Citizen Participation and Voluntary Action Abstracts*, and *Journal of Voluntary Action Research;* and a quarterly newsletter for members.

Association for Volunteer Administration (AVA)

P.O. Box 4584
Boulder, CO 80306
(303) 497-0238
Martha N. Martin, Exec. Sec'y.

AVA is a professional association of volunteer administrators, administrators of volunteer programs, educators, researchers and students, which works to stimulate the coordination of community volunteer services. It publishes a monthly *Newsletter/Update*, and the quarterly *Journal of Volunteer Administration.*

Business Committee for the Arts, Inc.

1775 Broadway, Suite 510
New York, NY 10019
(212) 664-0600
Judith A. Jedlicka, Pres.

The Business Committee for the Arts is a not-for-profit organization of business leaders which encourages business support to the arts through a variety of programs and activities designed for the business community.

Capital Research Center

1612 K St., N.W., Suite 605
Washington, DC 20006
(202) 822-8666

Capital Research Center provides data about public policy organizations and special interest groups that seek to expand public control and political regulation of private sector activities, and works to increase understanding of the not-for-profit world by holding conferences, seminars and briefings. It publishes *Organization Trends*, a monthly newsletter, as well as two monograph series: *Studies in Philanthropy* and *Studies in Organization Trends.*

Center for Arts Information   *1-7 p.m. M F*
625 Broadway
New York, NY 10012
(212) 677-7548   *212 - 787-6557*
Rita Roosevelt, Exec. Dir.
Contact: Jana Jevnikar, Assoc. Dir.

The Center for Arts Information acts as a national clearinghouse and management assistance center for the nonprofit arts. It offers free information and referral services on fundraising, guidelines for state and federal arts funding programs, arts administration, and related topics. Its library is open to the public by appointment only. CAI offers career seminars for artists, as well as workshops on fundraising and management for arts administrators. It publishes a quarterly newsletter, *For Your Information*, and a number of booklets on funding sources and other issues of interest to nonprofit arts groups.

The Center for Community Change
1000 Wisconsin Avenue, N.W.
Washington, DC 20007
(202) 342-0519
Pablo Eisenberg, Exec. Dir.

The core of the Center's operations continues to be substantive, on-site work with community organizations—low-income and minority—encompassing aid in planning, organizational development, public policy analysis, fundraising, and specific program areas such as housing, physical and economic development, job development and training, and community crime prevention. The assistance program is tailored to meet the individual and changing needs of local organizations. At the national level, the Center works with local and other groups to address public policy issues that have a direct impact on grassroots organizations and their constituencies. Both these thrusts are complemented by the Center's publications program, citizen monitoring efforts, and coalition building activities.

The Center for Effective Philanthropy
P.O. Box 10805, Salem Station
Winston-Salem, NC 27108
(919) 725-1483
Merrimon Cuninggim, Pres.

The Center for Effective Philanthropy is a nonprofit organization established to assist donors and foundations of all types in addressing their problems. CEP consultation services are available on a fee basis to individual foundations or to groups of grantmakers. In addition, CEP conducts studies and publishes reports on important issues confronting philanthropy. Their consultation services are designed to aid in organization, program development, personnel search, staff training, evaluation of programs and procedures, and analyses of management. Services are available to grantees only at the request of a foundation.

Center for Nonprofit Management
1052 W. 6th Street, Suite 700
Los Angeles, CA 90017
(213) 977-0372
Alan F. Kumamoto, Exec. Dir.
Contact: Patty Oertel

The purpose of the Center for Nonprofit Management is to assist other nonprofit organizations to develop and strengthen management of their organizations, programs, and assets in order to better serve and fulfill their nonprofit purposes. Primary programs include public seminars, management consulting, and a management information clearinghouse.

Center for Responsive Governance
1000 16th St., N.W., Suite 400
Washington, DC 20036
(202) 223-2400
Nelson M. Rosenbaum, Pres.

The Center is a nonprofit research and educational organization which specializes in issues of management and marketing for nonprofit institutions. It conducts an active research program on financial trends in the nonprofit sector, produces original studies on marketing and management issues, and publishes a wide range of periodicals, books, reports and training materials through its CRG Press division. It also operates the CRG Training Institute which offers national training conferences, advanced training seminars, and training workshops on marketing and management topics.

Citizens Forum on Self Government
55 W. 44th Street
New York, NY 10036
(800) 223-6004 or (212) 730-7930 in New York, Alaska, and Hawaii
William N. Cassella, Jr., Exec. Dir.

Citizens Forum is a non-profit, non-partisan association of concerned and active citizens sharing the common goal of making their state and local governments and organized citizen efforts more effective, representative, and responsive. The Forum maintains the CIVITEX database which contains brief descriptions of local problem-solving projects. CIVITEX is designed to provide local community organizations, companies, and government agencies with examples of effective community initiatives. The database is available to members of the Telecommunications Cooperative Network through the Dialcom electronic mail system. Citizens Forum will also conduct searches of CIVITEX on a fee basis. Citizens Forum publishes a monthly journal, *National Civic Review*, as well as numerous books and guides.

The Conference Board
845 Third Avenue
New York, NY 10022
(212) 759-0900
James T. Mills, Pres.

The Conference Board is a nonprofit business information service whose purpose is to assist senior executives and other leaders in arriving at sound decisions. Its 3,600 member organizations are primarily business concerns, but there are also a number of labor unions, colleges and universities, government agencies, libraries, and trade and professional associations that hold Associate membership. The Board operates extensive research, training, and publications programs in all areas of business management, including corporate philanthropy. It conducts an annual survey of corporate contributions and publishes a number of reports and bulletins on managing the contributions function, tax and legal aspects of corporate giving, and specific projects supported by corporations. Publications catalog available on request.

Council for Advancement and Support of Education (CASE)
11 Dupont Circle, Suite 400
Washington, DC 20036
(202) 328-5900
Dr. James L. Fisher, Pres.
Contact: Nancy Raley or Cynthia Snyder

CASE provides technical assistance support to institutional advancement professionals in educational fundraising, alumni administration, government relations, and public relations. Its services include conferences, workshops, seminars, and publications. CASE also serves as the National Clearinghouse for Corporate Matching Gift Information, providing corporations and nonprofit organizations with data and related services. *Currents* is the monthly magazine published by CASE.

Council for Financial Aid to Education, Inc. (CFAE)
680 Fifth Avenue
New York, NY 10019
(212) 541-4050
John R. Haire, Pres.

CFAE is a non-profit corporation that promotes voluntary support of colleges and universities by the private sector, especially business. It offers seminars for corporate contributions managers and advises corporations on such matters as designing matching-gift programs, establishing scholarship programs for employees' children, and awarding scholarships for research in disciplines of special interest. In collaboration with The Conference Board, CFAE gathers data on corporate charitable contributions and publishes numerous reports on corporate giving and support of education. CFAE maintains a clearinghouse and referral service for the business community, college and university fundraisers, and the general public. Publications list available on request.

Council on Foundations
1828 L Street, N.W.
Washington, DC 20036
(202) 466-6512
James Joseph, Pres.

Foundation Center 212-620-4230
-79 5th Ave 15-16th between 5th Floor
- 10:00-5:00

The Council on Foundations is a national membership organization of independent, community, operating, and public foundations, corporate grantmakers, and trust companies. The Council collaborates with 17 independent regional associations of grantmakers and some 25 groups of foundations with special interests. The Council works with its members to promote responsible and effective grantmaking; develop and maintain a supportive environment for philanthropy; encourage and support collaboration among grantmakers; and promote the formation of new foundations. It publishes a biweekly *Newsletter; Foundation News*, a bimonthly journal; and various handbooks.

Foundations and Donors Interested in Catholic Activities (FADICA)
1730 Rhode Island Ave, N.W., Suite 401
Washington, DC 20036
(202) 466-2999
Dr. Francis J. Butler, Pres.

FADICA is a nonprofit voluntary organization which provides foundations and other donors with independent analyses of present and future church needs. Its members share experience and operational and program concerns to improve foundation activities. FADICA serves the research and information needs of its members and promotes their collaboration. The association does not offer clearinghouse services to the public.

Fund Raising Institute
Box 365
Ambler, PA 19002
(215) 646-7019
Contact : Walter Balthauser, Editorial Director

FRI studies fundraising techniques used by nonprofit organizations and reports its findings in books and periodicals. The *FRI Monthly Portfolio* includes a newsletter, bulletin, and letter clinic. FRI offers occasional workshops on topics related to fundraising. All FRI publications, plus computer programs, audio-cassettes, fundraising systems and other material helpful to fundraisers are described in a free catalog, available on request.

Grantmakers in Health
275 Madison Avenue, Suite 1918
New York, NY 10016
(212) 725-0650
Catherine McDermott, Pres.

Grantmakers in Health is a resource center for foundations and corporations active in health philanthropy. Its activities include national and regional conferences on topics of interest in the health field, surveys, the development of an information clearinghouse, and the encouragement of collaborative giving in this area.

Grantsmanship Center
1031 S. Grand Avenue
Los Angeles, CA 90015
(213) 749-4721
Norton J. Kiritz, Exec. Dir.

The Grantsmanship Center is a national training organization and publisher of the technical assistance magazine for nonprofits, *The Grantsmanship Center News*. The Center produces approximately 40 other publications and conducts six different workshops in more than 50 cities across the country. Workshops cover such areas as grantsmanship, fundraising (without grants), proposal writing, business ventures for nonprofits, and computers in nonprofits.

Grantsmanship Institute
103 Biltmore, Suite 103
San Antonio, TX 78213
(515) 349-2444
Edward Leary, Exec. Dir.
Contact: Jessica Casias

The Grantsmanship Institute primarily provides grant-writing services to municipalities, countries, and nonprofit organizations seeking funds from federal and state agencies. Formerly based in the Washington, D.C. area, the Institute recently relocated to the sunbelt and now serves clients in Texas and bordering states. The Institute occasionally offers seminars on grant-writing techniques.

Hispanics in Philanthropy (HIP)
c/o The James Irvine Foundation
Steuart Street Tower, Suite 2305
San Francisco, CA 94105
(415) 777-2244
Contact: Luz Vega, Chair

HIP is a voluntary association of staff and trustees at philanthropic institutions who share an interest in how philanthropic policies and practices affect issues and concerns of Hispanic communities. It is devoted to helping philanthropic institutions respond more effectively to the needs of Hispanics. HIP's goals are to gain a more significant Hispanic representation on boards of trustees and staffs of private philanthropic organizations, and to facilitate and encourage grantsmanship information for nonprofit organizations that are controlled by Hispanics or primarily serve Hispanic communities.

Independent Sector
1828 L Street, N.W.
Washington, DC 20036
(202) 223-8100
Brian O'Connell, President

Independent Sector is an organization created to preserve and enhance our national tradition of giving, volunteering and not-for-profit initiative. Members include voluntary organizations, foundations, and corporations with national interest and impact on philanthropy and voluntary action. Key program areas include: *Public Education*, to improve the public's understanding of the independent sector; *Communication* within the sector to identify shared problems and opportunities; *Research*, to develop a comprehensive store of knowledge about the sector; *Government Relations*, to coordinate the multitude of interconnections between the sector and the various levels of government; *Encouragement of Effective Nonprofit Operations and Management*, to maximize service to individuals and society; and *Measurable Growth in Support of the Sector*, as manifested by increased giving and volunteering. IS publishes several newsletters for members, occasional papers, and special reports, such as *Dimensions of the Independent Sector*.

International Council of Voluntary Agencies (ICVA)
13, rue Gautier
21 Geneva, Switzerland
tel: 31.66.02

ICVA is the international association of non-governmental, nonprofit organizations active in the fields of humanitarian assistance and development cooperation. It was established in 1962 to promote development, growth, and improvement of voluntary agencies and their activities throughout the world. ICVA currently has five working groups or committees which focus on such issues as refugees and migration, voluntary agency cooperation and funding, and human development. It publishes a monthly newsletter, *ICVA News*.

The Lutheran Resources Commission-Washington (LRC-W)
1346 Connecticut Avenue, N.W., Suite 823
Washington, DC 20036
(202) 872-0110
Lloyd Foerster, Exec. Dir.

LRC-W is a grants consultation agency serving four participating denominations. It does not make grants. Upon church body authorization it consults with agencies on the development of competitive proposals and guides them to foundation, government, or corporate funding sources. LRC-W publishes a monthly resource bulletin, *NEWSBRIEFS*, and conducts semi-annual resource development conferences on grantsmanship and other fundraising techniques and issues for community-based groups, social service agencies, and other nonprofits.

The National Assembly of National Voluntary Health and Social Welfare Organizations, Inc.
1346 Connecticut Avenue, NW, Suite 424A
Washington, DC 20036
(202) 296-1515
Leonard W. Stern, Exec. Dir.

The National Assembly is an association of national, voluntary human service organizations. Its purpose is to facilitate communication and cooperation among member agencies, advancing the work of each member and the mission of the human service sector as a whole. The National Assembly provides opportunities for its members to develop and share information needed to lead and manage national, voluntary human services programs effectively; it promotes the implementation of public policies and programs and the development of resources that are responsive to the needs of human service organizations and those they serve; and it works to increase the public visibility, understanding and acceptance of the human service sector, member organizations, and the issues they represent. A significant affinity group is National Collaboration for Youth, composed of 14 national, youth-serving organizations, which sponsors programs and advocates social policies that respond to the needs of the nation's 6- to 18-year olds. The Assembly issues a variety of films, reports, guides, and directories for human service and advocacy organizations. Catalog available on request.

National Association for Hospital Development (NAHD)
8300 Greensboro Drive, Suite 1110
McLean, VA 22102
(703) 556-9555
Dr. William C. McGinly, Pres.
Contact: Ms. Ursula Ellis

NAHD, a nonprofit organization of over 1,400 hospitals and health care executives, works to advance professional competence and excellence in hospital resource development. It sponsors national and regional conferences, seminars, and institutes on managing development programs and specific fundraising techniques and concerns. Publications include the semi-annual *NAHD Journal*, *NAHD NEWS* (10/year), the *Development Primer Manual*, and occasional reports.

National Catholic Development Conference (NCDC)
86 Front Street
Hempstead, NY 11550
(516) 481-6000
George T. Holloway, Exec. Dir.

NCDC is the nation's largest association of religious fundraising organizations. Its services include national fundraising seminars and workshops; an annual conference for religious fundraisers; a resource library of books, periodicals, and tapes on fundraising and philanthropy; and a variety of publications including two monthly newsletters, *Dimensions* and *The Fund Raising Forum*, and reports on fundraising taxation, postal affairs, and other government activities.

National Center for Charitable Statistics
% Independent Sector
1828 L St., N.W.
Washington, DC 20036
(202) 233-8100
Virginia Hodgkinson, Exec. Dir.

NCCS works to improve the quality and quantity of data available about the charitable sector of this country through its own national database of national and local charitable organizations registered with the IRS and by encouraging data gathering efforts by federal and state government, voluntary organizations and the research community in general. On January 1, 1986, NCCS was officially merged with Independent Sector and is now operating as a program within that organization.

National Charities Information Bureau
19 Union Square West
New York, NY 10003
(212) 599-1744
Kenneth L. Albrecht, Pres.

NCIB evaluates national nonprofit organizations against its eight basic standards of responsible performance and advises contributors through its reports about individual agencies. It also works to increase the availability of public information about charities and has developed training materials to help charities, and the grantmakers who fund them, assess their own financial operations and management. It publishes the bimonthly *Wise Giving Guide* ($20/yr.) as well as pamphlets and brochures for nonprofit board members, managers, and donors.

National Committee for Responsive Philanthropy (NCRP)
2001 S Street, N.W.
Washington, DC 20009
(202) 387-9177
Robert O. Bothwell, Exec. Dir.

NCRP was incorporated in 1976 as an outgrowth of the Donee Group which had formed the previous year to advise the Filer Commission. Since its beginning, NCRP has been concerned about private philanthropy's accountability to the public, accessibility to grantseekers, and responsiveness to newer, non-traditional, private, nonprofit organizations. Foundations, corporate giving programs, United Ways, payroll deduction contributions programs, and the Combined Federal Campaign (the federal government charity drive) have been the focus of NCRP's efforts. NCRP publishes a quarterly newsletter and a variety of short reports.

National Executive Service Corporation
622 Third Avenue
New York, NY 10017
(212) 867-5010
Frank Pace, Jr., Chair and C.E.O.
Contact: L. Philip Ewald, Vice-President and Secretary

The mission of NESC is to organize and make use of retired corporate, professional, and academic executives for public and private benefit. It provides management improvement services to nonprofit organizations upon request by placing retired men and women as short-term volunteer consultants and by creating, testing, and developing specific programs in the fields of health, education, human services, religion, and the arts. It publishes a quarterly newsletter, *Helping Hands*, which reports on activities of locally-based, autonomous service corps.

National Network of Grantmakers
2000 P Street, N.W.
Washington, DC 20036
(202) 822-9236

The Network is an association of individuals involved in organized philanthropy who are committed to promoting social and economic justice through grantmaking. Its stated purposes are: to establish communication links across grantmaking sectors and provide a support network for individuals working on similar concerns in varied grantmaking settings; to convene formal and informal meetings of grantmakers and donees to discuss common issues; and to expand the resource base (human and financial) for social and economic justice activities.

National Society of Fund-Raising Executives
1511 K Street, N.W.
Washington, DC 20005
(202) 638-1395
J. Richard Wilson, CFRE, President
Contact: Mary Lou Coleman, Director of Education

NSFRE is a professional organization of more than 4,800 fundraising executives. Its purpose is to assist its members in their professional efforts by fostering ethical standards for the management, direction, and counseling of fundraising programs for nonprofit organizations and agencies; by providing a forum for the discussion of concerns common to the profession; and by developing and disseminating information cogent to the profession. NSFRE sponsors a variety of local and regional conferences and seminars on fundraising and publishes the *NSFRE Journal* and *NSFRE News*.

Nonprofit Management Association (NMA)

% The Center for Non-Profit Management
1052 W. 6th Street, Suite 500
Los Angeles, CA 90017
(213) 977-0372
Contact: Alan Kumamoto, Chair

The purpose of the NMA is to serve its members in their individual and organizational efforts to assist and improve the management of nonprofit organizations. The Association exists for the professional development of its members. It serves as a forum for exchange of its information and skills, develops suggested standards for service, and convenes periodic meetings to solve problems and set policy relating to the membership.

Philanthropic Advisory Service

The Council of Better Business Bureaus, Inc. (CBBB)
1515 Wilson Boulevard
Arlington, VA 22209
(703) 276-0133
Helen L. O'Rourke, Vice President for PAS
Contact: Elizabeth M. Doherty, Dir.

The Philanthropic Advisory Service, a division of the CBBB, evaluates charitable organizations that conduct national or international program services or fundraising activities. PAS informs the charitable organization of the results of the evaluation and acts as a donor information service to corporations, foundations, local Better Business Bureaus, and members of the general public who have questions about specific charities that are soliciting their contributions or volunteer time. PAS issues written reports about those charities about which it receives the most inquiries and encourages inquirers to make their own decisions about giving. PAS is open for telephone calls Monday thru Friday, 9-5; appointments for visits are necessary. PAS publishes a number of free brochures, including *Tips on Charitable Giving, Tips on Tax Deductions, CBBB Standards for*

Charitable Solicitations, and *Give but Give Wisely*, and a bimonthly newsletter, *Insight*.

Program on Non-Profit Organizations at Yale University (PONPO)
P.O. Box 154, Yale Station
88 Trumbull Street
New Haven, CT 06520
(203) 432-3864
Paul DiMaggio, Exec. Dir.

The Program on Non-Profit Organizations is an interdisciplinary research program based at the Institution for Social and Policy Studies, Yale University. Since the Program's first year of full-scale operations, scholars have been studying the impact of the American voluntary sector. As a contributor to greater knowledge of the nonprofit sector, PONPO seeks to build a substantial body of information, analysis, and theory relating to nonprofit organizations; to enlist the energy and enthusiasm of the scholarly community in research and teaching related to the world of nonprofit organizations; and to generate research that will assist decision makers, in and out of the voluntary sector, in addressing major policy and management dilemmas confronting the sector. PONPO issues a newsletter, *Research Reports*, available free of charge, and a series of Working Papers prepared by scholars working on PONPO projects.

The Society for Nonprofit Organizations
6314 Odana Rd., Suite 1
Madison, WI 53719
(608) 274-9777

This membership organization brings together professionals who serve the nonprofit sector. It publishes the bimonthly *Nonprofit World*, maintains an extensive resource center of materials focused on the nonprofit sector, provides fundraising training programs, and offers a variety of group benefits to members (including group insurance programs, publication and training seminar discounts, etc.). Individual memberships are $75; organizational memberships are $125.

The Support Center
1410 Q Street, N.W.
Washington, DC 20009
(202) 462-2000
Jonathon B. Cook, Managing Dir.
Contact: Richard LeBus,
   Dir. of Operations

Additional Locations:
53 West Jackson Blvd., Suite 652
Chicago, IL 60604
(312) 461-9300

75 Lily
San Francisco, CA 94102
(415) 552-7584

17 Academy Street
Newark, NY 07102
(201) 643-5774

3052 Clairmont Drive, Suite H
San Diego, CA 92117
(619) 275-9300

1117 N. Shartel, Suite 909
Oklahoma City, OK 73103
(405) 236-8109

3400 Montrose, Suite 721
Houston, TX
(713) 524-0076

86 Weybosset St, Suite 308
Providence, RI 02903
(401) 521-0710

The Support Center is a national network of management assistance centers located in 30 states. Its purpose is to provide reliable, economical management assistance to help other nonprofit organizations become more effective. The Support Centers offer assistance in strategic and operating planning, accounting and financial management, organizational design and staffing, legal and tax compliance, and resource development. The Support Centers provide management assistance through diagnostic and information services, on-site consultations and training, and a series of low-cost workshops offered regularly at each location.

Telecommunications Cooperative Network (TCN)
505 Eighth Avenue
New York, NY 10018
(212) 714-9780
Robert Loeb, Managing Dir.
Contact: June Bailen, Dir. of Membership

TCN is a not-for-profit cooperative designed to help nonprofits maximize use of new communications technologies and minimize communications expenditures. TCN's Long Distance Savings Program helps members achieve maximum cost-efficiency on long distance communications and includes group purchasing discounts on commercial long distance services. TCN's Computer Communications Center provides co-op discounts for use of electronic mail, access to on-line databanks, and participation in a computer communications network exclusively for nonprofits. Its Equipment Consulting Program helps nonprofits acquire the best computer or telephone systems for their needs at the lowest cost. A monthly newsletter is available to members.

United Way of America
810 N. Fairfax Street
Alexandria, VA 22314

(703) 836-1700
William Aramony, Pres.
Contact: Steve Paulachak

United Way of America provides national, regional, and local program support and consultation to over 1,200 local United Ways in the area of fundraising, budgeting, management allocation, planning and communications. Technical assistance is available through the National Agencies Division and training through the National Academy of Voluntarism. UWA publishes numerous newsletters, magazines, brochures, and an annual report.

Volunteer: The National Center for Voluntary Action
1111 N. 19th Street, Suite 500
Arlington, VA 22209
(703) 276-0542
Kerry Kenn Allen, Pres.

Volunteer seeks to encourage voluntarism in America by helping local communities and organizations manage their volunteer programs more effectively. It maintains a network of 400 affiliated volunteer centers, provides technical assistance to corporations with employee volunteer programs, sponsors a national conference on citizen involvement and volunteer administration, and develops motivational materials for volunteers. It publishes a bimonthly newsletter, *Volunteering*, and two quarterly publications, *Voluntary Action Leadership* and *Exchange Networks*. It also issues and distributes a number of publications on nonprofit management and volunteer program administration.

Volunteer Lawyers for the Arts (VLA)
1560 Broadway, Suite 711
New York, NY 10036
(212) 575-1150
Arlene Shuler, Exec. Dir.

Volunteer Lawyers for the Arts, a Manhattan-based organization with affiliates in 39 cities nationwide, provides the arts community with free legal assistance and practical information. Artists and organizations with low incomes or operating budgets may seek VLA's consultation in such areas as contracts, copyright, nonprofit incorporation and tax exemption, labor relations, insurance, loft problems, and trademark. VLA sponsors annual conferences for both artists and attorneys, biweekly nonprofit incorporation seminars for artists held at VLA's offices, and clinics and workshops conducted throughout the New York metropolitan area. VLA publishes legal guides for visual artists, writers, and other artists, guides to tax preparation and record keeping, and collections of journals on arts, entertainment, and communications law published in conjunction with the Columbia University School of Law.

Women and Foundations/Corporate Philanthropy
141 Fifth Avenue, Floor 7-S
New York, NY 10010
(212) 460-9253
Joanne Hayes, Pres.

WAF/CP is a membership organization of staff and trustees of grantmaking organizations working to increase the amount of money for programs benefitting women and girls and to advance the status of women within private philanthropy. It publishes a newsletter and occasional research reports on funding for women's programs and sponsors an annual conference for members.

Appendix F

Information on IRS Services

As part of its broad responsibility for administering and enforcing federal tax laws and related statutes, the Internal Revenue Service has primary responsibility for determining tax-exempt status for charitable organizations and ensuring the uniform interpretation and application of the federal tax laws governing exempt organizations and private foundations. The Employee Plans and Exempt Organizations Division, under the direction of Assistant Commissioner S. Allen Winborne, is charged with administering these functions within the IRS at the national level, while the seven IRS Regional Offices and the sixty IRS District Offices administer the internal revenue laws and provide taxpayer assistance at the local level.

Obtaining Tax-Exempt Status for Your Organization

All organizations seeking exemption from federal income tax must file an application with the Internal Revenue Service. IRS Publication 557, "Tax-Exempt Status for Your Organization," describes the exemption criteria and basic application procedures required, as well as the appeals process if the initial application is denied. Copies may be obtained free of charge by writing to the IRS Forms Distribution Center for your state at the addresses listed at the end of this appendix.

Obtaining Information on Private Foundations

Under federal tax law, the information returns filed annually with the IRS by private foundations (Form 990-PF) are public documents. The IRS requires that foundations make copies of their 990-PFs available in the foundations' principal offices for public inspection for 180 days after filing. (The filing date is four-and-a-half months after the end of the foundation's fiscal year, which is May 15 for the majority of foundations which operate on a calendar year.) In addition, copies of individual foundation returns can be ordered from the IRS for a fee or free inspection of any foundation return can be arranged through any IRS district office.

To examine returns at an IRS district office, write to your District Director (Attention: Taxpayer Service) and request the specific returns you wish to see. District Offices are listed at the end of this appendix or you can contact your local IRS office listed in the telephone book for the address or telephone number of the appropriate district office for your area.

To order copies of individual returns, send orders to: Philadelphia Service Center, Internal Revenue Service, P.O. Box 245, Bensalem, PA 19020, Attn: Photocopy Special Processing Unit-A, Drop Point 536. The IRS will make paper copies of returns for a charge of $1.00 for the first page of each return and 10¢ per page thereafter. In addition, returns can be ordered on "aperture cards"—tabulator cards on which a microfiche copy of the return is mounted. The charge for copies on aperture cards is $1.00 for the first card and 13¢ for each addition card for each return. Since each card holds up to 15 pages of a return, this format is significantly less expensive, but it does require a microfiche reader to view the material. In ordering IRS returns, include the following information for each foundation requested: full name, city and state location, desired year of return, and, if available, the Employer Identification Number (EIN). This number may be found for all foundations in The Foundation Center's publication, *The National Data Book*.

Unrelated Business Income Tax

Nonprofit organizations that are tax-exempt are required to pay taxes on gross income of $1,000 or more that is generated from an unrelated trade or business. These tax provisions are applied to any trade or business regularly carried on by a nonprofit organization that is not substantially related to carrying out the exempt purpose for which the organization exists. IRS Publication 598, "Tax on Unrelated Business Income of Exempt Organizations," explains these tax provisions with filing requirements and procedures and basic information on how to compute unrelated business taxable income. It may also be obtained free of charge from the IRS Forms Distribution Center for your state.

INTERNAL REVENUE SERVICE REGIONAL OFFICES

Central Region (Indiana, Kentucky, Michigan, Ohio, West Virginia)
  James Hallman, Commissioner
  550 Main St., Cincinnati, OH 45202
Mid-Atlantic Region (Delaware, Maryland, New Jersey, Pennsylvania, West Virginia)
  William D. Waters, Commissioner
  841 Chestnut St., Philadelphia, PA 19107
Midwest Region (Illinois, Iowa, Minnesota, Missouri, Montana, Nebraska, North Dakota, South Dakota, Wisconsin)
  Roger L. Plate, Commissioner
  1 N. Wacker Dr., Chicago, IL 60606
North Atlantic Region (Connecticut, Maine, Massachusetts, New Hampshire, New York, Rhode Island, Vermont)
  Charles H. Brennan, Commissioner
  90 Church St., New York, NY 10007
Southeast Region (Alabama, Arkansas, Georgia, Florida, Louisiana, Mississippi, North Carolina, South Carolina, Tennessee)
  Thomas A. Cardoza, Commissioner
  275 Peachtree St., N.E., Atlanta, GA 30043
Southwest Region (Arizona, Colorado, Kansas, New Mexico, Oklahoma, Texas, Utah, Wyoming)
  Richard C. Voskuil, Commissioner
  LB-70, 7839 Churchill Way, Dallas, TX 75271
Western Region (California, Hawaii, Idaho, Nevada, Oregon, Washington)
  Thomas Coleman, Commissioner
  525 Market St., San Francisco, CA 94105

INTERNAL REVENUE SERVICE DISTRICT OFFICES

Alabama 35233.................................... 500 22d St. S., Birmingham
Alaska 99501.. 310 K St., Anchorage
Arizona 85004..................................... 2120 N. Central Ave., Phoenix
Arkansas 77201 .... 700 W. Capitol Ave., Little Rock
California:
  Laguna Niguel 92677 .... 2400 Avila Rd.
  Los Angeles 90012 .... 300 N. Los Angeles St.
  Sacramento 95825............................. 2345 Fair Oaks Blvd.
  San Francisco 94102 .... 450 Golden Gate Ave.
  San Jose 95113 .... Suite 300, 1 N. 1st St.
Colorado 80265 .... 1050 17th St., Denver

Connecticut 06103 .... 135 High St., Hartford
Delaware 19801.................................... 844 King St., Wilmington
District of Columbia (part of Balti-
   more District
Florida 32202 .... 400 W. Bay St., Jacksonville
Georgia 30043 .... 275 Peachtree St. NE, Atlanta
Hawaii 96813 .... 300 Ala Moana Blvd., Honolulu
Idaho 83724... 550 W. Fort St., Boise
Illinois:
   Chicago 60604................................. 230 S. Dearborn St.
   Springfield 62701 .... 320 W. Washington St.
Indiana 46204...................................... 575 N. Pennsylvania, Indianapolis
Iowa 50309 .... 210 Walnut St., Des Moines
Kansas 67202 .... 412 S. Main, Wichita
Kentucky 40202 .... 601 W. Broadway, Louisville
Louisiana 70130 .... 500 Camp St., New Orleans
Maine 04330 .... 68 Sewall St., Augusta
Maryland 21201 .... 31 Hopkins Plaza, Baltimore
Massachusetts 02203 .... John F. Kennedy Federal Bldg., Boston
Michigan 48226.................................... 477 Michigan Ave., Detroit
Minnesota 55101 .... 316 N. Robert St., St. Paul
Mississippi 39269 .... 100 W. Capitol St., Jackson
Missouri 63101 .... 1114 Market St., St. Louis
Montana 59601..................................... 301 S. Park Ave., Helena
Nebraska 68102.................................... 106 S. 15th St., Omaha
Nevada 89509....................................... 300 Booth St., Reno
New Hampshire 03801 .... 80 Daniel St., Portsmouth
New Jersey 07102 .... 970 Broad St., Newark
New Mexico 87101 .... 517 Gold Ave. SW, Albuquerque
New York:
   Albany 12207 .... Clinton Ave. and N. Pearl St.
   Brooklyn 11201................................ 35 Tillary St.
   Buffalo 14202................................... 111 W. Huron St.
   Manhattan 10007 .... 120 Church St., New York
North Carolina 27401 .... 320 Federal Pt., Greensboro
North Dakota 58102.............................. 653 2d Ave. N., Fargo
Ohio:
   Cincinnati 45202 .... 550 Main St.
   Cleveland 44199 .... 1240 E. 9th St.
Oklahoma 73102 .... 200 NW 4th St., Oklahoma City
Oregon 97204 .... 1220 SW 3d Ave., Portland

Pennsylvania:
    Philadelphia 19106........................... 600 Arch St.
    Pittsburgh 15222 .... 1000 Liberty Ave.
Puerto Rico (*see* Foreign Operations   Carlos E. Chardon St., Hato Rey
    District)
Rhode Island 02903 .... 380 Westminster Mall, Providence
South Carolina 29201 .... 1835 Assembly St., Columbia
South Dakota 57401............................ 115 4th Ave. SE, Aberdeen
Tennessee 37203.................................. 801 Broadway, Nashville
Texas:
    Austin 78701 .... 300 E. 8th St.
    Dallas 75242 .... 1100 Commerce St.
    Houston 77042 .... 3223 Briorpark
Utah 84111 .... 465 S. 4th East, Salt Lake City
Vermont 05401.................................... 11 Elmwood Ave., Burlington
Virgin Islands (*see* Foreign Oper-   22 Crystal Glade, Charlotte Amalie, St.
    ations District)   Thomas
Virginia 23240..................................... 400 N. 8th St., Richmond
Washington 98174 .... 915 2d Ave., Seattle
West Virginia 26101............................. 425 Juliana St., Parkersburg
Wisconsin 53202 .... 517 E. Wisconsin Ave., Milwaukee
Wyoming 82001 .... 308 W. 21st St. Cheyenne
Foreign Operations District   1325 K St., NW, Washington, DC
    20225 ....

IRS FORMS DISTRIBUTION CENTERS

Alabama—Caller No. 848, Atlanta, GA   30370
Alaska—P.O. Box 12626, Fresno, CA   93778
Arizona—P.O. Box 12626, Fresno, CA   93778
Arkansas—P.O. Box 2924, Austin, TX   78769
California—P.O. Box 12626, Fresno, CA   93778
Colorado—P.O. Box 2924, Austin, TX   78769
Connecticut—P.O. Box 1040, Methuen, MA 01844
Delaware—P.O. Box 25866, Richmond, VA 23260
District of Columbia—P.O. Box 25866, Richmond, VA   23260
Florida—Caller No. 848, Atlanta, GA   30370
Georgia—Caller No. 848, Atlanta, GA   30370
Hawaii—P.O. Box 12626, Fresno, CA   93778
Idaho—P.O. Box 12626, Fresno, CA   93778
Illinois—P.O. Box 24711, 1500 E Bannister Rd., Kansas City, MO   64131

Indiana—P.O. Box 6900, Florence, KY 41042

Iowa—P.O. Box 24711, 1500 E. Bannister Rd, Kansas City, MO 64131

Kansas— P.O. Box 2924, Austin, TX 78769

Kentucky—P.O. Box 6900, Florence, KY 41042

Louisiana—P.O. Box 2924, Austin, TX 78769

Maine—P.O. Box 1040, Methuen, MA 01844

Maryland—P.O. Box 25866, Richmond, VA 23260

Massachusetts—P.O. Box 1040, Methuen, MA 01844

Michigan—P.O. Box 6900, Florence, KY 41042

Minnesota—P.O. Box 24711, 1500 E. Bannister Rd, Kansas City, MO 64131

Mississippi—Caller No. 848, Atlanta, GA 30370

Missouri—P.O. Box 24711, 1500 E. Bannister Rd, Kansas City, MO 64131

Montana—P.O. Box 12626, Fresno, CA 93778

Nebraska—P.O. Box 24711, 1500 E. Bannister Rd, Kansas City, MO 64131

Nevada—P.O. Box 12626, Fresno, CA 93778

New Hampshire—P.O. Box 1040, Methuen, MA 01844

New Jersey—P.O. Box 25866, Richmond, VA 23260

New Mexico—P.O. Box 2924, Austin, TX 78769

New York—

　　Western New York: P.O. Box 260, Buffalo, NY 14201

　　Eastern New York (including NY City): P.O. Box 1040, Methuen, MA 01844

North Carolina—Caller No. 848, Atlanta, GA 30370

North Dakota—P.O. Box 24711, 1500 E. Bannister Rd, Kansas City, MO 64131

Ohio—P.O. Box 6900, Florence, KY 41042

Oklahoma—P.O. Box 2924, Austin, TX 78769

Oregon—P.O. Box 12626, Fresno, CA 93778

Pennsylvania—P.O. Box 25866, Richmond, VA 23260

Rhode Island—P.O. Box 1040, Methuen, MA 01844

South Carolina—Caller No. 848, Atlanta, GA 30370

South Dakota—P.O. Box 24711, 1500 E. Bannister Rd, Kansas City, MO 64131

Tennessee—Caller No. 848, Atlanta, GA 30370

Texas—P.O. Box 2924, Austin, TX 78769

Utah—P.O. Box 12626, Fresno, CA 93778

Vermont—P.O. Box 1040, Methuen, MA 01844

Virginia—P.O. Box 25866, Richmond, VA 23260

Washington—P.O. Box 12626, Fresno, CA 93778

West Virginia—P.O. Box 636, Florence, KY 41042

Wisconsin—P.O. Box 24711, 1500 E. Bannister Rd, Kansas City, MO 64131

Wyoming—P.O. Box 2924, Austin, TX 78769

Foreign Addresses—Taxpayers with mailing addresses in foreign countries should send their requests for forms and publications to: IRS Distribution Center, P.O. Box 25866, Richmond, VA   23260.

Puerto Rico—Director's Representative, U.S. Internal Revenue Service, Federal Office Building, Chardon Street, Hato Rey, PR   00918

Virgin Islands—Department of Finance, Tax Division, Charlotte Amalie, St. Thomas, VI   00801

Appendix G

The Foundation Center Network

THE FOUNDATION CENTER is an independent national service organization established by foundations to provide an authoritative source of information on private philanthropic giving. In fulfilling its mission, the Center disseminates information on private giving through public service programs, publications and through a national network of library reference collections for free public use. The New York, Washington, D.C., Cleveland, and San Francisco reference collections operated by The Foundation Center offer a wide variety of services and comprehensive collections of information on foundations and grants. The Cooperating Collections are libraries, community foundations, and other nonprofit agencies that provide a core collection of Foundation Center publications and a variety of supplementary materials and services in subject areas useful to grantseekers.

Over 100 of the network members have sets of private foundation information returns (IRS Form 990-PF) for their states or regions which are available for public use. These collections are indicated by a • next to their names. A complete set of U.S. foundation returns can be found in the New York and Washington, D.C. collections. The Cleveland and San Francisco offices contain IRS returns for those foundations in the midwestern and western states, respectively.

Because the collections vary in their hours, materials, and services, it is recommended that you call each collection in advance. To check on new locations or current information, call toll-free 800-424-9836.

215

REFERENCE COLLECTIONS OPERATED BY
THE FOUNDATION CENTER

- The Foundation Center
79 Fifth Avenue
New York, New York 10003
212-620-4230

- The Foundation Center
1001 Connecticut Avenue, NW
Washington, D.C. 20036
202-331-1400

- The Foundation Center
Kent H. Smith Library
1442 Hanna Building
1422 Euclid Avenue
Cleveland, Ohio 44115
216-861-1933

- The Foundation Center
312 Sutter Street
San Francisco, California 94108
415-397-0902

COOPERATING COLLECTIONS

ALABAMA

- Birmingham Public Library
2020 Park Place
Birmingham 35203
205-226-3600

  Huntsville–Madison County Public
  Library
108 Fountain Circle
P.O. Box 443
Huntsville 35804
205-536-0021

- Auburn University at Montgomery
Library
Montgomery 36193 - 0401
205-271-9649

ALASKA

- University of Alaska,
Anchorage Library
3211 Providence Drive
Anchorage 99504
907-786-1848

ARIZONA

- Phoenix Public Library
Business and Sciences
Department
12 East McDowell Road
Phoenix 85004
602-262-4782

- Tucson Public Library
Main Library
200 South Sixth Avenue
Tucson 85701
602-791-4393

ARKANSAS

- Westark Community
College Library
Grand Avenue at Waldron Road
Fort Smith 72913
501-785-4241

- Little Rock Public Library
Reference Department

700 Louisiana Street
Little Rock 72201
501-370-5950

CALIFORNIA

Inyo County Library—
Bishop Branch
210 Academy Street
Bishop 93514
619-872-8091

• California Community Foundation
Funding Information Center
3580 Wilshire Blvd., Suite 1660
Los Angeles 90010
213-413-4042

• Community Foundation for
Monterey County
420 Pacific Street
Monterey 93942
408-375-9712

California Community Foundation
4050 Metropolitan Drive
Orange 92668
714-937-9077

Riverside Public Library
3581 7th Street
Riverside 92501
714-787-7201

California State Library
Reference Services, Rm. 309
914 Capital Mall
Sacramento 95814
916-322-0369

• San Diego Community Foundation
625 Broadway, Suite 1015
San Diego 92101
619-239-8815

• The Foundation Center
312 Sutter Street

San Francisco 94108
415-397-0902

Orange County Community
Developmental Council
1440 East First Street, 4th Floor
Santa Ana 92701
714-547-6801

• Penisula Community Foundation
1204 Burlingame Avenue
Burlingame, 94011-0627
415-342-2505

• Santa Barbara Public Library
Reference Section
40 East Anapamu
P.O. Box 1019
Santa Barbara 93102
805-962-7653

Santa Monica Public Library
1343 Sixth Street
Santa Monica 90401-1603
213-458-8603

Tuolomne County Library
465 S. Washington Street
Sonora 95370
209-533-5707

North Coast Opportunities, Inc.
101 West Church Street
Ukiah 95482
707-462-1954

COLORADO

Pikes Peak Library District
20 North Cascade Avenue
Colorado Springs 80901
303-473-2080

• Denver Public Library
Sociology Division
1357 Broadway
Denver 80203
303-571-2190

CONNECTICUT

• Hartford Public Library
    Reference Department
500 Main Street
Hartford 06103
203-525-9121

D.A.T.A.
880 Asylum Avenue
Hartford 06105
203-278-2477

D.A.T.A.
25 Science Park
Suite 502
New Haven 06513

DELAWARE

• Hugh Morris Library
University of Delaware
Newark 19717-5267
302-451-2965

FLORIDA

Volusia County Public Library
    City Island
Daytona Beach 32014
904-252-8374

• Jacksonville Public Library
Business, Science, and Industry
    Department
122 North Ocean Street
Jacksonville 32202
904-633-3926

• Miami–Dade Public Library
    Florida Collection
One Biscayne Boulevard
Miami 33132
305-579-5001

• Orlando Public Library
10 North Rosalind

Orlando 32801
305-425-4694

• University of West Florida
    John C. Pace Library
Pensacola 32514
904-474-2412

Selby Public Library
1001 Boulevard of the Arts
Sarasota 33577
813-366-7303

• Leon County Public Library
Community Funding Resources
    Center
1940 North Monroe Street
Tallahassee 32303
904-478-2665

Palm Beach County Community
    Foundation
324 Datura Street, Suite 311
West Palm Beach 33401
305-659-6800

GEORGIA

• Atlanta–Fulton Public Library
    Ivan Allen Department
1 Margaret Mitchell Square
Atlanta 30303
404-688-4636

HAWAII

• Thomas Hale Hamilton Library
    General Reference
University of Hawaii
2550 The Mall
Honolulu 96822
808-948-7214

Community Resource Center
The Hawaiian Foundation
Financial Plaza of the Pacific

111 South King Street
Honolulu 96813
808-525-8548

IDAHO

- Caldwell Public Library
1010 Dearborn Street
Caldwell 83605
208-459-3242

ILLINOIS

Belleville Public Library
121 East Washington Street
Belleville 62220
618-234-0441

DuPage Township
300 Briarcliff Road
Bolingbrook 60439
312-759-1317

- Donors Forum of Chicago
208 South LaSalle Street
Chicago 60604
312-726-4882

- Evanston Public Library
1703 Orrington Avenue
Evanston 60201
312-866-0305

- Sangamon State University Library
Shepherd Road
Springfield 62708
217-786-6633

INDIANA

Allen County Public Library
900 Webster Street
Fort Wayne 46802
219-424-7241

Indiana University Northwest
Library
3400 Broadway
Gary 46408
219-980-6580

- Indianapolis–Marion County Public
Library
40 East St. Clair Street
Indianapolis 46204
317-269-1733

IOWA

- Public Library of Des Moines
100 Locust Street
Des Moines 50308
515-283-4259

KANSAS

- Topeka Public Library
Adult Services Department
1515 West Tenth Street
Topeka 66604
913-233-2040

- Wichita Public Library
223 South Main
Wichita 67202
316-262-0611

KENTUCKY

Western Kentucky University
Division of Library Services
Helm-Cravens Library
Bowling Green 42101
502-745-3951

- Louisville Free Public Library
Fourth and York Streets
Louisville 40203
503-223-7201

LOUISIANA

* East Baton Rouge Parish Library
     Centroplex Library
  120 St. Louis Street
  Baton Rouge 70821
  504-389-4960

* New Orleans Public Library
     Business and Science Division
  219 Loyola Avenue
  New Orleans 70140
  504-596-2583

* Shreve Memorial Library
  424 Texas Street
  Shreveport 71101
  318-226-5894

MAINE

* University of Southern Maine
  Center for Research and
     Advanced Study
  246 Deering Avenue
  Portland 04102
  207-780-4411

MARYLAND

* Enoch Pratt Free Library
  Special Science and History
     Department
  400 Cathedral Street
  Baltimore 21201
  301-396-5320

MASSACHUSETTS

* Associated Grantmakers of
     Massachusetts
  294 Washington Street
  Suite 501
  Boston 02108
  617-426-2608

* Boston Public Library
  Copley Square
  Boston 02117
  617-536-5400

* Walpole Public Library
  Common Street
  Walpole 02081
  617-668-5497 ext.340

* Western Massachusetts Funding
     Resource Center
  Campaign for Human Development
     Chancery Annex
  73 Chestnut Street
  Springfield 01103
  413-732-3175 ext.67

* Grants Resource Center
  Worcester Public Library
  Salem Square
  Worcester 01608
  617-799-1655

MICHIGAN

* Alpena County Library
  211 North First Avenue
  Alpena 49707
  517-356-6188

* University of Michigan–Ann Arbor
     Reference Department
  209 Hatcher Graduate Library
  Ann Arbor 48109-1205
  313-764-1149

* Henry Ford Centennial Library
  16301 Michigan Avenue
  Dearborn 48126
  313-943-2337

* Purdy Library
  Wayne State University
  Detroit 48202
  313-577-4040

- Michigan State University Libraries
    Reference Library
  East Lansing 48824
  517-353-9184

- Farmington Community Library
  32737 West 12 Mile Road
  Farmington Hills 48018
  313-553-0300

- University of Michigan–Flint
    Library
  Reference Department
  Flint 48503
  313-762-3408

- Grand Rapids Public Library
    Sociology and Education Dept.
  Library Plaza
  Grand Rapids 49502
  616-456-4411

- Michigan Technological University
    Library
  Highway U.S. 41
  Houghton 49931
  906-487-2507

MINNESOTA

- Duluth Public Library
  520 Superior Street
  Duluth 55802
  218-723-3802

- Southwest State University Library
  Marshall 56258
  507-537-7278

- Minneapolis Public Library
  Sociology Department
  300 Nicollet Mall
  Minneapolis 55401
  612-372-6555

  Rochester Public Library
  Broadway at First Street, SE

Rochester 55901
507-285-8002

Saint Paul Public Library
90 West Fourth Street
Saint Paul 55102
612-292-6311

MISSISSIPPI

Jackson Metropolitan Library
301 North State Street
Jackson 39201
601-944-1120

MISSOURI

- Clearinghouse for Midcontinent
    Foundations
  Univ. of Missouri, Kansas City
  Law School, Suite 1-300
  52nd Street and Oak
  Kansas City 64113
  816-276-1176

- Kansas City Public Library
  311 East 12th Street
  Kansas City 64106
  816-221-2685

- Metropolitan Association for
    Philanthropy, Inc.
  5585 Pershing Avenue
  Suite 150
  St. Louis 63112
  314-361-3900

- Springfield–Greene County Library
  397 East Central Street
  Springfield 65801
  417-866-4636

MONTANA

- Eastern Montana College Library
    Reference Department

1500 N. 30th Street
Billings 59101-0298
406-657-2262

- Montana State Library
    Reference Department
1515 E. 6th Avenue
Helena 59620
406-444-3004

NEBRASKA

University of Nebraska, Lincoln
106 Love Library
Lincoln 68588-0410
402-472-2526

- W. Dale Clark Library
    Social Sciences Department
215 South 15th Street
Omaha 68102
402-444-4826

NEVADA

- Las Vegas—Clark County Library
    District
1401 East Flamingo Road
Las Vegas 89109
702-733-7810

- Washoe County Library
301 South Center Street
Reno 89505
702-785-4190

NEW HAMPSHIRE

- The New Hampshire Charitable
    Fund
One South Street
Concord 03301
603-225-6641

Littleton Public Library
109 Main Street

Littleton 03561
603-444-5741

NEW JERSEY

Cumberland County Library
800 E. Commerce Street
Bridgeton 08302
609-455-0080

The Support Center
17 Academy Street, Suite 1101
Newark 07102
201-643-5774

County College of Morris Masten
    Learning
Resource Center
Route 10 and Center Grove Road
Randolph 07869
201-361-5000 x470

- New Jersey State Library
    Governmental Reference
185 West State Street
Trenton 08625
609-292-6220

NEW MEXICO

Albuquerque Community
    Foundation
6400 Uptown Boulevard N.E.
Suite 500-W
Albuquerque 87110
505-883-6240

- New Mexico State Library
325 Don Gaspar Street
Santa Fe 87503
505-827-3824

NEW YORK

- New York State Library
    Cultural Education Center

Humanities Section
Empire State Plaza
Albany 12230
518-474-7645

Bronx Reference Center
New York Public Library
2556 Bainbridge Avenue
Bronx 10458
212-220-6575

Brooklyn in Touch
101 Willoughby Street
Room 1508
Brooklyn 11201
718-237-9300

• Buffalo and Erie County Public
Library
Lafayette Square
Buffalo 14203
716-856-7525

Huntington Public Library
338 Main Street
Huntington 11743
516-427-5165

• Levittown Public Library
Reference Department
One Bluegrass Lane
Levittown 11756
516-731-5728

SUNY/College at Old Westbury
Library
223 Store Hill Road
Old Westbury 11568
516-876-3201

• Plattsburgh Public Library
Reference Department
15 Oak Street
Plattsburgh 12901
518-563-0921

Adriance Memorial Library
93 Market Street
Poughkeepsie 12601
914-485-4790

Queens Borough Public Library
89-11 Merrick Boulevard
Jamaica 11432
718-990-0700

• Rochester Public Library
Business and Social Sciences
Division
115 South Avenue
Rochester 14604
716-428-7328

• Onondaga County Public Library
335 Montgomery Street
Syracuse 13202
315-473-4491

• White Plains Public Library
100 Martine Avenue
White Plains 10601
914-682-4488

NORTH CAROLINA

• The Duke Endowment
200 S. Tryon Street, Ste. 1100
Charlotte 28202
704-376-0291

Durham County Library
300 N. Roxboro Street
Durham 27701
919-683-2626

• North Carolina State Library
109 East Jones Street
Raleigh 27611
919-733-3270

• The Winston-Salem Foundation
229 First Union National Bank
Building

Winston-Salem 27101
919-725-2382

NORTH DAKOTA

Western Dakota Grants Resource
    Center
Bismarck Junior College Library
Bismarck 58501
701-224-5450

• The Library
  North Dakota State University
  Fargo 58105
  701-237-8876

OHIO

• Public Library of Cincinnati and
      Hamilton County
  Education Department
  800 Vine Street
  Cincinnati 45202
  513-369-6940

• The Foundation Center
  1442 Hanna Building
  1422 Euclid Avenue
  Cleveland 44115
  216-861-1933

  CALLVAC Services, Inc.
  370 South Fifth Street
  Suite 1
  Columbus 43215
  614-221-6766

  Lima–Allen County Regional
      Planning Commission
  212 N. Elizabeth Street
  Lima 45801
  419-228-1836

• Toledo–Lucas County Public
      Library

Social Science Department
325 Michigan Street
Toledo 43624
419-255-7055 ext.221

Ohio University–Zanesville
Community Education and
    Development
1425 Newark Road
Zanesville 43701
614-453-0762

OKLAHOMA

• Oklahoma City University Library
  NW 23rd at North Blackwelder
  Oklahoma City 73106
  405-521-5072

• The Support Center
  525 NW Thirteenth Street
  Oklahoma City 73103
  405-236-8133

• Tulsa City–County Library System
  400 Civic Center
  Tulsa 74103
  918-592-7944

OREGON

• Library Association of Portland
      Government Documents Room
  801 S.W. Tenth Avenue
  Portland 97205
  503-223-7201

  Oregon State Library
  State Library Building
  Salem 97310
  503-378-4243

PENNSYLVANIA

Northampton County Area
    Community College

Learning Resources Center
3835 Green Pond Road
Bethlehem 18017
215-865-5358

- Erie County Public Library
  3 South Perry Square
  Erie 16501
  814-452-2333 ext.54

- Dauphin County Library System
    Central Library
  101 Walnut Street
  Harrisburg 17101
  717-234-4961

  Lancaster County Public Library
  125 North Duke Street
  Lancaster 17602
  717-394-2651

- The Free Library of Philadelphia
  Logan Square
  Philadelphia 19103
  215-686-5423

- Hillman Library
  University of Pittsburgh
  Pittsburgh 15260
  412-624-4423

- Economic Development Council of
    Northeastern Pennsylvania
  1151 Oak Street
  Pittston 18640
  717-655-5581

  James V. Brown Library
  12 E. 4th Street
  Williamsport 17701
  717-326-0536

RHODE ISLAND

- Providence Public Library
    Reference Department
  150 Empire Street
  Providence 02903
  401-521-7722

SOUTH CAROLINA

- Charleston County Public Library
  404 King Street
  Charleston 29403
  803-723-1645

- South Carolina State Library
    Reader Services Department
  1500 Senate Street
  Columbia 29201
  803-758-3138

SOUTH DAKOTA

- South Dakota State Library
  State Library Building
  800 North Illinois Street
  Pierre 57501
  605-773-3131

  Sioux Falls Area Foundation
  404 Boyce Greeley Building
  321 South Phillips Avenue
  Sioux Falls 57102-0781
  605-336-7055

TENNESSEE

- Knoxville–Knox County Public
    Library
  500 West Church Avenue
  Knoxville 37902
  615-523-0781

- Memphis Shelby County Public
    Library
  1850 Peabody Avenue
  Memphis 38104
  901-725-8876

- Public Library of Nashville and
    Davidson County
  8th Avenue, North and Union Street
  Nashville 37203
  615-244-4700

TEXAS

Amarillo Area Foundation
1000 Polk
P. O. Box 25569
Amarillo 79105-269
806-376-4521

- The Hogg Foundation for Mental
  Health
  The University of Texas
  Austin 78712
  512-471-5041

- Corpus Christi State University
  Library
  6300 Ocean Drive
  Corpus Christi 78412
  512-991-6810

- Dallas Public Library
  Grants Information Service
  1515 Young Street
  Dallas 75201
  214-749-4100

- Pan American University
  Learning Resource Center
  1201 W. University Drive
  Edinburg 78539
  512-381-3304

- El Paso Community Foundation
  El Paso National Bank Building
  Suite 1616
  El Paso 79901
  915-533-4020

- Funding Information Center
  Texas Christian University Library
  Ft. Worth 76129
  817-921-7664

- Houston Public Library
  Bibliographic & Information Center
  500 McKinney Avenue
  Houston 77002
  713-224-5441 ext.265

- Funding Information Library
  507 Brooklyn
  San Antonio 78215
  512-227-4333

UTAH

- Salt Lake City Public Library
  Business and Science Department
  209 East Fifth South
  Salt Lake City 84111
  801-363-5733

VERMONT

- State of Vermont Department of
  Libraries
  Reference Services Unit
  111 State Street
  Montpelier 05602
  802-828-3261

VIRGINIA

- Grants Resources Library
  Hampton City Hall
  22 Lincoln Street, Ninth Floor
  Hampton 23669
  804-727-6496

- Richmond Public Library
  Business, Science, & Technology
  Department
  101 East Franklin Street
  Richmond 23219
  804-780-8223

WASHINGTON

- Seattle Public Library
  1000 Fourth Avenue
  Seattle 98104
  206-625-4881

- Spokane Public Library
  Funding Information Center

West 906 Main Avenue
Spokane 99201
509-838-3361

WEST VIRGINIA

- Kanawha County Public Library
  123 Capital Street
  Charleston 25301
  304-343-4646

WISCONSIN

- Marquette University Memorial
  Library
  1415 West Wisconsin Avenue
  Milwaukee 53233
  414-224-1515

- University of Wisconsin–Madison
  Memorial Library
  728 State Street
  Madison 53706
  608-262-3647

  Society for Nonprofit Organizations
  6314 Odana Road
  Suite One
  Madison 53719
  608-274-9777

WYOMING

- Laramie County Community
  College Library
  1400 East College Drive
  Cheyenne 82007
  307-634-5853

CANADA

Canadian Center for Philanthropy
3080 Yonge Street
Suite 4080
Toronto, Ontario M4N3N1
416-484-4118

ENGLAND

Charities Aid Foundation
14 Bloomsbury Square
London WCIA 2LP
01-430-1798

MARIANNA ISLANDS

Northern Marianas College
P.O. Box 1250 CK
Saipan, GM 96950

MEXICO

Biblioteca Benjamin Franklin
Londres 16
Mexico City 6, D.F.
525-591-0244

PUERTO RICO

Universidad Del Sagrado Corazon
M.M.T. Guevarra Library
Correo Calle Loiza
Santurce 00914
809-728-1515 ext.274

VIRGIN ISLANDS

College of the Virgin Islands Library
Saint Thomas
U.S. Virgin Islands 00801
809-774-9200 ext. 487

Appendix H

Services and Publications of The Foundation Center

THE FOUNDATION CENTER is a national service organization founded and supported by foundations to provide a single authoritative source of information on foundation giving. The Center's programs are designed to help grantseekers as they begin to select from some approximately 24,000 active U.S. foundations those which may be most interested in their projects. Among its primary activities toward this end are publishing reference books on foundations and foundation grants and disseminating information on foundations through a nationwide public service program.

Publications of The Foundation Center are the primary working tools of every serious grantseeker. They are also used by grantmakers, scholars, journalists, regulators, and legislators—in short, everyone seeking any type of factual information on foundation philanthropy. All private foundations actively engaged in grantmaking, regardless of size or geographic location, are included in one or more of the Center's publications. The publications are of three kinds: directories that describe specific foundations, characterizing their program interests and providing fiscal and personnel data; grants indexes that list and classify by subject recent foundation awards; and guides, brochures, and bibliographies which introduce the reader to funding research, elements of proposal writing, as well as other sources of information.

Foundation Center publications may be ordered from The Foundation Center, 79 Fifth Avenue, New York, NY 10003. For more information about any aspect of the Center's program or for the name of the Center's library collection nearest you, call toll-free (800) 424-9836.

THE FOUNDATION DIRECTORY, 10TH EDITION

The Foundation Directory has been widely known and respected in the field for 25 years. It includes the latest information on all foundations whose assets exceed $1 million or whose annual grant total is $100,000 or more. The new 10th Edition is the biggest ever: 4402 foundations are included, five hundred of which are new to the *Directory* this year, and 720 of which are corporate foundations. *Directory* foundations hold over $63 billion in assets and award $4.1 billion in grants annually, accounting for 92% of all U.S. foundation dollars awarded in 1983 and 1984.

Each *Directory* entry now contains more precise information on application procedures, giving limitations, types of support awarded, the publications of each foundation, and foundation staff—all this in addition to such vital data as the grantmakers' giving interests, financial data, grant amounts, addresses and telephone numbers. The Foundation Center works closely with foundations to ensure the accuracy of the information provided—foundation response to requests for information for the 10th Edition increased dramatically over previous editions.

The *Directory* includes indexes by foundation name; subject areas of interest; names of donors, trustees, and officers; geographic location; and the types of support awarded. Also included are analyses of the foundation community by geography, asset and grant size, different types of foundations, trends in foundation establishment, and information on the effects of inflation on the field since 1975.

10th Edition, Oct. 1985. 928 pages. ISBN 0-87954-132-6. $65

COMSEARCH PRINTOUTS

This popular series of computer-produced guides to foundation giving derived from The Foundation Center Database is now issued in four separate categories:

COMSEARCH: Broad Topics

This series indexes and analyzes recent foundation grants in 24 broad subject categories. Each listing includes all grants in the particular subject area reported to The Foundation Center during the preceding year, along with an index listing name and geographic location of organizations which have received grants, a geographic index arranged by state of the organization which received grants, and a key word index listing descriptive words and phrases which link a foundation's giving interests with your organization's field. *COMSEARCH: Broad Topics* includes grants for:

Arts & Cultural Programs
Business & Employment
Children & Youth
Higher Education
Hospitals & Medical Care Programs
Museums
Science Programs
Social Science Programs
Women & Girls
International & Foreign Programs
Minorities
Religion & Religious Education
Public Health
Public Policy & Political Science
Recreation
Community & Urban Development
Elementary & Secondary Education
   (Public & Private Schools)
Matching & Challenge Support
Film, Media, & Communications
Crime & Law Enforcement
Environmental Law, Protection &
   Education
Family Services
Medical & Professional Health
   Education
Physically & Mentally Disabled

Series published annually in June. $35 each

COMSEARCH: Subjects

This series includes 65 specially focused subject listings of grants reported to The Foundation Center during the preceding year. Listings are arranged by the state where the foundation is located and then by foundation name, and include complete information on the name and location of the grant recipient, the amount awarded, and the purpose of the grant. *COMSEARCH: Subjects* may be purchased as a complete set on microfiche or individually by particular subject area of interest in paper or microfiche form. A full list of categories follows:

232   FOUNDATION FUNDAMENTALS

Order Number/Title

Communications
   3. Language, Literature &
      Journalism
   4. Publications

Education
   15. Adult & Continuing Education
   17. Student & Professional
       Internships
   18. Higher Education—Capital
       Support
   19. Higher Education—
       Endowments
   20. Higher Education—Faculty and
       Professorships
   21. Higher Education—Fellowships
   22. Scholarships, Student Aid
       & Loans
   23. Library & Information Services
   24. Educational Research
   25. Vocational Education, Career
       Development & Employment
   26. International Studies, Education
       & Exchange
   27. Teacher Training

Health
   30. Health & Medical Care—Cost
       Containment
   32. Medical Research &
       Advancement
   33. Dentistry
   34. Nursing
   37. Mental Health
   39. Alcohol & Drug Abuse
   40. Cancer Care & Research
   41. Hospices
   42. Abortion, Birth Control &
       Family Planning
   43. Children & Youth—Health
       Programs
   44. Children & Youth—Medical
       Research

Cultural Activities
   46. Humanities Programs
   47. Theater
   48. Music Schools & Music
       Education
   49. Orchestras & Musical
       Performances
   50. Architecture, Historical
       Preservation & Historical
       Societies
   51. Dance

Population Groups
   64. Boys
   65. Blacks
   66. Hispanics
   67. Blind & Visually Impaired
   68. Deaf & Hearing Impaired

Science & Technology
   74. Mathematics
   75. Biology & Genetics
   76. Agriculture & Farming
   77. Chemistry
   79. Computer Science & Systems
   80. Energy
   81. Engineering

Social Sciences
   85. Business Education
   86. Economics
   88. Law Schools & Legal Education
   89. Psychology & Behavioral
       Sciences

Welfare
   90. Peace Initiatives & Arms Control
   91. Legal Services
   92. Housing & Transportation
   93. Community Funds
   95. Child Abuse
   97. Community Centers
   98. Young Men's & Women's
       Associations
   99. Food & Nutrition

101. Animal Welfare & Wildlife
102. Rural Development
104. Camps & Camperships
105. Parks, Gardens & Zoos
106. Refugee & Relief Services
107. Volunteer Programs
108. Homeless

109. Human Rights
Other
110. Nonprofit Management
111. Philanthropy & Nonprofit Sector Research
112. Governmental Agencies
114. Conferences & Seminars

Series published annually in June. $225 microfiche set; $17.50 per subject on paper; $6 per subject on microfiche.

COMSEARCH: Geographics

This series provides customized listings of grants received by organizations in two cities, eleven states, and seven regions. These listings make it easy to see which major foundations have awarded grants in your area, to which nonprofit organizations, and what each grant was intended to accomplish. Listings are available for Washington D.C., New York City, California, Illinois, Massachusetts, Michigan, Minnesota, New Jersey, New York State (excluding New York City), North Carolina, Ohio, Pennsylvania, Texas, the Northeast (Maine, New Hampshire, Rhode Island, Vermont, Connecticut), Southeast (Florida, Georgia, Alabama, Mississippi, Louisiana, South Carolina, Tennessee), Northwest (Alaska, Washington and Oregon), the Rocky Mountains (Arizona, New Mexico, Colorado, Utah, Nevada, Idaho, Montana, Wyoming), South Atlantic (Delaware, Maryland, Virginia), Central Midwest (Indiana, Iowa, Kansas, Kentucky, Missouri), Upper Midwest (Nebraska, North Dakota, South Dakota, Wisconsin).

Series published annually in June. $28 each

COMSEARCH: Special Topics

These are the three most frequently requested special listings from the Center's computer database. The three special listings are:

- The 1,000 Largest U.S. Foundations by Asset Size,
- The 1,000 Largest U.S. Foundations by Annual Grants Total,
- The nearly 1,400 Operating Foundations that Administer Their Own Projects or Programs.

Series published annually in June. $17.50 each

THE FOUNDATION GRANTS INDEX ANNUAL, 15TH EDITION

The Foundation Grants Index Annual lists the grants of $5,000 or more awarded to nonprofit organizations by about 444 foundations. It is the most thorough

subject index available to the actual grants of major U.S. foundations, including the top 100 grantmakers.

The 15th Edition is the largest annual *Index* ever, with an expanded analyt-
ical introduction, an improved and enlarged subject index, and more grant descriptions than ever before—more than 36,000 grants of $5,000 or more made
to nonprofit organizations reported to the Center in 1984 and 1985. The volume
is arranged alphabetically by state, then by foundation name. Each entry includes the amount and date of the grant, name and location of the recipient, a
description of the grant, and any known limitations of the foundation's giving
pattern. The grants are indexed by subject and geographic location, by the
names of the recipient organizations, and by a multitude of key words describing all aspects of each grant. These grants total over $2 billion and represent
about 40% of all foundation giving, making this the most comprehensive grants
compilation available.

The Foundation Grants Index Annual is the reference used by educators, librarians, fundraisers, medical personnel, and other professionals interested in
learning about foundation grants. It shows you what kind of organizations and
programs the major foundations have been funding.

15th Edition, 1986. 848 pages. ISBN 0-87954-160-1. $44

THE FOUNDATION GRANTS INDEX BIMONTHLY

This unique subscription service keeps your fundraising program up-to-date,
bringing you important new information on foundation funding every other
month. Each issue of *The Foundation Grants Index Bimonthly* brings you descriptions of over 2,000 recent foundation grants, arranged by state and indexed
by subjects and recipients. This enables you to zero in on grants made in your
subject area within your geographic region. You can use the *Bimonthly* to target
potential sources of funding for medical schools in Washington D.C., for example, modern dance troupes in New York, or any other combination of factors.

The *Bimonthly* also contains updates on grantmakers, noting changes in
foundation address, personnel, program interests, and application procedures.
Also included is a list of grantmakers' publications—annual reports, information brochures, grants lists, and newsletters. *The Foundation Grants Index Bimonthly* is a trusted current-awareness tool used by professional fundraisers.

Annual subscription $24/ 6 issues/ISSN 0735-2522

NATIONAL DATA BOOK, 10TH EDITION

Lists the approximately 24,000 currently active grantmaking foundations in the
U.S. in one easy-to-use volume arranged by state in descending order by their

annual grant totals. A separate alphabetical index to foundation names is also included. Foundation entries include name, address, and principal officer, plus full fiscal data (market value of assets, grants paid, gifts received, and fiscal period) and an indication of which foundations publish annual reports. The *National Data Book* will help you find the address of any active U.S. foundation, locate all foundations in a particular city or state, identify all foundations in a particular city or state, identify all foundations that issue annual reports, and profile foundation assets or giving levels by state or region.

2 vols. Annually in January. ISBN 0-87954-156-3. $55

SOURCE BOOK PROFILES
Source Book Profiles is an annual subscription service offering detailed descriptions of the 1,000 largest foundations, analyzing giving patterns by subject area, type of support, and type of recipient. The service operates on a two-year publishing cycle, with each one-year series covering 500 foundations. Each quarterly installment includes 125 new profiles as well as information on changes in address, telephone, personnel, or program, and a revised, cumulative set of indexes to all 1,000 foundations covered in the two-year cycle by name, subject interest, type of grants awarded, and city and state location or concentration of giving.

1986 Series / $275 annual subscription / ISBN 0-87954-157-1
1985 Series / $265 annual subscription / ISBN 0-87954-128-8
1984 Cumulative Volume (500 Profiles) / $250 / ISBN 0-87954-096-0

CORPORATE FOUNDATION PROFILES, 4TH EDITION
This volume includes comprehensive analyses of approximately 250 of the nation's largest company-sponsored foundations, with full subject, type of support, and geographic indexes. Summary financial data is provided for approximately 475 additional corporate foundations. Entries are drawn from *Source Book Profiles* and include address and telephone number, complete information about the parent company, financial data, an analysis of the foundation's giving program, and information regarding the foundation's policies, guidelines, and application procedures.

4th Edition Nov. 1985. ISBN 0-87954-135-0. $55

FOUNDATION GRANTS TO INDIVIDUALS, 5TH EDITION
The only publication devoted entirely to specialized foundation grant opportunities for qualified individual applicants. The 5th Edition provides full descrip-

tions of the programs for individuals of over 950 foundations. Entries also include foundation addresses and telephone numbers, names of trustees and staff, financial data, and sample grants. This volume can save individuals seeking grants countless hours of research. The fully revised 5th Edition is scheduled for publication in fall 1986.

5th Edition, 1986. 243 pages. ISBN 0-87954-158-X. $18

AMERICA'S VOLUNTARY SPIRIT: A BOOK OF READINGS

In this thoughtful collection, Brian O'Connell, President of INDEPENDENT SECTOR, brings together 45 selections which celebrate and examine the richness and variety of America's unique voluntary sector. O'Connell researched nearly 1,000 selections spanning over 300 years of writing to identify those speeches, articles, chapters, and papers which best define and characterize the role that philanthropy and voluntary action play in our society. Contributors as diverse as de Tocqueville and John D. Rockefeller, Thoreau and Max Lerner, Erma Bombeck and Vernon Jordan are unified in a common examination of this unique dimension of American life. The anthology includes a bibliography of over 500 important writings and a detailed subject index.

October 1983. ISBN 0-87954-079-6 (hardcover). $19.95
ISBN 0-87954-081-8 (softcover). $14.95

PHILANTHROPY IN AN AGE OF TRANSITION
The Essays of Alan Pifer

This is a collection of essays by one of the most respected and well-known individuals in philanthropy. In these essays, Alan Pifer analyzes issues of great concern to all Americans; the responsibilities of higher education, charitable tax deductions, women in the work force, the financial straits of the nonprofit sector, the changing age composition of the American population, bilingual education, the progress of blacks, and more. The essays have been collected from the annual reports of Carnegie Corporation, from 1966-82, some of the most turbulent years in American history.

Alan Pifer is President Emeritus of Carnegie Corporation of New York where he was President for over seventeen years.

270 pages. April 1984. ISBN 0-87954-104-0. $12.50

THE BOARD MEMBER'S BOOK
by Brian O'Connell, President, INDEPENDENT SECTOR

Based on his extensive experience working with and on the boards of voluntary organizations, Brian O'Connell has developed this practical guide to the essential functions of voluntary boards. O'Connell offers practical advice on how to be a more effective board member and how board members can help their organizations make a difference. This is an invaluable instructional and inspirational tool for anyone who works on or with a voluntary board. Includes an extensive reading list.

208 pages. May 1985. ISBN 0-87954-133-4. $16.95

MANAGING FOR PROFIT IN THE NONPROFIT WORLD
by Paul B. Firstenberg

How can service-oriented nonprofits expand their revenue bases? In this title in our series on nonprofit management, author Paul B. Firstenberg shares his view that a vital nonprofit is an entrepreneurial nonprofit. Drawing upon his 14 years of experience as a professional in the nonprofit sector—at the Ford Foundation, Princeton, Tulane, and Yale Universities, and Children's Television Workshop—as well as his extensive for-profit experience, Firstenberg outlines innovative ways in which nonprofit managers can utilize the same state-of-the-art management techniques as our most successful for-profit enterprises.

WORKING IN FOUNDATIONS: CAREER PATTERNS OF WOMEN AND MEN
by Teresa Jean Odendahl, Elizabeth Trocolli Boris, and Arlene Kaplan Daniels

This publication is the result of a groundbreaking study of foundation career paths of women and men undertaken by Women and Foundations/Corporate Philanthropy with major funding from Russell Sage Foundation. This book offers a detailed picture of the roles and responsibilities of foundation staff members, employment opportunities in philanthropy, and the management styles and grantmaking processes within foundations.

115 pages. April 1985. ISBN 0-87954-134-2. $12.95

ASSOCIATES PROGRAM

"Direct line to Fundraising Information"
The Associates Program puts important facts and figures on your desk through a toll-free telephone reference service helping you to:

- identify potential sources of foundation funding for your organization,
- gather important information to target and present your proposals most effectively.

Your annual membership in the Associates Program gives you vital information on a timely basis, saving you hundreds of hours of research time.

- Membership in the Associates Program puts important funding information on your desk, including information from:
  —foundation annual reports, information brochures, press releases, grants lists, and other documents
  —IRS 990-PF information returns for all 24,000 U.S. foundations—often the only source of information on small foundations
  —books and periodicals chronicling foundation and philanthropic history and regulations
  —files filled with news clippings about foundations
  —The Foundation Center's own publications: *Foundation Directory* and *Supplement, Foundation Grants Index*—annual and bimonthly, *Source Book Profiles, Corporate Foundation Profiles, National Data Book, COMSEARCH Printouts, Foundation Fundamentals, Grants to Individuals*, and *Special Topics*.

- The Associates Program puts this vital information on your desk through a *toll-free telephone call*. The annual fee of $300 for the Associates Program grants you 10 free calls or 2½ hours worth of answers per month.

- Membership in the Associates Program allows you to request *custom searches* of the Foundation Center's *computerized databases* which contain information on all 24,000 active U.S. foundations.

Thousands of professional fundraisers find it extremely cost effective to rely on the Center's Associates Program. Put our staff of experts to work for your fundraising program. For more information call TOLL-FREE 800-424-9836.

FOUNDATION CENTER COMPUTER DATABASES

Foundation and Grants Information Online
As the only nonprofit organization whose sole purpose is to provide information on philanthropic activity, The Foundation Center offers three important databases online—Foundation Directory, Foundation Grants Index, and National Foundations. The databases correspond in form and content to the printed volumes: *The Foundation Directory, The Foundation Grants Index*, and the *National Data Book*. Online retrieval provides vital information on funding sources, philanthropic giving patterns, grant application guidelines, and the financial status of foundations to:

Nonprofit organizations seeking funds   Researchers
Grantmaking institutions   Journalists
Corporate contributors   Legislators

Searches of the Center's databases can provide comprehensive and timely answers to your questions, such as . . .

- Which New York foundations support urban projects? Who are their officers and trustees?
- What are the program interests of the ten largest corporate foundations? Which ones publish annual reports?
- Which foundations have given grants in excess of $100,000 in the past two years for continuing education for women?
- Which foundations would be likely to fund a cancer research project at a California hospital?
- Which are the ten largest foundations in Philadelphia by annual grants amount?
- What are the names and addresses of smaller foundations in the 441 zip code area?

The Center's up-to-date and authoritative data is available online through DIALOG Information Services. For additional information about how you may have access to Foundation Center databases, Call TOLL-FREE 800-424-9836.